THE
FEDERAL
BUDGET

THE
FEDERAL
BUDGET

POLITICS, POLICY, PROCESS

Allen Schick

THE BROOKINGS INSTITUTION
Washington, D.C.

Library of Congress Cataloging-in-publication data

Schick, Allen.
   The federal budget: politics, policy, process / Allen Schick
         p.   cm.
   Includes bibliographical references and index.
   ISBN 0-8157-7734-5 (c1)   — ISBN 0-8157-7733-7 (pa)

   1. Budget—United States.   I. Title.
   HJ2051.S3424 1994
   353.0072'221—dc20   94-521
                                                  CIP

9 8 7 6 5 4 3 2 1

The paper used in this publication meets the minimum requirements of the
American National Standard for Information Sciences—Permanence of Paper
for Printed Library Materials, ANSI Z39.48—1984

Typeset in Palatino and Helvetica

Composition by Marcotte/Wagner Design
Potomac, Maryland

Printed by R. R. Donnelley and Sons Co.
Harrisonburg, Virginia

Foreword

Determining the federal budget is one of the most important political processes of our time. The budget has become the measuring rod by which much contemporary legislation is judged and presidential performance is often assessed. It is both opportunity and obstacle, as was demonstrated by Bill Clinton's success in reducing the deficit and his failure to reform health care financing. The budget's importance is partly a matter of size: it allocates more than $1.5 trillion a year in spending, an amount equal to almost one-quarter of the nation's gross domestic product. But the importance is also a matter of programs and policies, for the budget is one of the principal means by which government priorities are established or redirected.

Another side to the budget is less well known, but no less significant. Budgeting entails complex rules and procedures that affect government policies and their outcomes. As concern has mounted over the size of the budget deficit, these rules have become more prominent and constraining. In this book Allen Schick, a visiting fellow in the Brookings Governmental Studies program, explains how budgeting works at each stage of executive and legislative action, from preparation of the president's budget through the appropriation and expenditure of funds, and assesses the effects of the procedures on budget politics and policies. He shows why the budget is both controlled and out of control, and contends that many of the reforms proposed to deal with these problems will not accomplish their stated objectives.

The author wishes to thank Thomas Mann, Charles Schultze, and Joseph White, who read all or parts of the manuscript. Robert Keith of the Congressional Research Service assisted in assembling documents and exhibits and explaining some of the recent innovations in budgetary practice. Ingeborg Lockwood provided administrative support and Eric Messick verified the book for factual accuracy. Theodore Noell provided research assistance, James Schneider edited the book, Norman Turpin designed the text, Jeanne Wagner typeset it, Carlotta Ribar proofread it, and Julia Petrakis compiled the index.

The views expressed in this book are those of the author and should not be ascribed to any of the persons acknowledged above, or to the trustees, officers, or staff members of the Brookings Institution.

Bruce K. MacLaury
President

Washington, D.C.
November 1994

Contents

CONTENTS

Chapter 1

Budgeting at the Close of the Twentieth Century

The federal budget is an enormously complex undertaking. It demands the active participation of the president and most members of Congress and the efforts of tens of thousands of staff persons in the executive and legislative branches. It entails thousands of big and small decisions, regard for countless rules and procedures, and conflict over how the government raises and spends public funds. The process could hardly be otherwise because so much is at stake when budget decisions are made. The budget controls more than $1.5 trillion a year in spending, an amount equal to almost one-quarter of the nation's gross domestic product. Federal budget receipts are about one-fifth of GDP. The budget deficit, which results from the imbalance between revenues and expenditures, makes the federal government the largest single borrower in capital markets.

The budget is, however, much more than a matter of dollars. It finances federal programs and agencies that are important means by which the government establishes and pursues national objectives. The budget assists millions of households in meeting basic expenses, and it provides a safety net for the sick and the elderly. It enables the country to invest in its future through physical improvement, such as highway construction, and human improvement, such as education and training. It signals to allies and adversaries the role of the United States in the world. And it is one of the principal instruments by which the federal government steers economic activity and stabilizes household incomes.

With so much at stake, it is not surprising that budgeting is a difficult and contentious process. Allocating more than $1 trillion a year is anything but a routine task, for as big as the budget is, there is never enough money to satisfy all the claims on it. To budget is to fight over money and to fight over the things that money buys. The conflict sprawls between the Democratic and Republican parties (and often within them as well) and between the legislative and executive branches. Budgeting causes friction among congressional committees, and between those who make tax policy and those who control spending.

As the scope of this conflict has expanded and the budget has grown and become more important in the economic and political life of the United States, it has attracted more attention. Thousands of budget makers and influencers now work in Washington, many on the staffs of members of Congress or congressional committees and many more representing national corporations, trade associations, state and local governments, and other groups mobilized to expand or protect their share of the budget's largess. News media of all types cover budget issues and

1

actions, reporting on developments in both executive suites and legislative chambers. In some years the budget is the president's agenda as well as the vehicle for much of Congress's legislative effort, a large part of which is packaged into an omnibus revenue and spending bill. In national politics, it seems, now is the age of budgeting.

But as the budget has grown, it has become more constraining and less supple and responsive. An end-of-the-century president inheriting a $1.5 trillion budget may have fewer easy options than did predecessors who worked with budgets that had not yet reached $100 billion. A generation ago, in 1970, I collaborated in the Brookings Institution project, Setting National Priorities. The title and tone of that series optimistically intimated that by means of the budget the government could set priorities and establish policies each year and mold the economy and federal programs to achieve its objectives. The budget was an empowering process; it enhanced the capacity of the government to govern. Today the budget often appears to be a limiting process, imprisoned in old priorities that narrow the opportunities available to the government. The budget crowds out genuine choice; it forces tomorrow's programs to give way to yesterday's decisions.

How can this be? How can the budget be both bigger and weaker? How can it have more resources but less capacity, more programs but fewer options, more effort to control spending but less effective control? A full consideration of these questions would lead to an inquiry into the condition of American national government in the late twentieth century. Budgeting is not the only process that has suffered a loss in capacity; governing also has come upon hard times. It has been weakened by a long period of divided power, a loss of public trust and confidence, a mismatch between what Americans want of government and what they are willing to give it in political and financial support, conflict over the role of the government in the economy, social ills that seem irremediable through governmental action, and more. Budgeting cannot be confident and efficacious when government is not.

To say that the federal government and the machinery of budgeting are weaker than they once were is not to conclude that initiative or change is impossible. Ronald Reagan demonstrated in 1981 and Bill Clinton in 1993 that governing and budgeting are potent forces for redirecting national policies and reallocating public resources. They showed that the budget can be made into an instrument of change, that the opportunities to govern can be expanded, and that the processes of budgeting can be deployed in pursuit of the administration's objectives. They took advantage of the rules and procedures of budgeting to press ahead, even when the easiest course might have been to settle for much less than they finally got. Both presidents invested a lot of scarce political capital in their first budget, with the result that they had much less with which to fight subsequent budget battles.

Inaugural years such as 1981 and 1993 offer bigger opportunities for budgetary action than do the more routine years of a presidency. But every budget provides some opportunities for government to chart its course and mobilize resources for desired ends. To do so, it must come to grips with critical budget issues of the times. As the next century approaches, these issues include the persistent deficit, the adequacy of the tax structure, the ongoing shrinkage in defense forces, limits on discretionary spending, and the built-in escalation of medicare and other entitlements. This is not a full list of the issues vexing the federal budget; it does not include the many choices that the president and Congress make each year in deciding which programs to fund and how much to allot. The handful of issues discussed here are the ones the president and Congress return to year after year, the ones by which the performance of contemporary leaders and institutions is judged.

This chapter examines each of these issues from the perspective of the early years of the Clinton presidency. For each, the discussion focuses on actions already taken, particularly those incorporated in the 1993 budget legislation, and the outlook for the years ahead.

The Deficit

For the foreseeable future, one issue looms above all others: the huge federal deficit. It constrains presidential and congressional actions and has spawned complex rules that affect all budget legislation, as well as some measures that have only an incidental impact on the budget.

Two weeks before he left office in January 1993, George Bush issued budget projections indicating a $327 billion deficit for the 1993 fiscal year then in progress, lower deficits for each of the next three years, and markedly higher deficits near the end of the century. Clinton's first official projections, presented to Congress after he had been in office for a month, showed even higher deficits in 1995 and subsequent fiscal years. Clinton's projections, like Bush's, assumed that no changes would be made in budget policy.

Clinton's options at the start of his presidency would have been far broader if the budget had increments to parcel out rather than deficits to cut. With increments he could have financed the ambitious new programs and expansions he talked about during the 1992 presidential campaign: a new national service corps, more money for Head Start and other children's programs, and the expansion of job training, welfare reform, investment in new technologies, and more. With the budget awash in red ink, Clinton was barred by both the politics and the rules of budgeting from proposing actions that would add to the deficit. It was not tenable for him to insist that coveted initiatives be funded despite the budget's dire condition. Nor could he wish away the deficit the way Ronald Reagan did—with rosy economic forecasts that overestimated future revenue and underestimated the program cuts or tax increases needed to close the budget gap.

Clinton entered office following half a dozen years of prevarication about the deficit (induced by unworkable deficit reduction rules) by politicians of both parties and both branches. He could not risk discrediting his new administration by pretending that the deficit would go away by itself. And he could not assume that journalists,

who had become increasingly skeptical about budget promises and more knowledgeable about the budget's arithmetic than they had been when Reagan came to Washington, would ignore bad news. He also had to reckon with second-guessers at the Congressional Budget Office who had become accustomed to challenging the president's numbers.

Clinton turned the constraints of high deficits into an opportunity to bolster the government's tax resources and to shift some funds from inherited programs to his initiatives. In a February 17, 1993, address to Congress, he described unending deficits as a political albatross that had to be removed so that his administration could get on with its work. "Large deficits," his "A Vision of Change for America" warned, "have virtually assured that each legislative session has been dominated by the deficit debate, encouraging budgetary quick fixes that have shortchanged the nation's long-term public investment and created a deficit of trust."

Clinton's inaugural budget called for almost $500 billion in deficit reduction from fiscal years 1994 to 1998 through a combination of tax increases and spending cuts. The proposed reductions were calculated against a baseline that assumed future spending increases would keep pace with inflation and participation in various entitlement programs would expand. Some critics of the Clinton plan complained that the estimates of deficit reduction were exaggerated, but regardless of how they were viewed, the proposal promised major decreases in the deficit.

To win enactment, Clinton's plan survived a series of close calls in the House and the Senate. It had to go through two rounds of votes, one on the overall plan, another on implementing legislation. Both rounds drew solid Republican opposition, but congressional Democrats held ranks during the major votes, and the plan passed by a comfortable margin. The House and Senate then got down to the business of enacting specific tax and spending changes to meet Clinton's $500 billion target. Because some of the proposals were unacceptable to conservative Democrats, the

3

president had to accept changes in his package. The give-and-take between the White House and congressional Democrats produced a 219-213 majority in the House and a 50-49 tiebreaking vote by the vice president in the Senate. These close votes were repeated, 218-216 in the House and 51-50 in the Senate, when Congress approved the conference report on the deficit reduction bill.

Although Congress made some major changes, the enacted legislation reduced the deficit by approximately the amount that Clinton had requested. The Congressional Budget Office estimated that the baseline deficit had been lowered by $433 billion over five years, beginning with a $33 billion reduction in fiscal year 1994 and building up to $143 billion four years later (table 1-1).

Despite this accomplishment, Clinton has not put the deficit problem behind him. The longer he serves as president, the greater the likelihood that he will have to seek additional reductions. In fact, the problem is likely to persist long after he has left office. In 1994 the CBO forecast that the deficit will remain between $170 billion and $200 billion through the rest of this century and then increase in the early years of the next century, reaching $365 billion in 2004, more than double the estimate for the mid-1990s. This forecast assumes sustained but moderate economic growth and no change in revenue or spending policies. It does not take into account the potentially enormous costs of health care reform.

The further ahead one looks, the more dismal the outlook becomes. Although projections extending twenty or more years ahead are very uncertain, the pressure on future budgets cannot be doubted. When the first wave of baby boomers retires, federal pension and health care spending will soar, and social security, which now has an annual surplus, will incur sizable deficits. The baby boomers will not affect the budget for another fifteen to twenty years, but there is a good chance that the next drive to reduce the deficit will come in Clinton's second term, if he has one. The battle is likely to be tougher than the one fought in 1993.

The deficit has many causes but few solutions. It has been blamed on a weak economy, the surging cost of health care, protracted conflict between the president and Congress over the budget, and the mixed messages sent politicians by voters who want more from government but are unwilling to pay more. Regardless of the causes, no solution will be durable unless it includes significant revenue increases. Clinton recognized this in 1993; he and his successors will face the same predicament in the future.

Taxes

Despite ups and downs, revenues have been a remarkably stable share of GDP for a long time: 18.3 percent of GDP in 1960, before the Great Society and the Vietnam War, and 18.3 percent in 1993. But although this revenue base may have been adequate thirty years ago, it is not today. Medicare and medicaid did not exist in 1960, nor did food stamps, supplemental security income, earned income tax credits, federal support of elementary and secondary education, and dozens of other programs that now have secure niches in the federal budget. The elderly constituted a smaller proportion of the population, and the benefits provided them were a smaller proportion of federal spending. Interest on the national debt was a much smaller burden. And although defense expenditures made up a much larger share of both GDP and total expenditures, their decrease has been more than made up by increases in other expenditures. It is possible to compile a list of program cuts that would bring federal spending into alignment with revenues, but there is no possibility that Congress will approve enough reductions to cover the structural shortfall in revenues.

That shortfall was at least 3 percent of GDP—more than $180 billion—when Clinton became president. This crude estimate is based on a simple assumption: that the ratio of spending to GDP will not, under any foreseeable scenario, fall below the lowest level reached in the almost two decades that the congressional budget process has been in operation. That level—

Table 1-1. Budgetary Impact of 1993 Deficit Reduction Legislation, Fiscal Years 1994-98
Billions of dollars

Actions	1994	1995	1996	1997	1998	Five-year total
			Revenue increases			
Increased tax rate on high-income individuals[a]	15.4	22.8	25.7	24.6	26.3	114.8
Motor fuels taxes	4.4	4.5	7.4	7.5	7.5	31.3
Repeal of medicare tax cap	2.8	6.0	6.4	6.8	7.2	29.2
Increase in taxable portion of social security benefits	1.9	4.6	5.3	6.0	6.7	24.6
Increased corporate tax rate	4.4	2.8	2.9	3.1	3.2	16.4
Other[b]	-2.5	2.7	3.8	12.7	8.2	24.4
Total revenue increases	26.4	43.5	51.5	60.7	58.5	240.6
			Spending cuts			
Medicare[a]	2.1	5.5	11.6	16.4	20.2	55.8
Federal employee benefits	0.4	0.8	2.9	3.7	4.0	12.0
Medicaid	*	1.0	1.6	2.1	2.5	7.1
Other mandatory programs	1.2	1.7	3.5	4.6	5.4	16.4
Discretionary spending caps[a]	0	0	7.7	23.0	37.9	68.5
Spending increases[b]	(0.2)	(2.2)	(4.8)	(6.9)	(7.4)	(21.6)
Total program cutbacks	3.5	7.0	22.5	42.9	62.6	137.9
			Other deficit reduction			
Lower debt service[a]	0.9	3.4	7.5	13.6	21.3	46.8
FCC electromagnetic spectrum auction	1.7	1.8	1.7	1.0	1.0	7.2
Total deficit reduction	32.6	55.5	83.3	118.1	143.4	432.9

Source: Congressional Budget Office, *The Economic and Budget Outlook: An Update* (September 1993), table 2-2.
* Less than 0.5 billion.
   a. Four items, the tax on high-income individuals, lower medicare expenses, discretionary spending caps, and lower debt service, account for two-thirds ($286 billion) of the net deficit reduction.
   b. Spending increases are shown in parentheses because they add to the deficit; they are netted in the totals.

21.3 percent of GDP–was achieved in fiscal years 1977 and 1978.

The inadequacy of the revenue base received repeated legislative attention during the Reagan and Bush presidencies. Between 1982 and 1990 Congress enacted a dozen tax increases that augmented fiscal year 1990 revenue by $250 billion. But these measures were preceded by a huge tax reduction in 1981 that subtracted more than $300 billion from fiscal 1990 revenue. So all the tax increases enacted from 1982 to 1990 did not restore the revenue forgone by the 1981 legislation. When Clinton became president in 1993, the government would have had more revenue if Congress had done nothing by way of tax legislation during the previous dozen years. Of course, it would have been politically impractical for Congress to have been so inactive. But the point remains that Clinton inherited a smaller revenue base than Reagan did.

Clinton's options for expanding the revenue base were limited by his campaign pledge not to raise taxes for the middle class. He would, he had promised, generate new revenue by making millionaires and multinational corporations pay their fair share. As president, however, he quickly learned (if he did not already know) that he would have to produce much more additional revenue than could be extracted from these sources.

The deficit reduction package Clinton prepared strayed from his campaign promises but still paid lip service to them. According to the CBO, most of the new money was to come from high-income earners, redefined to include couples with taxable incomes higher than $140,000 ($115,000 for individuals). The marginal tax rate for taxpayers in this bracket would be raised from 31 percent to 36 percent. Those with taxable incomes above $250,000 faced a 10 percent surcharge that could boost their highest marginal rate to 39.6 percent. Clinton also proposed a hike in the corporate income tax rate, expansion of the medicare tax to cover all earned income, and an expansion of the portion of social security benefits subject to taxation. These and other increases on business and high-income earners accounted for

more than five-sixths of the additional revenue the president sought. The remainder was to come from a broad-based tax on the heat content of coal, oil, and other energy sources.

Clinton previewed the energy tax increase in a prime-time television address on February 15, 1993, two days before his deficit reduction plan was officially presented to Congress. He had hoped, he told middle-class Americans, to avoid taxing them more. "I've worked harder than I've ever worked before in my life to meet that goal. But I can't–because the deficit has increased so much, beyond my earlier estimates and beyond even the worst official government estimates from last year. We just have to face the fact that to make the changes our country needs, more Americans must contribute today."

Clinton's choice was not as clear cut as he portrayed it. Although the energy tax would have provided only a small part of the revenue, it generated most of the controversy in Congress. The House passed a watered-down version, but some important Democratic senators refused to vote for it, jeopardizing passage of all the budget legislation. Congress finally dumped the new energy tax and settled for a small increase in the tax on motor fuels.

The 1993 tax legislation boosted federal revenue by about 1 percentage point of GDP, enough to cover one-third of the estimated revenue shortfall. The deepening deficits projected for the end of this century and the beginning of the next indicate that the 1993 tax increases will not suffice. Taxes probably will be raised again, although not right away. The odds are that Clinton will defer major new tax legislation until the political system has digested the financial implications of the 1993 legislation and until he has enough political strength to tackle the issue.

When the necessity for increasing taxes is once again a prominent budgetary issue, it will be difficult to confine the increase to the most wealthy Americans. To produce enough new revenue, it will be necessary to tax a broad swath of the population. As the 1993 battles demonstrated, this will not be an easy task.

Defense Spending

President Clinton steered his deficit reduction legislation through Congress by claiming that every dollar of tax increase would be matched by a dollar of spending reduction. The actual ratio was tilted toward more taxes, even if savings in debt service are counted as spending cuts (table 1-1). The proportion of deficit reduction achieved through tax actions would be substantially greater if only program reductions were counted as spending cuts.

During his presidency, Clinton faces four problems that dramatically affect spending: the pace at which defense spending is reduced, limitations on discretionary spending, the growth of entitlements, and health care costs. Of these, defense offers the easiest means to achieve spending reductions, but many of the easy cuts were made before Clinton arrived. New defense spending peaked in fiscal year 1985; adjusted for inflation, it has decreased every year since then. Adjusted for inflation, it was 28 percent below the peak when Clinton became president and 35 percent below the peak eighteen months later. Fiscal year 1994 was the ninth consecutive year of attrition in the defense budget (table 1-2). The drop-off has been particularly sharp in defense procurement, which lost two-thirds of its buying power between 1985 and 1994. This decline was not immediately reflected in production levels because the Defense Department drew on unspent resources appropriated in previous years. By the early 1990s, however, these resources had been depleted and procurement plummeted.

The decrease in defense dollars has been accompanied by a shrinkage in defense forces. Table 1-3 shows that these forces have gone through cycles of expansion and contraction since 1980. The buildup began in the late 1970s and accelerated when Ronald Reagan became president. In 1987 the army had more divisions, the air force more air wings, and the navy more combat vessels than they had had seven years earlier. High budget deficits, reports of wasteful defense spending, and shifts in public opinion led to a halt

in the buildup in the late Reagan years. With the end of the cold war during the Bush administration, the Pentagon undertook a planned decrease in its force structure. The fiscal year 1994 column in table 1-3 shows the force programmed by the Defense Department near the end of the Bush presidency. This force would have had 33 percent fewer army divisions, 46 percent fewer active air wings, and 20 percent fewer ships than had been operational during the peak years. The final column in table 1-3 shows the force structure planned in the "bottom-up review" conducted by the Defense Department during President Clinton's first year. It shows further attrition in all defense forces with the exception of the Marine Corps, which is scheduled to grow slightly. However, the decrease planned by Clinton is smaller than that achieved by Bush.

Beyond a certain point, it is increasingly difficult to shrink defense forces without crippling the ability of the United States to respond to world events. Although the bottom-up review did redefine defense missions, it assumed that this country will continue to have worldwide responsibilities that would require large, mobile, and technologically advanced forces.

Discretionary Spending

Defense accounts for half of all discretionary spending, the portion of the budget controlled by annual appropriations decisions. Discretionary programs have been a shrinking part of federal spending for many years. They now account for 35 percent of total outlays, only half the share they had in the early 1960s. By the turn of the century, they are likely to comprise less than 30 percent of federal spending. As table 1-4 shows, both total discretionary spending and discretionary domestic spending have decreased as a share of GDP.

Discretionary domestic spending is now slightly lower than defense spending but is expected to surpass it by the end of the century. Real (inflation-adjusted) discretionary domestic spending was reduced at the start of the Reagan era, regained some resources and stabilized in later

Table 1-2. Defense Outlays, Selected Years, 1960-90, and Estimated, 1995, 1999

Year	Current dollars (billions)	Constant FY 1987 dollars (billions)	Change from previous period (percent)	Defense as part of total outlays (percent)	Defense as part of GDP (percent)
1960	48	220	-16	52	9.5
1965	51	204	- 7	43	7.5
1970	82	263	29	42	8.3
1975	87	184	-30	26	5.7
1980	134	187	2	23	5.1
1985	253	261	40	27	6.4
1990	299	273	5	24	5.5
1995[a]	271	207	-24	18	3.9
1999[a]	258	175	-16	14	2.9

Source: *Budget of the United States Government, Fiscal Year 1995, Historical Tables*, table 6.1.
a. Estimated. The amounts for fiscal years 1995 and 1999 are based on President Clinton's proposed budget for fiscal year 1995.

Reagan years, and rose by about 15 percent during the Bush years. The surprising upturn between 1989 and 1993 was due to Bush's ineffectiveness in budget matters and to the 1990 deficit reduction deal negotiated by Richard Darman. In that deal congressional negotiators accepted dollar limits on discretionary domestic expenditures and changes in certain budget rules in exchange for substantial increases in discretionary expenditures for 1991-93. At the time the agreement was sealed, it was estimated to allow $45 billion in spending increases during the three fiscal years. Table 1-4 shows that actual increases were greater.

The discretionary spending caps were initially set for each of the five fiscal years through 1995, but it was widely assumed that they would be relaxed or removed after the 1992 election. Retaining the original caps would have squeezed discretionary spending during fiscal years 1994 and 1995. But instead of relaxing the caps, Congress tightened them in 1993 and extended them through fiscal 1998. The CBO data in table 1-1 indicate that (excluding debt service) 47 percent of the spending cuts achieved in the 1993

deficit legislation came from the new limits on discretionary spending. One should not be surprised if Congress extends the caps beyond the scheduled 1998 expiration or if it caps expenditures at a level lower than the one set in 1993.

The prospective impact of the caps is evident in table 1-4. If real domestic outlays do decline in 1997-99, total real discretionary spending might be lower at the end of the century than it was at any time during the Reagan presidency. Even more startling, discretionary domestic spending would be a smaller percentage of GDP than it was in the early 1960s before the Great Society programs were launched.

These prospects pose substantial budget problems for President Clinton and Congress. During the 1992 campaign Clinton advocated many program initiatives that would add to discretionary domestic spending. The fiscal year 1994 budget was Clinton's first, and the first in which the spending caps did not accommodate program expansion. Because the president could not find extra room in the discretionary budget for his programs while continuing existing ones, he had to cut back funding for some

Table 1-3. Defense Force Structure, Selected Fiscal Years, 1980-99

Forces	1980	1985	1990	1994	Bottom-up review, 1999
Army divisions (active)	16	18	18	12	10
Marine divisions	3	3	3	3	3
Navy ships	479	541	546	413	347
Tactical air wings (active)	26	25	24	13	13
Active duty personnel (thousands)	2,050	2,152	2,069	1,621	1,453

Source: Congressional Research Service, *Defense Budget for FY 1994: Data Summary* (1993).

established programs. This necessity played into his hands, for it justified a budget prepared by a Democratic president that by his count retrenched more than 150 programs. But even with the proposed cutbacks his budget exceeded the preset discretionary spending limits, and the Senate and House Appropriations Committees scaled back some of his initiatives to preserve existing programs. After Congress completed action on the fiscal 1994 budget, the White House estimated that the president had received 69 percent ($11.5 billion of the $16.7 billion) of the requested increase. However, some high priorities, such as education and training programs, received less than half of the increase sought by the president.

In 1994 the CBO estimated that in fiscal year 1995 the caps will be $4 billion below the amount needed to maintain real spending levels, but the gap will widen to $56 billion in fiscal year 1998. To meet a shortfall equal to approximately 10 percent of total discretionary spending, Clinton will face harder program choices than he did during his first two years in office. The 10 percent reduction he promised in the federal work force–252,000 employees–will go part of the way toward meeting the shortfall, but additional steps will have to be taken.

Entitlements

The pressure on discretionary spending is largely caused by incessant increases in spending for entitlements, which now comprise more than 50 percent of total expenditures, and are expected to exceed $1 trillion a year before the turn of the century. Although current budget rules make limits on discretionary spending independent of the amount spent on entitlements, the unrelenting growth in mandatory spending has inevitably spilled over to discretionary accounts. In 1994, for example, the Senate rejected proposals to reduce the deficit by cutting entitlements; it voted instead to lower the discretionary caps.

No recent president has had much success in reining in entitlements, although several have tried. Virtually all the budget reconciliation measures enacted since 1980 have claimed some savings in entitlements, most often in medicare expenditures. These cutbacks have usually been achieved through freezes or other limitations on payments to providers or by raising fees to users rather than by cutting services or benefits. Presidents and Congress have taken credit for substantial savings at the same time that program expenditures have escalated.

Because elected politicians like to provide pro-

Table 1-4. Discretionary Domestic Spending, Selected Fiscal Years, 1963-93, and Projected 1996 and 1999
Billions of dollars unless otherwise specified

Year	Discretionary outlays		Discretionary domestic outlays	Real discretionary domestic outlays[a]	Discretionary domestic outlays	
	Percent of total outlays	Percent of GDP			Percent of total outlays	Percent of GDP
1963	70	13.4	19	80	17	3.3
1966	70	12.8	30	113	22	4.1
1969	66	13.1	35	114	19	3.7
1972	58	11.6	49	132	21	4.3
1975	49	10.8	67	139	20	4.4
1978	48	10.1	106	176	23	4.9
1981	45	10.4	137	173	20	4.6
1984	45	10.3	135	149	16	3.7
1987	44	10.0	147	147	15	3.3
1990	40	9.2	183	162	15	3.3
1993	39	8.6	228	186	16	3.6
1996[b]	34	7.4	263	197	17	3.5
1999[b]	30	6.3	269	185	15	3.1

Source: *Budget of the United States Government, Fiscal Year 1995, Historical Tables*, tables 8.1, 8.2, 8.3, 8.4.
a. The decline projected in real discretionary domestic outlays near the end of the century assumes that current limits in discretionary spending will not be raised or superseded by emergency appropriations. If the caps remain in effect, discretionary spending will rise less than the rate of inflation.
The discretionary spending limits apply to the totals; they do not distinguish between defense, international, or domestic programs. Within the limits, more spending on one of the categories would mean less for the others.
b. Estimated.

grams but must cut spending, they have devised budgetary tools that enable them to accomplish both ends. For discretionary spending they have set dollar limits on totals without voting on specific program cuts; for entitlements they have cut assumed spending increases while allowing expenditures to rise. An understanding of how they manage this feat requires an understanding of budgetary arithmetic, especially baseline projections, which is the subject of the next chapter.

Given the agility with which budget makers have produced substantial savings while avoiding severe program cuts and allowing costs to increase, the president and Congress should be able to continue this practice for many years. Indeed, as entitlement spending rises so, too, will the savings they claim to have achieved.

There is, however, one problem. Expenses for some entitlement programs are projected to rise so steeply in the years ahead that, if nothing is done, they will claim a greater share of the federal budget and of national income and doom efforts to constrain the deficit. This likelihood applies especially to medicare and medicaid, the principal health care entitlements in the federal budget.

Health Care Reform

The Congressional Budget Office has projected that if current policies are continued, federal spending will increase $1 trillion dollars between fiscal years 1994 and 2004. Almost half this amount ($438 billion) will be accounted for by medicare and medicaid. And with the higher interest payments attributable to these programs included, their share of the increase would be greater than 50 percent. If the projections are reasonably accurate, the budget's future will be determined by trends in health care costs.

In health care programs, it is one thing to claim savings but quite another to control costs. The need for cost control was one of the factors that impelled President Clinton to place health care reform at the top of his domestic policy agenda. He submitted an ambitious reform package to Congress in the fall of 1993, a little more than a month after it approved his deficit reduction plan. The proposal would change both the financing and organization of health care by requiring employers to pay at least 80 percent of the premiums for a prescribed package of benefits and by establishing regional alliances to manage competition among health care providers. All Americans would be cov-ered, regardless of their medical, financial, or work status. The details of this complex scheme need not concern us here, but its budgetary implications must.

As proposed by Clinton, much of the new health care system would be off budget. He reasoned that because the premiums paid by employers and workers and the expenditures by alliances for the purchase of health care services would neither enter nor leave the U.S. treasury, they should not be counted in the federal budget. The Congressional Budget Office, however, took the position that inasmuch as the payments to and by the health care alliances would be mandated by the federal government, they should be budgeted as federal receipts and expenditures.

Congress, of course, failed to act on the Clinton proposal. But regardless of whether some more modest reform is passed in the next Congress, future budgets will be hostage to health care costs. As these costs continue to be propelled upward by technological advances, medical inflation, and the aging of the population, the odds are that Bill Clinton will not be the last president to face a crisis in the health care system. Nor will he be, therefore, the last president to face a crisis in federal budgeting.

Chapter 2

The Arithmetic
of Budgeting

Every budget is a compilation of numbers on the revenues, expenditures, borrowing, and debt of the government. The federal budget has millions of these numbers, computed according to rules and practices that have accumulated over the years. The rules do not always conform to the way finances are accounted for by other American governments or by businesses. Many are not recognized in law or in accounting principles, but they nevertheless determine how revenues and expenditures are tallied in the federal budget.

The first step in interpreting or using the budget must be to understand what the numbers mean. In federal budgeting, not every dollar taken in is counted as a receipt, nor is every dollar paid out counted as an outlay. To say therefore that the government collects $1.3 trillion or spends $1.5 trillion a year is to mean that these are the official totals generated according to the budget rules currently in effect. Different rules would produce different totals.

This chapter explains the basic rules and practices of budgetary arithmetic. The chapter considers the scope of the budget and its basic building blocks–revenues, budget authority, and outlays–then focuses on facets of budgeting in which estimates and assumptions are critical, such as constructing baselines, measuring the budgetary impact of legislation, and projecting the effects of economic conditions.

The Politics of Budgetary Arithmetic

The arithmetic of budgeting is political arithmetic; it influences budgetary actions and outcomes. Even when the numbers are compiled strictly in accordance with technical rules and established practices, as is usually the case, they have political consequences. They influence public perceptions about the budget, such as the size of the deficit. They may influence the behavior of officials by making one type of transaction more or less expensive than another, and they may impede or facilitate the passage of legislation by increasing or reducing the estimated budgetary impact of a pending measure.

Although the rules for recording revenues and expenditures have always been important, recent efforts to control federal spending and the deficit have given them added prominence. How outlays are counted may determine whether particular expenditures are within current budget rules or in violation of them. Enforcing the rules is rarely straightforward, for it often depends more on the behavior of individuals and businesses than on the actions of government. Each budget sets forth amounts to be spent during the next year on medicaid, food stamps, unemployment assistance, social security, and other benefit programs. These amounts are not firm numbers. They are based on assumptions about future economic conditions, the number of persons who will participate in the programs, and the payments each person will receive. The budget says more about the numbers in it than about the underlying assumptions, but the assumptions are where political influence has broadest scope.

The rules and assumptions are entrusted to budget staffs in the executive and legislative branches: the president's Office of Management and Budget and the Congressional Budget Office. These staffs often coordinate their work, and each agency has a strong interest in upholding the integrity of the budget process, but neither can avoid being entangled in the political world of budgeting in which it operates. As a key unit in the Executive Office of the President, OMB cannot openly take positions counter to the policies announced by the White House. As a congressional staff agency responsible to many committees and members, CBO must vigilantly guard its independence. On many routine matters of budgetary arithmetic CBO and OMB agree, but major conflicts occasionally explode into the open.

One such clash occurred over President Clinton's proposed health care reforms. OMB estimated that if enacted the president's reforms would reduce the budget deficit by almost $60 billion in fiscal years 1995-2000. Looking at the same proposals, CBO concluded that they would add $70 billion to the deficit. The wide difference between the two estimates derived from differing assumptions about the future cost of health care.

Both OMB and CBO claimed that their estimates were free of political influence. Even if this were so, the numbers they generated had important political consequences. OMB's optimistic estimate enabled Clinton to reconcile the twin objectives of health care reform and deficit reduction; CBO's more cautious numbers compelled congressional committees to revise the legislation before taking it to the floor.

With so much riding on the assumptions and the numbers, it matters whose estimates are given greater credence in the budget process. By law, OMB is the budget's official scorekeeper; it measures the budgetary impact of legislation. In practice, CBO has the upper hand when the numbers pertain to pending legislation. The Budget Enforcement Act of 1990 states that OMB's estimates of the budgetary impact of enacted legislation shall be authoritative. Before enactment, however, Congress almost always defers to CBO's judgment on these matters.

Having two scorekeepers is not just a matter of getting a second opinion. The arrangement is a by-product of the American separation of powers. Congress is determined to maintain its independence in budgetary matters. But it is in the interest of the president to base his budget on numbers produced by his staff rather than by Congress's budget experts. When Bill Clinton became president, he assumed that because Democrats controlled both the executive and legislative branches there would be no need for separate budget scorekeeping, and he vowed in his February 1993 budget speech to Congress to rely on CBO assumptions and data in estimating the deficit reduction that his budget would produce. "Let's at least argue about the same set of numbers," Clinton urged, "so the American people will think we're shooting straight with them." Within a few months, however, the administration was using its own budget and economic assumptions, which differed from those issued by CBO.

Budgetary arithmetic, like much else in budgeting, is an amalgam of procedures and politics. To assume that the numbers are manipulated to serve political interests would ignore the remarkable extent to which entries in the budget are determined by technical rules. But to assume that the numbers materialize out of a politics-free process would ignore the extent to which budget makers try to shape the amounts to their liking. The balance between politics and process varies with different facets of budgeting. Where the numbers represent actual transactions, technical rules predominate; where they represent assumptions about future conditions, there is greater scope for political influence. Because the budget is increasingly in the form of assumed

13

rather than actual transactions, political arithmetic has become more important than it was a generation ago.

Scope of the Budget

The president's budget for the 1995 fiscal year estimated that the federal government would spend $1.52 trillion. It also estimated that the government would spend $300 billion less–$1.22 trillion. Both sets of numbers were right. The first figure was calculated on a unified basis; the second counted only on-budget outlays. How much the budget adds up to depends on what is included. By some counts, the totals are much higher than those in the broadest measures reported by the government.

In 1968 the federal government adopted the principle of a unified budget that accounts for all revenues and expenditures. This principle, enunciated by the President's Commission on Budget Concepts, was adopted to facilitate use of the budget as an instrument of economic policy and to enable the government to establish priorities among programs financed by different sources or managed by different federal entities.

The unified budget includes federal and trust funds, operating and investment expenditures, the transactions of most government-owned enterprises, and direct and guaranteed loans. But despite its broad scope, the budget does not provide a truly comprehensive account of federal revenues and expenditures. Certain funds and transactions are excluded.

General, Special, and Trust Funds

The budget consists of three main groups of funds: general, special, and trust funds. General funds are not earmarked by law for specific purposes. In the general fund, therefore, there is no express link between revenues and expenditures. Almost all income taxes are paid into the general fund, which is also financed by excise taxes, certain other receipts, and borrowing. The general fund pays for national defense, interest on the public debt, and the operating expenses of most federal agencies. It accounts for almost two-thirds of total federal revenue and three-quarters of total outlays. The budget deficit is concentrated in the general fund.

Special funds are earmarked for particular purposes, but they are not designated by law as trust funds. Most special funds, such as the Land and Water Conservation Fund and the National Wildlife Refuge Fund, are financed by user fees or other special collections. Although special funds are accounted for separately, the budget combines them with general funds under the label federal funds. The government does not pay any interest if it uses the balance in the special funds.

Trust funds are restricted by law to designated programs or uses. The funds receive most of their revenues from earmarked taxes, such as social security taxes and medicare premiums. Unlike the general fund, which habitually runs a deficit, the trust funds have surpluses that are borrowed by the federal government and for which it pays prevailing interest rates (table 2-1). These funds held more than $1 trillion in balances at the start of the 1994 fiscal year, and are expected to approach $2 trillion by the end of the century. The federal government borrows these balances and pays more than $80 billion in interest (out of the general fund) to the trust funds each year.

On-Budget and Off-Budget Entities

The principle of a unified budget dictates that federal and trust funds be combined in the budget. Nevertheless, Congress has excluded social security and the Postal Service from official computations of the deficit and other budget totals. It gave off-budget status to these entities to guard against diversion of their resources to deficit reduction or other uses. Thus the budget reports two deficits: the on-budget deficit, which excludes social security and the Postal Service, and the consolidated or unified deficit, which includes them. Most references to the deficit in government reports and the news media include the off-budget entities.

Table 2-1. Income, Outgo, and Balances of Major Trust Funds, Fiscal Year 1993 and Estimated for 1999
Billions of dollars

Trust fund	1993				1999			
	Balance[a]	Interest income[b]	Total income	Outgo	Balance[a]	Interest income[b]	Total income	Outgo
Social security (OASDI)	374	27	351	305	823	48	510	414
Medicare (hospital insurance)	126	11	95	92	173	12	149	138
Medicare (supplementary medical insurance)	23	2	61	54	20	1	113	110
Federal civilian employees' retirement	319	26	63	35	487	31	73	46
Military retirement	98	10	35	26	138	12	38	33
Highway trust	23	2	20	19	22	1	25	24
Airports and airways	13	1	4	7	17	1	8	7
Unemployment	37	3	41	40	61	3	33	29
All other	68	2	34	29	86	3	31	28
Total	1,080	82	702	602	1,827	111	977	825

Source: *Budget of the United States Government, Fiscal Year 1995, Analytical Perspectives,* table 18.4.
a. Fund balance at the end of the fiscal year.
b. The interest earned by the trust funds is also budgeted as interest paid by federal funds. This interest is netted out in calculating budget totals.

Capital and Operating Expenditures

Capital and operating expenses are commingled in the budget. In contrast to the practice of state and local governments, investment and current expenditure are not segregated. Both expenditures for the current operation of government agencies and for the acquisition of buildings, roads, weapons, or other physical assets are budgeted as outlays. Proposals have been made from time to time to divide the budget into current expenditures and capital investment, but they have not been adopted. The budget does, however, provide supplementary information on investment outlays.

The main reason for unifying the budget a quarter of a century ago was to improve its usefulness as an instrument of economic policy. If capital and operating accounts were separated, the two budgets would have to be combined to assess the total fiscal impact of government policy. Establishing a capital budget would give rise to issues that might add or subtract billions of dollars from the amounts classified as investments. For example, should the capital budget be limited to investments in physical and financial assets or should it be expanded to include investments in education and training or research and development that are expected to yield benefits in future years? State governments, which have had extensive experience in capital budgeting, generally apply a restrictive test, but the federal government might face enormous pressure to include a broad range of investments in "human capital."

Government-Owned or Government-Sponsored Corporations

The federal government owns and operates some multi-billion-dollar enterprises, including the Postal Service, the Government National Mortgage Association, the Pension Benefit Guaranty Corporation, and the Overseas Private Investment Corporation. Corporations owned in whole or in part by the federal government are included in the budget on a net basis; that is, expenses are subtracted from revenues to show the net budgetary impact. In 1993, for example, the Postal Service had $50 billion in gross outlays, but only $1.4 billion was included in the consolidated budget.

The budget presents two business-type statements for most corporations, one on revenue and expense, the other on financial condition. The statements of financial condition resemble commercial balance sheets; they show the assets, liabilities, and equity in the corporation. Because these statements are based on accrual or commercial accounting standards that differ from the principles applied to federal agencies, they cannot be combined with regular budget schedules.

In contrast to government-owned corporations, government-sponsored enterprises are excluded from the budget because they are deemed to be private entities. The federal government does not have any equity in GSEs, most of which receive financing from private sources. Most of these enterprises engage in credit activities; they borrow funds in capital markets and lend them to finance agricultural, housing, education, and other programs. There are about a dozen GSEs, including the Student Loan Marketing Association (Sallie Mae), the Federal National Mortgage Association (Fannie Mae), the Federal Home Loan Mortgage Corporation (Freddie Mac), and the farm credit banks (table 2-2).

Although the GSEs serve government objectives and issue obligations that are implicitly guaranteed by the federal government (some have a standby line of credit at the Treasury), their budgets are not reviewed by the president or Congress. Financial schedules of the government-sponsored enterprises are published in the budget but are not included in the totals.

Direct and Guaranteed Loans

The government participates in two types of loan transactions. It makes direct loans to borrowers and it guarantees loans made by other lenders. The Federal Credit Reform Act of 1990 changed the budgetary treatment of both types of loans from a cash basis, in which disbursements are recorded as outlays, to the subsidized cost of the loans.

The new system requires that funds be budgeted and appropriated to cover the estimated costs of the loans. The subsidy cost is defined in the 1990 act as "the estimated long-term cost to the government of a direct loan or a loan guarantee, calculated on a net present-value basis, excluding administrative costs." The net present value is calculated by discounting estimated future cash flows (disbursements by the government and payments to it) of each loan account to the present, using a discount rate equal to the interest paid by the Treasury on loans of comparable maturity. In general, loans may be obligated or guaranteed only to the extent that Congress has appropriated funds to cover the subsidy cost.

Estimating the subsidy cost is a complex process that is done annually for each credit account. The process is designed to separate the subsidized portion–the cost to the government–from the unsubsidized portion, the amount that will be repaid, recovered, or not defaulted. Distinguishing between the subsidized and unsubsidized portions of loans entails three types of accounts: *Program accounts* receive appropriations for the subsidy cost of loans and for associated administrative expenses. *Financing accounts* handle all cash inflows and outflows of loans made or guaranteed since fiscal

Table 2-2. Government-Sponsored Enterprises

Enterprise	Function
AGRICULTURE	
Banks for cooperatives	These banks were established by the government and are owned by farmers' cooperatives. The banks obtain funds from sales of bonds (which are not guaranteed by the government) and lend funds to agriculture and rural utility cooperatives.
Farm credit banks	These banks make short-term production and long-term real estate loans to farmers and ranchers, using funds obtained through the sale of bonds (not guaranteed by the government) to the public.
Federal Agricultural Mortgage Corporation (Farmer Mac)	Farmer Mac was established in 1987 to provide a secondary market for farm and rural housing mortgages. It guarantees or purchases pooled securities backed by pools of eligible loans. Its funds come mostly from private sources, but it has a line of credit at the Treasury.
BANKS AND SAVINGS AND LOANS	
Financing Corporation (FICO)	FICO was set up in 1987 to function as a financing vehicle for the savings and loan industry, using borrowed funds and other money. FICO's authority to borrow was terminated in 1991.
Resolution Funding Corporation (REFCORP)	The sole purpose of REFCORP, which was established in 1989, was to borrow billions of dollars and to remit the proceeds to the Resolution Trust Corporation, an enterprise included in the budget.
EDUCATION	
Student Loan Marketing Association (Sallie Mae)	Sallie Mae was established in 1972 to expand student loan funds by purchasing insured student loans, making advances to lenders of these loans, and other secondary market activities.
College Construction Loan Insurance Association (Connie Lee)	Connie Lee was established in 1986 to guarantee bonds and loans for constructing and renovating college facilities.
HOUSING	
Federal National Mortgage Association (Fannie Mae)	Fannie Mae, established in 1938, provides a secondary market for residential mortgages. Its primary activity is to purchase these mortgages and to pool them into secondary instruments. It assists in financing about one-sixth of these mortgages.
Federal Home Loan Mortgage Corporation (Freddie Mac)	Freddie Mac, established in 1970, serves as a conduit for the flow of funds from capital markets to mortgage lenders by maintaining a secondary market for mortgage-backed securities. It participated in almost $1 trillion of loan transactions in 1993.
Federal home loan banks	These banks were chartered by the government in 1932. They facilitate access to housing and community development by making advances to member savings and loan associations, credit unions, and others.

Source: *Budget of the United States Government, Appendix, Fiscal Year 1995*, pp. 1029-42.

Table 2-3. Accounting for Direct and Guaranteed Loans

Description	Program account	Financing account	Liquidating account
Purpose of account	Receives appropriation for subsidy budget authority	Handles all cash flows for loans and guarantees	Handles all loans made before fiscal year 1992
Budget status	Subsidy cost included in budget	Means of financing (not included in receipts or outlays)	Cash receipts and payments included in budget
Cash inflows	Receives appropriation for subsidy budget authority and administrative expenses. Has permanent indefinite budget authority for subsidy reestimates	Receives subsidy payment from program account Borrows unsubsidized part of loans from Treasury Collects repayments, fees, and interest from borrowers. Receives interest on reserves held by Treasury.	Collects repayments, interest, and fees on old loans
Cash outflows	Pays subsidy outlays to financing account	Disburses new loans. Repays borrowings to Treasury with interest. Pays defaults and interest subsidies on guaranteed loans	Does not make any new loans. Pays defaults and interest subsidies on old loans

year 1992 (when the new system took effect). *Liquidating accounts* handle cash flows deriving from loans made before 1992. Table 2-3 explains the budgetary status of these types of accounts.

Although the new rules are complex and involve assumptions about the volume and timing of future defaults, recoveries, and payments, there is also a political dimension to the credit budgeting system. In shifting from a cash basis to a subsidized basis, the 1990 reform made direct loans less expensive and guaranteed loans more

costly. In the past the entire amount paid out in direct loans was budgeted as an outlay; now, however, only the subsidized portion of the loan is outlayed in the budget. For guaranteed loans the old system did not record outlays until a default occurred and the government made good on its obligation. Now estimated outlays are recorded in advance. Although it is too early to tell, the change in the budgeted cost of the two types of loans may well lead to an increase in direct lending and a decrease in guaranteed loans.

Revenues and Expenditures

The federal budget has various conventions for computing revenues and expenditures. These practices affect not only the amounts entered in the budget but also the behavior of participants in the budget process and budget outcomes.

Receipts

Money collected by the government in the exercise of its sovereign power is recorded as a budget receipt; money received by the government in the conduct of business-type operations is counted as an offsetting collection. Borrowed funds are not counted as a receipt, and repayment of debt is not counted as an outlay. The $1 trillion in revenues collected each year comes mostly from taxes, but customs duties, fines, and compulsory user fees also contribute. Business-type revenue comes from the sale of assets, the operation of government enterprises, and certain voluntary user charges. This income does not appear on the revenue side of the budget but is netted against outlays, usually those of the account or agency that collects the money. Some of these collections are deducted from total budget outlays.

Counting income as an offsetting receipt rather than as a revenue does not affect the size of the deficit, but it may, under some interpretations, make room in the budget for additional spending within the expenditure caps now in effect (see chapter 3). To the extent that offsetting receipts permit additional spending within the caps, the administration and federal agencies have an incentive to make greater use of them.

Budget Authority and Outlays

The federal government has an obligations-based budget system. The key points of decision and control relate to the obligations that agencies are authorized to incur, not to the outlays disbursed during the year. When Congress appropriates money, it gives agencies *budget authority* to enter into obligations. Budget authority may also

be provided in any other legislation that enables an agency to incur obligations. *Obligations* occur when agencies enter into contracts, execute purchase orders, employ personnel, or take any action that commits the government to the payment of funds. Some obligations such as those resulting from loan guarantees are contingent on default or some other occurrence; the subsidy cost of these contingencies is included in the definition of budget authority. *Outlays* occur when obligations are paid off through checks, electronic fund transfers, or cash.

Money that first becomes available for obligation in a particular fiscal year is counted as *new budget authority*. In programs that have permanent appropriations, new budget authority becomes available each year without congressional action. By law, for example, all income of the social security trust fund and most other trust funds is available for obligation; but only the amount obligated in a fiscal year is counted as new budget authority.

Although outlays generally receive greater public attention because of their bearing on the deficit, the provision of budget authority is usually the key point at which Congress controls federal spending. Congress does not directly control the annual outlays of federal programs or agencies; rather, it regulates outlays indirectly by providing new budget authority. Each year's outlays derive principally from new budget authority, but a portion also derives from budget authority carried over from previous years. For example, President Clinton's budget for fiscal year 1995 estimated that outlays would total $1.52 trillion. More than three-quarters of this amount, about $1.18 trillion, was estimated to come from new budget authority for that fiscal year. The remainder ($335 billion) was estimated to come from budget authority provided in previous years (exhibit 2-1).

Budget authority and outlays can be thought of as akin to deposits and withdrawals in bank accounts. When Congress provides budget authority, it deposits financial resources in an agency's account. When obligations are incurred, the encumbered resources are no longer available for other purposes. When bills are paid and outlays occur, resources are withdrawn from the account.

The relation of budget authority and outlays varies among federal programs and depends on the rate at which new budget authority is disbursed. In programs with high spendout (outlay) rates, most new budget authority is expended during the fiscal year for which the funds were provided; when the spendout rate is low, most of the outlays occur in later years. Budget authority provided for salaries and other operating expenditures typically has high spendout rates; resources provided for procurement or construction have relatively low rates. For example, more than 90 percent of the new budget authority appropriated for military personnel is spent during the first year, but less than 5 percent of the new money voted for shipbuilding is used in the year for which it is provided. Regardless of the spendout rate, the outlays set forth in the budget for the current or future fiscal years are merely estimates of the amounts to be disbursed. Actual payments are often higher or lower.

The statistical relationship of budget authority and outlays provides useful clues to program trends. When new budget authority is increasing faster than outlays, more resources are being supplied than are being consumed, and program spending is likely to increase. When, however, budget authority is flat or contracting but outlays are expanding, program spending is decreasing because resources are being used faster than they are being replenished. (This pattern does not apply to trust funds.) Figure 2-1 shows trends in defense spending from 1976 to 1994. Budget authority rose sharply during the early 1980s, followed by leveling off and then decline later in the decade. When defense budget authority was rising, the gap between it and outlays widened. But when growth in budget authority ceased, outlays continued to rise and the gap narrowed. By the late 1980s, outlays exceeded new budget authority, signaling the shrinkage in defense resources that continued into the next decade.

Figure 2-1. Defense Spending, Fiscal Years 1976-94
Billions of dollars

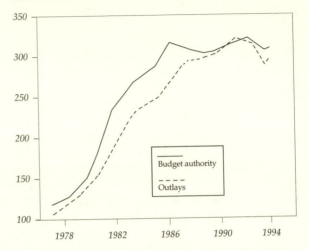

Source: *Budget of the United States Government, Fiscal Year 1995, Historical Tables*, tables 3.2, 5.1.

Baseline Projections

In considering revenue or spending legislation, Congress must be able to measure the impact of its actions on the budget. This task is relatively simple for programs funded in annual appropriations; Congress can compare the amounts provided to the previous year's appropriation or to the president's request for the next year. But the task is difficult when Congress acts on revenue or entitlement legislation; in these cases, it must take account of exogenous factors, principally the condition of the economy and the behavior of those affected by its decisions. The revenue yield of tax legislation depends on the volume of economic activity and on adjustments by taxpayers to changes in the tax laws. The cost of entitlement legislation depends on variables such as inflation and unemployment rates, demographic and income trends, and the extent to which eligible persons avail themselves of services. Future conditions can only be assumed at the time Congress acts on revenue and entitlement legislation. These are the areas of budget-

Exhibit 2-1. Budget Authority and Outlays, Fiscal Year 1995
Billions of dollars

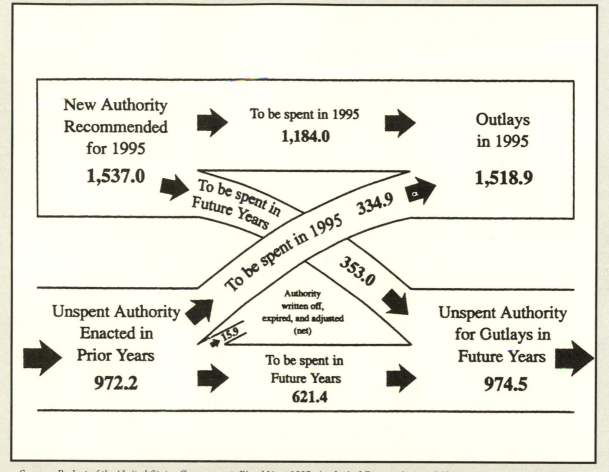

Source: *Budget of the United States Government, Fiscal Year 1995, Analytical Perspectives*, p. 268.

(a) This exhibit shows the relationship of total new budget authority and total outlays in the fiscal year 1995 budget. It shows that not all budget authority is spent in the year for which it is provided, and part of each year's outlays derives from budget authority provided in previous years. The flow of outlays from budget authority is measured by the spendout rate (also called the outlay rate).

(b) Total new budget authority typically exceeds total outlays for a fiscal year because programs with long lead times, such as construction, spend most resources in out years, not in the year for which they were provided, and trust funds, such as social security, build up balances that are held in reserve for future expenditure.

(c) Unspent budget authority carried into future years consists of both obligated and unobligated balances. Most obligated balances are for contracts, most unobligated balances are in trust funds.

(d) The outlays in this diagram (and in most budget schedules) are only estimates of the amounts to be spent. Actual outlays for a fiscal year vary, sometimes significantly, from the estimate.

ing where assumptions rather than actual numbers are all-important in computing the effects of legislative or executive decisions.

Assumptions about future revenues and expenditures are incorporated in baseline projections prepared by CBO or OMB. The projections, usually for each of the next five years, are based on the assumption that current policy will continue in effect. The baseline incorporates assumptions about inflation as well as projected workload changes mandated by law, such as an increase in the number of persons receiving social security payments. It does not include discretionary workload changes, such as an increase in the number of patent applications processed by the Patent Office.

Once the baseline has been projected, any executive or legislative action that would cause revenue or spending to deviate from the baseline is measured as a policy change. Table 2-4 provides a hypothetical example of baseline projections and of how they are used in estimating the budgetary impact of legislation. This illustration deals only with expenditures, but the same method is used for measuring policy changes in federal revenues.

In the hypothetical case, baseline spending would increase from $100 million in the current year to $141 million five years later. The $41 million increase is assumed; it is not the increase that will occur over the next five years. The actual increase will be $41 million only if the assumptions underlying the baseline–4 percent annual inflation and 3 percent annual workload increases–materialize.

Making these assumptions entails a great deal of uncertainty about the future budget implications of current policy. In many programs OMB and CBO have used similar assumptions and their baseline projections have been similar. But in a few cases, the agencies have used different starting points and have ended up with very different baselines. Defense and health care financing have been two of the most contentious areas, defense because of disagreement over what constitutes current defense policy, health care

because of difficulties in predicting changes in the cost and utilization of medical services.

In a world of perfect information, future revenues and spending would be equal to baseline projections, plus or minus the budgetary effects of policy changes. But information about the future is far from perfect, so actual revenues and spending often diverge significantly from projected levels. Despite the uncertainty and the errors, however, the legislative process cannot wait until the future is known; the best Congress can do is to act on the basis of the assumptions and projections available to it.

In the hypothetical example shown in table 2-4, policy changes would reduce projected spending below baseline levels. The estimated reductions amount to $3.08 million in the first year and grow to $19.15 million in the fifth. Deficit reduction is conventionally measured as the cumulative effect of these policy changes over a five-year period. In this example, the estimated savings from policy changes add up to $53 million over five years.

The typical deficit reduction results in spending higher than the current level but less than the baseline. When this occurs, politicians can portray their actions both as a spending cut and as a spending increase. They can use the baseline to demonstrate that the deficit has been cut, and they can use current spending levels to demonstrate that programs have been protected. Making the case both ways is no small feat; it enables cross-pressured politicians to satisfy Americans' conflicting demands for smaller deficits and less spending on the one hand and bigger programs on the other.

The 1993 deficit reduction package illustrates how the president and Congress produce big savings while minimizing program cutbacks. According to CBO, medicare accounted for $56 billion (over five years) of deficit reduction. That is a lot of money, and it would seem to have violated the pledge President Clinton made to Congress on February 17, 1993, when he launched his deficit reduction drive. "Let me be clear. There will also be no new cuts in medicare.... Let me repeat this because I know it matters to a

Table 2-4. Hypothetical Baseline Projections and Policy Changes, Fiscal Years 1994-98
Millions of dollars

Projections and changes	1994	1995	1996	1997	1998
Initial projection	100.00	107.12	114.74	122.91	131.66
Assumptions					
4 percent inflation	4.00	4.28	4.59	4.92	5.27
3 percent workload increase	3.12	3.34	3.58	3.83	4.11
Estimated increase	7.12	7.62	8.17	8.75	9.38
Baseline projections	107.12	114.74	122.91	131.66	141.04
Policy changes					
Cap inflation increase at 2 percent	-2.00	-4.20	-6.63	-9.30	-12.23
Change laws so that workload rises an estimated 2 percent	-1.08	-2.30	-3.67	-5.20	-6.92
Total policy changes	-3.08	-6.50	-10.30	-14.50	-19.15
Projected spending	104.04	108.24	112.61	117.16	121.89

lot of you on both sides of the aisle. This plan does not make a recommendation for new cuts in medicare benefits for any beneficiary." Had Clinton failed to protect medicare, the deficit legislation would not have been enacted.

How did the president and Congress manage to pare so much without cutting benefits? Medicare proved that the job is not as difficult as one might think. About $50 billion came from reductions in baseline payments to providers, some of which would probably not be counted as cuts if more reasonable standards were used. For example, fees for surgical services were allowed to rise 8.6 percent in 1994, far above general inflation and even above medical inflation, but below the 12.2 percent allowed by formula. Payments to hospitals were reduced by 7.4 percent, compared to a 10 percent reduction in effect for 1993-95. The scorekeepers at the Congressional Budget Office recorded this smaller reduction as a multi-billion-dollar saving because baseline projections were higher. Several billion dollars more were saved by

extending the requirement that medicare part B premiums recoup 25 percent of program costs. The spending cuts produced by these bookkeeping tactics and some other extensions and tinkerings with medicare payments permitted a smattering of medicare improvements in the deficit reduction measure.

Like other features of budgeting, the baseline was developed for technical reasons–to measure policy change–but it also serves political ends. It influences public perceptions about the budget, gives budget makers incentives to cut the deficit in certain ways rather than in others, and protects some programs against inflation. In the case of entitlements, it transforms the decision facing the president and members of Congress from how much should spending be increased? to how much should spending be cut? This transformation enables politicians to claim more credit for cutting the deficit while making it more difficult for them to cut the deficit.

So much of the baseline hinges on the assumptions used in making the projections that there is ample scope for politicians to generate numbers more to their liking. They can meet deficit reduction targets through temporary savings rather than through structural changes in programs. They can schedule cutbacks in the next few years while deferring spending increases to later years, beyond the period for which baseline projections are drawn. By the time budget projections are made for these later years, the spending increases are part of the baseline (because they were previously enacted into law).

Baselines weaken the president's role in budgeting, for they provide a benchmark for congressional action that is wholly independent of his recommendations. The baseline does not move up or down a single dollar if the president asks for more or less. In measuring the impact of revenue or spending legislation in terms of the baseline, Congress does not even have to know what the president has recommended.

Economic Assumptions

Assumptions about the future performance of the economy are among the main variables in constructing budget baselines. These also are among the most turbulent and uncertain variables, especially during transitional periods when the economy is moving into or out of recession.

The relationship of the budget and the economy is reciprocal. Budget policy influences economic conditions, and economic performance influences budget outcomes. The size of the budget and the deficit, the structure and amount of taxes, and the pattern of expenditure influence the rate of economic growth, employment levels, price changes, and interest rates. In making budget decisions, the president and Congress must be mindful of the potential effects on these measures of economic performance.

They also must take account of the effects of current and prospective economic conditions on the budget. They must make assumptions about nominal and real economic growth, short-term and long-term interest rates, and inflation and unemployment trends. The president's budget

forecasts economic performance for the current and next five calendar years, and his revenue, spending, and deficit estimates are based on these economic assumptions. Congress is not bound by the president's assumptions; it usually relies on CBO's forecast.

Because the budget is predicated on assumptions, the extent to which the president's or Congress's budget policies materialize depends strongly on whether the assumptions prove accurate. Major discrepancies between assumed and actual economic conditions will translate into significant variances between expected and actual budget results. Table 2-5 shows the budget's sensitivity to unforeseen changes in economic conditions. Deviation of the economy from the assumed path will lead to higher or lower revenues, outlays, and the deficit. Much of the adjustment of the budget to economic change is automatic; it occurs without presidential or congressional action, and it occurs whether it is welcome or not. Revenues are particularly sensitive to the rate of economic growth; outlays are sensitive to the interest rate on government debt.

Even a temporary deviation from the expected economic course will have lingering effects. According to the OMB estimates (from which table 2-5 is drawn), if actual economic growth were 1 percentage point less than forecast in 1994, but reached projected levels in each of the next five years, the fiscal year 1999 deficit would nevertheless be $30 billion higher than the level projected five years earlier. Over the full six years the cumulative deficit would be more than $130 billion above projections. Almost three-quarters of this overrun would be due to revenue shortfalls.

The effect on the budget becomes greater the longer the economy varies from its expected course. If economic growth were 1 percentage point less in each of the six years, the cumulative deficit would be $350 billion higher than the original projections. And the variance from budgeted levels widens each year the economy stagnates. One percentage point lower growth would subtract an estimated $7 billion from federal revenues in the first year and $107 billion in the sixth year; a

Table 2-5. Budget Sensitivity to Changes in Economic Assumptions, Fiscal Years 1994-99
Billions of dollars

Assumption	1994	1995	1996	1997	1998	1999
Real growth: 1 percentage point less than projected in 1994; growth as projected in later years[a]						
Receipts	-7	-14	-17	-17	-18	-19
Outlays	1	5	7	8	10	12
Deficit increase	8	19	23	25	28	30
Real growth: 1 percentage point less than projected each year, 1994-99						
Receipts	-7	-22	-40	-60	-82	-107
Outlays	0	1	2	5	9	15
Deficit increase	7	22	43	66	92	122
Inflation: 1 percentage point more than projected each year, 1994-99						
Receipts	7	21	38	56	75	96
Outlays	1	4	9	16	24	31
Deficit reduction	-6	-18	-29	-40	-51	-65
Interest rates: 1 percentage point more than projected each year, 1994-99						
Receipts	1	2	2	3	3	3
Outlays	5	15	21	27	32	44
Deficit increase	5	13	19	24	29	41

Source: *Budget of the United States Government, Fiscal Year 1995, Analytical Perspectives*, table 1.6. Totals may not add up due to rounding.
a. Assumes half percentage point rise in unemployment rate.

1 percentage point rise in interest rates would add $5 billion to federal outlays in the first year and $44 billion in the sixth year.

The president and Congress are thus hostage to the performance of the economy. Because that performance cannot be known when the budget is prepared, there are bound to be errors in the projections. But because budget plans depend on economic conditions, there may be an incentive to assume more favorable conditions than are likely. This bias was especially pronounced during the late 1980s, when the Gramm-Rudman-Hollings procedures discussed in chapter 3 threatened the automatic cancellation of budgetary resources if the projected deficit exceeded target levels set in law. Politicians were able to avoid putting favored programs on the chopping block by (among other means) projecting a more favorable economic outlook than was warranted.

Even when there is no effort to manipulate economic forecasts for political advantage, it is extremely difficult to foretell when a recession will arrive, how deep or lasting it will be, or its impact on the budget. The deficit tripled (from $74 billion to $208 billion) during the recession of the early 1980s and doubled (from $152 billion to $290 billion) during the recession of the early 1990s.

The economy has the last word, even when it is growing. There is a strong correlation between the rate of economic growth and the size of budget deficits (figure 2-2). Fast growth is associated with small deficits, slow growth with large ones. This linkage was evident during the almost eight years between the end of the Reagan era recession in 1982 and the onset of the Bush era recession in 1990. Although these years were the longest peacetime expansion in U.S. history, large deficits persisted because the growth was weak.

The persistence of deficits led many observers to conclude that the president and Congress had done little to remedy the imbalance between revenue and expenditure. In fact, however, many changes were enacted in tax and spending laws between 1980 and 1990 in a vain effort to vanquish the deficit. According to congressional budget reconciliation reports, more than $1 trillion was pared from baseline deficits during these years. Although the amounts may have been overstated, there can be no doubt that elected politicians wrestled repeatedly with the deficit problem and until 1994 had little to show for their exertions.

The lesson of recent budget history is that cutting expenditures and increasing taxes does not suffice to close the gap when the economy fails to grow quickly enough. This lesson does not mean that active deficit control is futile, only that its success depends on the economy. The budget can grow out of the deficit only when the economy is sufficiently vigorous to produce incremental revenues that rise faster than the built-in escalation in expenditures.

This conclusion strongly implies that the budget is the passive recipient of the economy's good or bad news. But isn't it also the case, as was stated at the beginning of this section, that the budget helps shape the economy? Doesn't the budget determine its own fate by influencing the pace of economic expansion and thus the size of the deficit as well? During the long period of economic vigor in the 1960s,

the prevailing sentiment was that well-guided and timely budget policy would steer the economy on a high-growth, low-inflation course. The idea was that deficits should be fine-tuned to suit changing economic conditions. They should be allowed to increase when the economy is weak and needs stimulus, and they should be curtailed when the economy is vigorous and needs restraint.

Following this script requires great confidence in the capacity of the government to manage the economy. During the past two decades, confidence in fiscal management has been eroded by chronic deficits that have grown when the economy has been weak and have persisted when the economy has recovered. Confidence has also been eroded by growth that was lower in the 1970s than in the 1960s, and lower yet in the 1980s, and by rigidities in the budget that have made it difficult for politicians to get the deficit reductions they profess to want. Use of the budget as an instrument of economic policy has also been undermined by conflict over what should be done. Some economists insist that the size of the deficit is of little consequence; others are concerned that big deficits will lead to a less bountiful future than would be possible if the United States had saved and invested more. With consensus lacking, elected officials find it difficult to take decisive action on the deficit. Why bother when the economy is underperforming and the deficit does some good by propping up demand?

Cutting the deficit entails clear short-term costs–tax increases or spending cuts–to produce problematic long-term gains–a more productive future. This may be an appropriate trade-off for economists, but it is not attractive for politicians who face election every few years and are more responsive to today's voters than to tomorrow's. Given the political costs of acting, it is remarkable that so much has been done to ease the deficit.

Not enough, however, for politicians to put the deficit problem behind them or to liberate

Figure 2-2. Economic Growth and Budget Deficits, Four-Year Averages, Fiscal Years 1961-92[a]

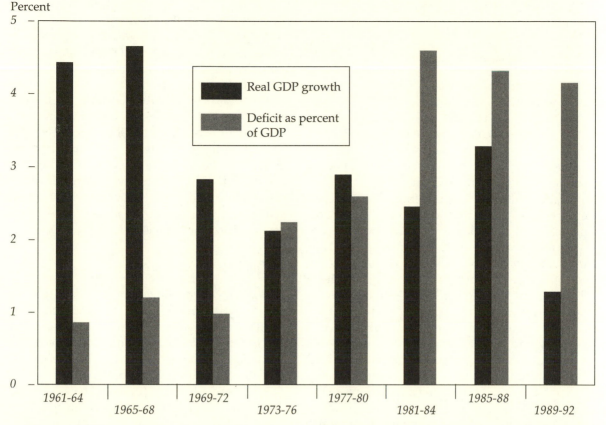

Sources: *Budget of the United States Government, Fiscal Year 1995, Historical Tables*, table 1.1; *Economic Report of the President, January 1994*, table B-2.

a. The four-year periods shown here approximately correspond with presidential terms. However, the budget data are by fiscal year, while the GDP data are by calendar year.

the budget from the clutches of economic confusion and weakness. As long as the large deficit persists, the budget cannot be actively used to invigorate the economy. But as long as the economy is not vigorous, it will not supply sufficient fiscal dividends to liquidate the deficit.

Measuring the Deficit

In this and the previous chapter the deficit has been taken to be whatever is officially reported in the budget. The reported deficit is not the only measure of the deficit, nor is it the one that most

Americans have in mind when they think about the deficit. The deficit is commonly defined as the difference between the amount the government takes in and the amount it spends. This is not the way the deficit is measured in the federal budget. The deficit is the difference between receipts and outlays as they are recorded in the budget. Several of the arithmetic issues discussed in this chapter affect the size of the deficit. To the extent receipts and outlays are not budgeted on a cash basis, neither is the deficit. To the extent certain activities are excluded from the budget, they also are excluded from calculation of the deficit. The reported deficit varies by many billions of dollars, depending on what is included or excluded. The five measures shown in figure 2-3 are all commonly used in budgeting.

The Consolidated Deficit

On a consolidated basis the budget deficit peaked at $290 billion in fiscal 1992; it is now about $100 billion lower. The consolidated basis is the broadest measure shown in figure 2-3, but it does not include all payments for which the government may be liable. It includes the off-budget entities, all trust funds, and both capital and operating accounts, but not government-sponsored enterprises. With the exception of direct and guaranteed loans, the consolidated budget recognizes receipts and outlays in the fiscal period during which cash is received or paid. It does not recognize contingent liabilities, such as those incurred in insuring bank deposits and private pensions, nor does it recognize the future outlays that will result from the obligation to pay social security and medical expenses. The amounts involved in potential future claims on the federal treasury are truly gargantuan. By some estimates, the unfunded accrued liabilities of federal retirement and health care programs exceed $6 trillion.

To rectify the failure of the budget to recognize direct or contingent obligations before they come due, some have urged that the present value of future costs of pension guarantees, deposit insurance, GSEs, and other arrangements for which the government will eventually have to make payments be budgeted as an outlay. Others have suggested that future obligations be recorded in supplementary schedules or in financial statements but not in the budget totals.

The On-Budget Deficit

The on-budget deficit excludes social security and the Postal Service and is about $60 billion greater (approximately the amount of the annual social security surplus) than the amount reported on a consolidated basis. The off-budget status of social security and the Postal Service is designed to protect them from deficit reduction pressures in the rest of the budget. By itself, however, off-budget status makes little difference, though social security's special status is reinforced by being exempt from reconciliation and sequestration, the government's main tools for compelling deficit reduction.

Because social security is so large, excluding it from the deficit impairs the budget's utility as a measure of fiscal impact. How can the budget's impact on the economy be assessed when one-fifth of the government's revenues and outlays are excluded? In fact, social security is almost always included in both government and news references to the budget. By law, social security is excluded; in practice, it is included.

The Federal Funds Deficit

Social security, along with all other trust funds, is excluded from the federal funds deficit, which is $100 billion higher than the consolidated deficit. In the early 1990s the federal funds deficit approached $400 billion; it has since receded to less than $300 billion, but is projected to rise in the years ahead. Federal funds is the entrenched deficit, the deficit that does not go away in good times and balloons in bad times. It is the deficit that persists because Americans do not want to pay for the government they want to have. As long as huge imbalances persist in federal funds–which is to say, as far ahead as projections have been made–federal budgeting will be hobbled by deficits.

In the consolidated budget the federal funds deficit is partly offset by surpluses in the trust funds. This accounting practice has given rise to complaints that social security and other trust funds are being invaded to finance the current expenses of government and they therefore will not be available to pay future benefits. The truth is a bit more complicated than that. The government does borrow trust fund balances, but it pays prevailing interest rates on the money. In fact, half of the $450 billion increase in social security balances projected in table 2-1

Figure 2-3. Alternative Measures of the Deficit, Fiscal Years 1983, 1988, 1993, 1995
Billions of dollars

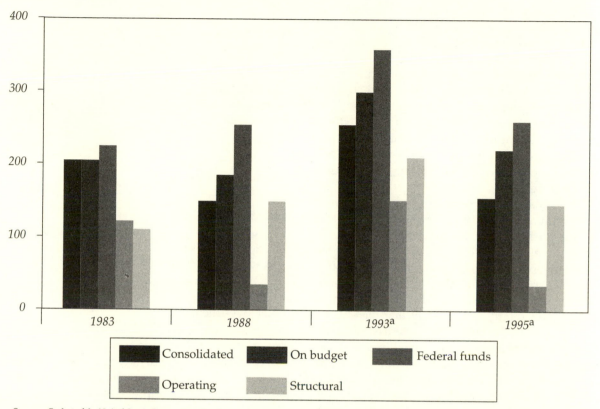

Sources: *Budget of the United States Government, Fiscal Year 1995, Historical Tables,* tables 1.1, 1.4, 9.1; and Congressional Budget Office, *The Economic and Budget Outlook, Fiscal Years 1995-1999,* tables 1-2, E-1.
    a. Estimated.

is attributable to the interest the government will turn over to this trust fund. The interest payments add to the federal funds deficit and trust fund surpluses, but have no effect on the consolidated deficit.

The problem with social security is not today's surplus but tomorrow's shortfall. Under current policy, the surplus will vanish early in the next century as millions of baby boomers retire. Even if, as is highly likely, the government repays the money it has borrowed, social security will have difficulty meeting all its commitments. This looming deficit will not be solved by quarantining social security from the federal budget.

The Operating Deficit

The operating deficit measures the gap between current receipts and expenditures; it excludes capital investment from the calculation. As shown in figure 2-3, capital investment is investment in physical assets, such as roads and buildings; it does not include research and development or investment in human capital through education and training.

Although the federal government does not presently have a separate capital budget, the 1993 National Performance Review recommended that the budget "recognize the special nature and long-term benefits of investments through a separate capital budget." NPR proposed a limited definition of capital expenditure that would have excluded investment in military weapons and facilities, as well as certain domestic investments. A definition that covers all investment in physical capital would remove $120 billion from the operating deficit. Expanding the definition to include research and development would slice another $70 billion and (excluding depreciation charges) would produce a balanced operating budget. Going further and shifting investment in education and training to capital accounts would yield a substantial surplus in the operating budget. Table 2-6 compares the alternative definitions of capital investment.

Subtracting the gross amount invested in physical or human capital from operating expenditure would greatly understate the deficit in the operating budget. It is also appropriate to charge the operating budget for depreciation and write-off of capital assets. If these adjustments were made, the operating deficit would differ from the consolidated deficit only to the extent that there was a net change in the stock of capital assets. If the government had a separate capital budget in fiscal 1995, the operating budget would record an estimated $68 billion expense for depreciation.

The federal government is not ready for a full-fledged capital budget. Before separating investment and operating expenditure, it will be necessary to resolve definitional issues and to develop accounting principles and procedures for measuring net changes in the capital stock. Inasmuch as the different measures are more than $100 billion apart, it will take considerable work to produce agreement.

The Structural Deficit

The final measure in figure 2-3 differs from the previous three in that it depends on variables outside the scope of the budget rather than on rules of budgetary accounting. The structural deficit is a measure of what the gap between revenues and expenditures would be if the economy were operating at full potential. When the economy is operating below potential, as it has been in most of the

Table 2-6. Federal Investment Outlays, Fiscal Year 1995

Billions of dollars

Type of investment	Amount	Cumulative
Construction		
Direct nondefense	14.9	14.9
National defense	5.0	19.9
Grants to states and localities	36.5	56.5
Acquisition of equipment		
Direct nondefense	7.0	63.5
National defense	55.4	118.9
Land and structures	0.8	119.8
Research and development		
Nondefense	30.3	150.1
National defense	39.4	189.5
Education and training	44.6	234.0
Total investment outlays	234.0	...
Less depreciation	-68.0	...
Net investment outlays	166.0	...

Source: *Budget of the United States Government, Fiscal Year 1995, Analytical Perspectives*, tables 8.5, 8.8.

past decade, the gap widens because revenues are lower and outlays are higher than potential levels. During 1992, for example, CBO estimated the actual deficit to be $84 billion higher than the structural deficit. It should be noted that CBO excludes certain financing shocks, such as contributions by other countries to pay for the Persian Gulf War and expenditures from insuring bank and savings and loan deposits, from its calculation of the structural deficit.

The size of the structural deficit depends on how the potential of the economy is measured. CBO defines this potential in terms of the unemployment rate that is consistent with nonaccelerating inflation. It currently estimates this rate to be 5.5 percent, meaning that if unemployment were to drop below this rate, inflation would probably accelerate.

The structural deficit is an analytical tool, though some have suggested that it also be used as an instrument to control deficits. It is useful in distinguishing between deficits due to the performance of the economy and those due to government policy. Since 1983 the structural deficit has consistently been more than $100 billion, indicating that the overall deficit would remain very high even if the economy were to reach full potential.

Conclusion

How the deficit is measured depends on how the budget is defined. At issue is a matter that cannot be resolved by replacing one measure of the deficit (or of the budget) with another. The budget has multiple measures of the deficit because the budget has multiple uses. Each measure tells a different story; none sees the budget from all perspectives. A budget that calculates the deficit on the basis of cash flows provides essential information on the financing needs of government and is a budget that politicians can understand and deal with. A cash budget, however, is not a useful measure of future claims on the government. For this purpose, the budget must accrue future costs by estimating their net present value, as is now done for loans, or through some other method.

Neither the cash nor accrual basis fully gauges the interaction of the budget and the economy or measures the net change in human or physical capital. For these purposes, specialized measures provided by the capital and structural budgets are appropriate.

Although there are many ways to tell the budget's story, there can be only one way for deciding the budget. Of all the means of measuring the deficit, only one can be the basis on which the budget is decided. If Congress decides to control the cash deficit, that measure will be paramount and Congress cannot control on the basis of the structural deficit. The first three measures shown in figure 2-3 are cash based. The consolidated federal funds and on-budget deficits tell the same story; they differ in which chapters are left out. But they can and do exist side by side in the budget. At this stage of their development, the operating and structural measures provide supplementary data; they inform budget makers but are not a basis for decision and control. They are not likely to gain a greater toehold in budgeting as long as cash-based accounting remains preeminent.

Chapter 3

Mapping the Federal Budget Process

Budgeting differs from many other government responsibilities in that its tasks must be completed each year. No matter how difficult the choices or uncertain the outlook, the president must submit a budget each year and Congress must make appropriations. If the president and Congress decide that the time is not ripe to act on a particular legislative proposal, they can lay it aside until more information is available or an agreement has been hammered out. But they cannot default on their responsibility to deal with the budget each year. If they did, federal programs and agencies would shut down for lack of money and the work of government would come to a halt.

Budgetary procedures regulate conflict by parceling out tasks and roles, establishing expectations and deadlines for action, and limiting the scope of issues that are considered. Conflict is dampened by the routines of budgeting, the repetitive tasks that are completed with little change year after year, and the behavior of participants. Budget makers generally display a willingness to compromise that is often lacking when other kinds of matters are in dispute.

The rules of budgeting affect the outcomes. How much is taxed and spent, who pays and who benefits, which programs grow and which shrink--these and other matters are influenced by formal procedures and informal behavior. Throughout this book, therefore, the discussion shifts back and forth between the process and the politics of budgeting. No explanation of budgeting is complete unless it takes both into account.

The process and the politics revolve around two main institutions of government power: the presidency and Congress. The evolution of federal budgeting has been a long contest for political power; the weapons used by the combatants have been the rules and procedures of budgeting. For two hundred years these institutions have vied for power of the purse, with the advantage sometimes held by one and sometimes by the other. The struggle over the past two centuries has resulted in parallel budget processes in the executive and legislative branches.

The evolution not only bequeathed budgetary roles to the president and Congress, it also left the federal government with two budget processes, one centered on annual appropriations, the other dispersed among many entitlement programs. The two are sometimes merged to compile a budget for the entire federal government. But on key matters, such as the route taken by legislation in Congress and the rules of deficit control, the processes go their separate ways.

The final section of this chapter introduces the annual budget process and the roles of the many participants in federal budgeting. The brief description points the way to the much fuller discussion in chapters 4 through 9.

Table 3-1. Federal Receipts, Outlays, Deficit, and Public Debt, Selected Fiscal Years and Periods, 1789-1995[a]
Billions of dollars

Fiscal years	Revenues	Outlays	Surplus or deficit	Public debt[b]
1789-1900	16	17	-1	1
1910	1	1	*	1
1920	7	6	*	24
1930	4	3	1	16
1940	7	9	-3	43
1950	39	43	-3	219
1960	92	92	*	237
1970	193	196	-3	283
1980	517	591	-74	709
1990	1,031	1,253	-221	2,410
1993	1,154	1,408	-265	3,247
1995[c]	1,354	1,519	-165	3,646

Sources: *Historical Statistics of the United States: From Colonial Times to 1970*, series Y 335-338; and *Budget of the United States Government, Fiscal Year 1995, Historical Tables*, tables 1.1, 7.1.
*Less than $0.5 billion.
a. Amounts shown are on a unified or consolidated budget basis. They include social security, other trust funds, and other off-budget transactions. The amounts for 1789-1900 are the total receipts, outlays, deficit, and public debt accumulated during this period. The amounts shown for other years are the receipts, outlays, surplus or deficit, or public debt recorded for the relevant fiscal year.
b. The public debt is the portion of the gross federal debt held by the public. It does not include the portion of the federal debt held by government accounts, such as the social security trust funds. At present, the gross federal debt is about $1.3 trillion higher than the public debt.
c. Estimated.

The Evolution of Federal Budgeting

The history of federal budgeting is intertwined with the growth of the nation's revenues, expenditures, and deficits. Large federal budgets and huge deficits are a recent development (table 3-1). The first Congress in 1789 appropriated only $639,000 to cover the expenses of the new government. This amount is now spent by the federal government every ten or fifteen seconds. The growth of government transformed budgeting from a Congress-centered activity to one in which both it and the president have prominent roles, and from a process that (except for wartime) usually produced balanced budgets into one in which deficits are common. These transformations are associated with three periods of federal budgeting. The first, stretching from 1789 to 1921, began with small government and rare deficits and ended with a much enlarged government and financial difficulties. The second began with the Budget and Accounting Act of 1921, which gave the president a central role in managing the nation's finances, and ended with a vastly larger government and efforts to make Congress more responsible for budget policy. The third period began with the Congressional Budget Act of 1974 and includes the Gramm-Rudman-Hollings legislation in 1985 and 1987 and the Budget Enforcement Act of 1990.

Legislative Dominance, 1789-1921

The Constitution gives Congress the power to levy taxes and provides that funds may be drawn from the treasury only pursuant to appropriations made by law. The Constitution does not specify how these legislative powers of the purse are to

Table 3-2. Impact of War on Federal Spending, Selected Fiscal Years, 1811-1975
Millions of current dollars

War	Prewar level[a]		Wartime peak[a]		Percentage change	Postwar low[a]		Percentage change
War of 1812	8	(1811)	35	(1814)	331	22	(1817)	-37
Mexican-American War	28	(1846)	57	(1847)	106	45	(1849)	-21
Civil War	67	(1861)	1,298	(1865)	1,850	358	(1867)	-72
Spanish-American War	366	(1897)	605	(1899)	65	521	(1900)	-14
World War I	713	(1916)	18,493	(1919)	1,678	6,358	(1920)	-50
World War II	9,468	(1941)	92,712	(1945)	879	59,232	(1946)	-36
Korean War	42,562	(1950)	76,101	(1953)	79	68,444	(1955)	-10
Vietnam War	118,528	(1964)	183,640	(1969)	55	332,332	(1975)	81

Sources: *Historical Statistics of the United States: Colonial Times to 1970*, series Y 335-338, Y 457-465; and *Budget of the United States Government, Fiscal Year 1993, Historical Tables*, tables 1.1, 3.1.
   a. Fiscal year in parentheses.

be exercised, nor does it expressly provide any role for the president in financial matters or for a federal budget process. In fact, the concept of budgeting was imported from Europe more than a century after the Constitution was adopted.

In the early years of American government, revenue and spending legislation, as well as other financial matters, were concentrated in the House Ways and Means and the Senate Finance Committees. Federal revenues and spending grew sporadically during the nineteenth century. Growth spurts, usually occasioned by war (table 3-2) were followed by periods of stability. Federal spending tripled during the War of 1812, doubled during the Mexican-American War, and increased twentyfold during the Civil War. Spending receded after each war, but still remained well above prewar levels. Total spending usually was stable between wars. For example, the government spent $358 million in 1867 (the first full fiscal year after the Civil War) and $366 million in 1897 (the last year before the Spanish-American War). The government typically accumulated debt during wartime, was burdened by high interest payments after a war, and gradually undertook new expenditures as debt was retired and interest charges decreased. The paydown of the public debt was made possible by revenues (mostly from tariffs) that were ample

to cover expenditures during peacetime. With budgets consistently at or near balance, the public debt dropped from $2.8 billion in 1866 to $1.3 billion in 1900.

Remarkably, financial balance was achieved despite the lack of a budget system that coordinated all legislative or executive revenue and expenditure action. As long as the federal government was small and its financial operations stable, a budget was not considered necessary. Two related developments, however, brought this comfortable situation, in which the government achieved satisfactory outcomes without a coordinated process, to a close. One was the fragmentation of congressional action, the other the growth of federal spending and peacetime deficits.

The first step in fragmenting legislative action occurred as a by-product of the Civil War, which greatly added to the financial burdens of government. Both the House (1865) and the Senate (1867) separated spending and revenue jurisdiction and assigned spending to newly established appropriations committees. The second step, which occurred late in the nineteenth century, was the assignment of half the appropriations bills to various legislative committees, with the result that the appropriations committees no longer had jurisdiction over all federal spending. The dispersion of appropriations control led to higher spending, especially in those bills in the jurisdiction of legislative committees.

Legislative fragmentation was mirrored by decentralization in the executive branch. The president had a limited role in overseeing financial operations. Most agencies submitted their spending estimates directly to the relevant congressional committees without having their requests reviewed by him. Agency requests were compiled in an annual *Book of Estimates*, but little policy control was exercised over the amounts requested. Fragmentation and the progressive increase in federal spending (which doubled between 1894 and 1914) as the United States expanded social and regulatory programs and became more active in international matters led to persistent deficits. Spending exceeded revenues in eleven of the seventeen years between 1894 and 1910. Then came World War I. Federal spending soared from $700 million in 1914 to more than $18 billion five years later, and the public debt exploded from $1 billion to $25 billion. Shortly after the war, Congress turned to the president to coordinate financial decisions. The key legislation was the Budget and Accounting Act of 1921, which established the executive budget system that is still in operation. This and other landmarks in federal budgeting are listed in table 3-3.

Presidential Budgeting, 1921-74

The 1921 act did not directly alter the procedures by which Congress made revenue and spending decisions (although it did spur the House and Senate to return jurisdiction over all spending bills to the appropriations committees). The main impact was in the executive branch. The president was required to submit a budget to Congress each year, and the Bureau of the Budget, renamed the Office of Management and Budget (OMB) in 1970, was established to assist him in carrying out his budget responsibilities. These responsibilities were organized around an elaborate executive budget process in which agency requests were reviewed by the president's budget staff. Agencies were barred from submit-

ting their budgets directly to Congress, as they had in the past. Under the new procedures the president and his budget aides decided how much would be requested.

In effect, the 1921 act made the president an agent of congressional budget control. Congress, it was expected, would coordinate its revenue and spending decisions, and thereby eliminate deficits, by acting on comprehensive recommendations from the president. Although the 1921 act does not bar Congress from appropriating more than the president requests, the expectation was that it would weigh his recommendations in making its own budget decisions.

The Budget and Accounting Act had immediate success in controlling federal finance. Taxes were reduced, and both spending and the public debt declined during the 1920s (table 3-1). These accomplishments may have been partly due to the conservative temperament of postwar America, but they also were the result of the fiscal discipline imposed by the new budget system. Throughout the 1920s the president's budget office maintained a tight grip on agency spending.

Then came the Great Depression, and with it the New Deal and a vast expansion in the scale of government. On the eve of the depression in 1929, federal spending was only 3 percent of GDP; a decade later it was 10 percent. Although expenditures tripled, revenues failed to keep pace, and the government incurred substantial deficits. World War II, however, brought a massive inflow of revenue as Congress enacted a broad-based income tax with high rates. As a result, federal revenues were seven times higher in 1945 than they had been five years earlier. Following the pattern set after previous wars, Congress lowered taxes but retained sufficient additional revenue to enlarge government programs. Although outlays averaged 18 percent of GDP during the 1950s, the surge in revenues enabled the president to produce budgets that were at or near balance.

The additional revenues and expanded government enabled the president to use the budget to develop an annual legislative program and to manage federal agencies. It became customary in

Table 3-3. Milestones in Federal Budgeting, 1789-1990

Year	Event	Significance
1789	Constitution	Gives Congress the power to levy taxes and requires appropriations by Congress before funds are disbursed
1802-67	Committee structure	House Ways and Means Committee established as standing committee in 1802; House Appropriations Committee established in 1865. Senate Finance Committee established in 1816; Senate Appropriations Committee in 1867
1837, 1850	House and Senate rules	House and Senate bar unauthorized appropriations
1870, 1905-1906	Antideficiency Act	Requires apportionment of funds to prevent overexpenditure
1921	Budget and Accounting Act	Provides for an executive budget; establishes the Bureau of the Budget and the General Accounting Office
1939	Reorganization Plan No. 1	Transfers Bureau of the Budget to the new Executive Office of the President and expands the bureau's role
1967	President's Commission on Budget Concepts	Adoption of the unified budget, including trust funds
1974	Congressional Budget and Impoundment Control Act	Establishes the congressional budget process, House and Senate budget committees, and the Congressional Budget Office. Also establishes procedures for legislative review of impoundments
1980	Reconciliation process	Reconciliation used for the first time at start of congressional budget process
1985, 1987	Gramm-Rudman-Hollings Acts	Set deficit reduction targets and sequestration procedures
1990	Budget Enforcement Act	Shifts from fixed to adjustable deficit targets, caps discretionary spending, establishes pay-as-you-go rules for revenues and direct spending, and establishes new budgeting rules for direct and guaranteed loans
1990	Chief Financial Officers Act	Provides for a chief financial officer in all major agencies to oversee financial management and integrate accounting and budgeting

the 1950s for the president to compile a set of legislative proposals each year in tandem with the formulation of the annual budget. The president's budget staff actively used the budget process to improve the management of federal programs and agencies. With the budget's increased share in GDP, the president became increasingly active in steering the economy and keeping it on a high-growth, low-inflation course. Despite the steady rise in federal spending--real outlays doubled between 1949 and 1966--the booming economy enabled the government to balance its books or hold deficits sufficiently low that they did not give rise to budget difficulties.

The Vietnam War and the growth of mandatory expenditures brought this idyllic period in federal budgeting to an end. Because the war was unpopular, Congress was reluctant to pay for it with tax increases. It did enact a small surtax, and the additional revenue produced a small surplus in fiscal year 1969, but the tax expired and deficit spending resumed before the war ended. Attitudes toward the deficit were conditioned by distaste for the war. Rather than considering the deficit an appropriate means of financing military operations, as it had been thought of in previous wars, many Americans regarded it as evidence of an abandonment of fiscal responsibility. To make matters worse, when the war ended, federal spending did not recede and the budget did not return to balance. In fact, there was no postwar year in which federal spending did not surpass the wartime peak. There was a small drop in the ratio of expenditures to GDP, but not enough to balance the budget.

The post-Vietnam pattern differed from the budgetary patterns after previous wars because the composition of federal spending had changed. Past spending had been determined by annual presidential and congressional actions. In the past, when war ended, Congress appropriated less for military purposes, cut some or all of the taxes levied to finance the war, and applied surplus funds to domestic programs. After the Vietnam War, however, an expanding share of the budget went for mandatory payments--social security, medicare and medicaid, food stamps, and other entitlements--that had to be made regardless of the government's financial condition. Less than one-quarter of total spending a generation ago, entitlement payments are now more than one-half (table 3-4). After Vietnam the increase in these payments exceeded the decrease in defense expenditures. Between 1969 and 1973, defense spending declined by $6 billion, but payments to individuals soared by $50 billion. Instead of a post-Vietnam peace dividend, the budget was hobbled by large and persistent deficits.

With an increasing share of the budget driven by eligibility rules and payment formulas, the president's budget became more a means of estimating the future cost of existing obligations than of deciding the program and financial policies of the government. The president's budget capacity was also weakened by the Vietnam War, which undermined confidence in his leadership and soured his relationship with Congress. President Nixon warred with Congress over budget priorities and the impoundment of funds. Spurred by belief that the budget was out of control and that the president could not lead, Congress sought to bolster its own role in budgeting.

Grappling with the Deficit, 1974-94

Congress's quest for its own budget process culminated in the Congressional Budget Act of 1974, which President Nixon signed into law less than a month before he was driven from office by the Watergate scandal. This measure provided for Congress to adopt a budget resolution that sets forth budget totals and functional allocations. The budget resolution is the only occasion for Congress to vote on the size of the deficit, total spending, and budget priorities.

In bolstering Congress's budget capacity, the legislation did not alter the formal role of the president. As before, the president submits a budget each year, and Congress can defer to his recommendations if it wishes to do so. Now, however, Congress has the option of relying on its own

Table 3-4. Federal Payments to Individuals, Selected Programs, Fiscal Years 1970, 1980, 1990, and Estimated, 1994, 1997

Program	1970	1980	1990	1994	1997
Outlays (billions of dollars)					
Social security (OASDI)	30	117	246	317	336
Federal retirement	3	15	31	36	38
Supplemental security income	0	6	11	24	28
Medicare (HI)	5	24	66	102	183
Medicaid	3	14	41	87	106
Food stamps	1	9	15	26	27
Family support (AFDC)	4	7	12	16	17
Veterans' assistance	5	11	14	19	19
Total payments for individuals	65	279	584	830	994
Percent of total federal outlays	33	47	47	56	59
Recipients (millions)					
Social security	26	35	39	42	45
Medicare (HI)	n.a.	28	33	36	38
Medicaid	15	22	25	36	39
Food stamps	9	19	19	27	27
Family support (AFDC)	7	11	11	14	17

Sources: *Budget of the United States Government, Fiscal Year 1995, Analytical Perspectives*, p. 204; and *Budget of the United States Government, Fiscal Year 1995, Historical Tables*, tables 11.3, 6.1.

n.a. Not available.

budget resolution rather than on the president's budget for guidance on revenue and expenditure decisions. The budget resolution retains the congressional processes for enacting revenue and spending legislation, but it provides a framework within which the many separate measures affecting federal finances can be considered. Congress can assess the financial implications of revenue appropriations and other spending measures in the light of the policies adopted in its budget resolution.

The Congressional Budget Act did not ordain that the budget be balanced, nor did it bar Congress from adopting resolutions that have big deficits. Nevertheless, the act was spurred by the expectation that deficits would be smaller if Congress expressly had to vote for them. This expectation has not been fulfilled. The economy went into a tailspin just about the time that Congress began implementing the new process, so that the deficit was much higher than had been incurred before 1974. During the first decade (fiscal years 1976-85) of the new process, the budget deficit averaged more than $110 billion a year. It had been $15 billion a year during the previous decade. The deficit averaged 3.8 percent GDP during the decade; in the previous decade it averaged 1.4 percent.

The soaring deficit had various causes: economic stagflation during the 1970s, the built-in escalation in entitlement expenditures, and President Reagan's success in prodding Congress to cut taxes at the same time it was boosting defense expenditures. Whatever the cause, no one could claim that having Congress vote on a budget resolution generated lower deficits.

As the budget crisis deepened in the 1980s–the deficit averaged more than $200 billion a year during fiscal years 1983-86–Congress established annual targets to reduce the deficit. The Balanced Budget and Emergency Deficit Control Act of 1985, commonly referred to as the Gramm-Rudman-Hollings (GRH) Act, called for the progressive reduction in the deficit in each fiscal year from 1986 through 1990 and for a balanced budget in 1991. It also provided for the cancellation of budget resources if the projected deficit exceeded the target by more than an allowed amount. Congress amended the law in 1987 and postponed the target year for a balanced budget to 1993.

Despite the threat of sequestration–the withholding of funds when deficit targets have been exceeded–the deficit exceeded the GRH target in each fiscal year from 1986 through 1990. The law was defective in a number of ways. It did not require that the actual deficit be within the target, only that the deficit projected at the start of the fiscal year be within that year's allowed level. An increase in the deficit during the fiscal year, whether because of estimation errors, changes in economic conditions, or new policies, did not require compensatory action to offset the increase, even if the actual deficit exceeded the target. Reliance on projected rather than actual deficits led to manipulation of budget estimates, bookkeeping tricks in lieu of genuine savings, and deficits much higher than had been budgeted.

Budget Enforcement Rules

One of the lessons Congress derived from the failure of GRH is that it is futile to set fixed dollar limits on annual deficits. Fixed limits can be overtaken by unforeseen developments such as the recession that began in the summer of 1990. To contain the deficit, Congress concluded, it is necessary to control the amount of revenue raised and money spent. In line with this reasoning, the Budget Enforcement Act of 1990 established a new deficit control process that distinguishes between discretionary spending, controlled by annual appropriations decisions, and direct spending, controlled by substantive legislation outside the jurisdiction of the appropriations committees. The BEA rules were to be effective only for fiscal years 1991-95, but they were subsequently extended through fiscal year 1998, and there is a strong probability that they will be extended for additional years.

BEA has three sets of rules: adjustable deficit targets, caps on discretionary spending, and pay-as-you-go (PAYGO) rules for revenues and direct spending.

The Gramm-Rudman-Hollings law set targets that were not adjusted for changes in economic conditions or for reestimates of program expenditures. BEA, however, gives the president the option of adjusting the maximum deficit amount when he submits his budget to Congress. President Clinton exercised this option for both the 1994 and the 1995 fiscal years, thereby eliminating the possibility that funds would be sequestered because the maximum deficit amount had been exceeded. In effect, under the rules now in place, whatever the deficit is is what it is permitted to be. Removal of direct control of the deficit has not, however, ushered in an anything goes era in federal budgeting: strong controls are imposed on the revenue and spending decisions that affect the size of the deficit.

One of these controls pertains to the one-third of federal spending that is controlled by annual appropriations. This discretionary spending includes virtually all defense expenditures, the operating costs of most federal agencies, and many of the grants made each year to state and local governments. Discretionary spending does not include the many billions of dollars appropriated each year for entitlement programs. These *appropriated entitlements* are classified as direct rather than discretionary spending because they are controlled by the legislation that establishes eligibility criteria and payment formulas. Appropriations for entitlements must be sufficient to finance the payments the government is obligated to make. The appropriations committees do not have discretion to fund these entitlements at

Table 3-5. Discretionary Spending Limits, Fiscal Years 1994-98[a]
Billions of dollars

Limits	Baseline projection and outlays	1994	1995	1996	1997	1998
Original statutory caps	Ba	510.8	517.7	519.1	528.1	530.6
	OL	534.8	540.8	547.3	547.3	547.9
Adjustments, special allowances	Ba	2.9	2.9	0	0	0
	OL	3.4	2.7	1.2	0.5	0.1
IRS, IMF, debt forgiveness	Ba	0.2	0.2	0	0	0
	OL	0.4	0.4	0	0	0
Changes in inflation	Ba	-9.5	-11.8	n.a.	n.a.	n.a.
	OL	-5.8	-8.8	n.a.	n.a.	n.a.
Credit reform and other changes	Ba	8.6	9.8	0	-0.1	-0.1
	OL	2.8	3.9	-0.2	-0.2	-0.3
Emergency appropriations	Ba	2.3	0	0	0	0
	OL	8.2	3.2	0.4	0	0
Discretionary limits, February 1994	Ba	515.3	518.7	519.1	528.0	530.0
	OL	543.8	542.4	548.6	547.8	547.7
President's fiscal year 1995 budget	Ba	n.a.	515.3	517.7	520.3	526.0
	OL	n.a.	542.4	546.1	547.8	544.4

Source: *Budget of the United States Government, Fiscal Year 1995, Analytical Perspectives, Preview Report*, tables 14.1, 14.2, 14.3.

n.a. Not available

a. Early in each session, OMB and CBO issue sequestration preview reports estimating discretionary spending limits with the adjustments prescribed by law. In August the two agencies issue update reports to reflect the impact of legislation enacted up to that point in the session. They issue final sequestration reports after the session has concluded.

This table sets forth the original spending limits enacted in 1990 for fiscal years 1994 and 1995 and in 1993 for fiscal years 1996-98. It also shows the adjustments made as of February 1994 in the limits for each of these years. Additional adjustments will be made for the later years in subsequent sequestration reports. By the time Congress makes appropriations for fiscal 1996 and beyond, the spending limits will differ from those displayed here.

levels that differ from those mandated by law.

For each year through fiscal year 1998 BEA sets a dollar limit on total discretionary budget authority and outlays (table 3-5). The limits may be adjusted for emergency spending and certain other factors; if they are not adjusted, total discretionary spending will be frozen at approximately fiscal year 1993 levels for each of the next five years. If appropriations cause the limits on either budget authority or outlays to be breached, the president must sequester sufficient budget resources to compensate for the excess spending. Under BEA rules, a uniform percentage would be taken from all discretionary programs, projects, and activities. If the excess spending were to occur during the last quarter of the fiscal year

(between July 1 and September 30), the next year's discretionary spending limits would be reduced by the amount of the excess.

Only two tiny sequesters have been applied to discretionary spending during the first four fiscal years (1991-94) that the caps have been in place. Congress has been determined to stay within the caps, even to the extent of turning down some of President Clinton's spending proposals. Doing so was not difficult during the early years of BEA because the caps were set at a sufficiently high level to accommodate expected spending. But now that the caps have been frozen at 1993 levels through 1998, they are likely to be increasingly onerous.

The final set of BEA rules pertains to the PAYGO (pay-as-you-go) parts of the budget, revenues and direct spending. The basic rule is that legislation increasing direct spending or decreasing revenues must be fully offset so that the deficit is not increased. Direct spending consists mostly of entitlement programs that have either annual or permanent appropriations, but it also includes other budgetary resources (such as control authority for the highway trust fund) provided outside the appropriations process.

PAYGO does not require any offsetting action when the change in revenue or spending occurs pursuant to existing law, such as a drop in revenue caused by a weakening economy or an increase in medicare payments caused by inflation in health costs. Nor does PAYGO bar Congress from passing revenue or spending legislation that would add to the deficit. Rather, it requires that the deficit increase caused by such legislation be fully offset by legislation raising revenues or cutting direct spending, or by the sequestration of funds from certain direct spending programs. In practice, however, Congress has been unwilling to approve direct spending legislation unless it has already decided how the deficit increase would be offset. In 1994, for example, action on the GATT (General Agreement on Tariffs and Trade) Treaty was delayed because the measure would have reduced tariff revenue.

A determination of whether a PAYGO sequestration is required is made after each session of Congress. At that time OMB, which makes the official estimates of the impact on the budget of enacted legislation, calculates the net impact on the deficit of revenue and direct spending legislation enacted during the session. PAYGO scorecards show the effects for a multiyear period going back to legislation enacted in 1991 and projecting the impact on each year's budget through 1998 (table 3-6). Social security legislation and other direct spending or revenue legislation designated by the president and Congress as emergency measures are excluded from estimates of the deficit impact. If OMB were to find a net increase in the deficit, nonexempt direct spending programs would be sequestered by a uniform percentage. Because most direct spending is exempted from sequestration, the brunt of any mandated cutback would fall on a few programs.

Although PAYGO has not curtailed deficits resulting from existing revenue or spending laws, it has had a marked effect on new legislation. Since it went into effect in the 1991 session, Congress and the president have applied the emergency designation only sparingly. In fact, Congress blocked the use of PAYGO to expand direct spending by decreeing that the savings achieved in the 1993 deficit reduction legislation should not be included in PAYGO computations. A complete reckoning of what has happened since the rules were devised in 1990 would show that Congress has achieved substantial deficit reduction by increasing revenue and cutting direct spending under existing law while also offsetting any deficit increases resulting from new legislation.

The deficit control rules established by the Budget Enforcement Act are the most recent step in the evolution of federal budgeting. They will not be the last. Other proposals to revise federal budget practices are discussed in chapter 10.

The Annual Budget Process

Each reform has layered federal budgeting with distinctive roles, rules, and procedures. The various processes added over the years revolve around an annual budget cycle that begins with the formulation of the president's budget in the executive branch, then moves to Congress, which has four separate processes for making budget decisions, and then on to agencies as they implement their approved budgets. The cycle concludes with the review and audit of expenditures. Table 3-7 provides a timetable of the major steps in the process. It represents an ideal; it assumes that each stage is completed on schedule, something that has rarely happened in the past fifteen years. But the basic steps are repeated from year to year with little change, even though particular procedures may vary in accord with the style of the president and his relations with Congress or in response to changes in political or economic conditions.

Table 3-6. Deficit Impact of Pay-As-You-Go (PAYGO) Legislation, Fiscal Years 1993-98[a]
Millions of dollars

			Impact on baseline deficit				
Legislation	1993[b]	1994	1995	1996	1997	1998	1993-98
Legislation enacted in 1991 and 1992							
OMB estimate	-2,676	-910	-803	...	...	...	-4,389
CBO estimate	-2,676	-910	-803	...	...	...	-4,389
Legislation enacted in 1993							
Phaseout of programs for wool and mohair							
OMB estimate	0	0	-47	-103	-183	-181	-514
CBO estimate	0	0	-57	-103	-176	-169	-505
Unemployment Compensation (P.L. 103-152)							
OMB estimate	0	853	-164	-429	-286	-383	-409
CBO estimate	0	1,070	-137	-285	-270	-372	6
National Defense Authorization (P.L. 103-163)							
OMB estimate	0	52	47	43	41	45	228
CBO estimate	0	13	3	5	6	8	35
Naval Vessels Transfer Act (P.L. 103-174)							
OMB estimate	0	-27	-17	-15	-11	-6	-75
CBO estimate	0	-27	-17	-15	-11	-6	-75
All other 1993 legislation							
OMB estimate	-20	6	13	31	29	4	63
CBO estimate	-20	16	8	28	28	3	63
Subtotal: bills enacted in 1993							
OMB estimate	-20	884	-168	-473	-410	-521	-707
CBO estimate	-20	1072	-198	-370	-423	-536	-475
Total: all bills enacted as of December 3, 1993							
OMB estimate	-2,696	-26	-971	-473	-410	-521	-5,097
CBO estimate	-2,696	162	-1001	-370	-423	-536	-4,864

Source: Office of Management and Budget, *Final Sequestration Report to the President and Congress for Fiscal Year 1994* (December 1993), table 7.
a. Effects on the deficit of all revenue and direct spending legislation enacted since the 1991 session.
   In addition to periodic sequestration reports, OMB must report to Congress within five days after the enactment of direct spending or revenue legislation on the budgetary impact of that measure.
   An OMB estimate that an increase in the deficit due to revenue or direct spending legislation has not been fully offset would trigger a sequestration. The report excerpted here estimates that PAYGO legislation enacted in 1993 decreased the deficit for 1993-98 by $700 million.
   b. The Omnibus Reconciliation Act of 1993 reduced the deficit for fiscal years 1994-98 (according to OMB) by almost $500 billion. However, that act provided that these savings were to be excluded from the PAYGO computations.

Chapters 4 through 9 of this book discuss each of the processes in detail. The present discussion introduces each process and describes a few of its salient features.

The President's Budget

Preparation of the executive budget involves the three sets of participants whose principal functions are listed in table 3-8. These are federal agencies, which request funds; the Office of Management and Budget, which reviews the requests and compiles the budget; and the president, who is responsible for submitting a budget to Congress in early February each year. Budget preparation generally begins in a decentralized manner, with each agency using its own procedures and guidelines for assembling its request. Some presidents such as Bill Clinton issue policy directives through OMB to guide agencies in compiling their budgets; others such as George Bush do not become engaged in the process until agencies have made their submissions.

The process takes eight to ten months in most agencies, longer in some of the largest. At the time they are preparing the new budget, agencies also are implementing the budget for the year in progress and seeking funds from Congress for the fiscal year immediately ahead. Because of the long lead times, agencies assemble their budgets with great uncertainty about the conditions that will prevail when the funds actually become available.

Agency work on the budget is concentrated during the spring and summer of the year preceding its submission to Congress. OMB examines agency requests in the fall, after which it notifies them (via a passback) of its recommended spending levels for their programs. Agencies have a brief period during which they may appeal to the president for more than was recommended by OMB. Once the appeals have been decided, the budget is printed and submitted to Congress.

The Congressional Budget Resolution

Congressional action on the budget involves the four sets of committees whose functions are listed in table 3-9. Each set of House and Senate committees has custody over one of the four types of congressional budget actions: the annual budget resolution, revenue measures, authorizing legislation, and appropriations bills. In performing these tasks, Congress is aided by several legislative staff agencies (table 3-10).

The budget committees produce a resolution that is an internal framework for Congress; it has no legal effect. Its principal purpose is to guide Congress in its consideration of revenue and spending measures. The budget resolution, which covers a five-year period, sets forth budget totals and functional allocations. In addition, the resolution often contains reconciliation instructions directing certain House and Senate committees to report legislation that conforms existing revenue or spending laws to the policies adopted in the budget resolution. Legislation developed by committees pursuant to these instructions is packaged in an omnibus reconciliation bill (commonly labeled the deficit reduction bill), which is considered by the House and Senate under special procedures that expedite its passage.

Revenue Measures

The budget resolution is Congress's only means of considering the whole budget, albeit in highly aggregated terms. All other budget-related actions deal with particular revenue or spending matters. Although Congress takes some action affecting revenues just about every year, it has no regular schedule for taking up major tax legislation. In some years it hardly does anything; in a few it makes truly significant changes in the tax laws.

Revenue legislation is in the jurisdiction of the House Ways and Means and the Senate Finance Committees, two of the oldest and most powerful committees in Congress. The Ways and Means Committee usually acts first because the Constitution stipulates that revenue measures shall originate in the House. Although the Senate takes up the measure after the House, it often makes major changes, setting the stage for the conference at which much of Congress's tax legislation is written.

43

Table 3-7. Timetable of the Fiscal Year 1995 Budget

Period	Activities
1993	
March-June	Development of budget guidelines and preliminary policies; call for estimates issued by agency budget office to operating units
July-September	Agencies formulate detailed requests, which are submitted to OMB
October-December	OMB reviews agency requests and issues passbacks; agency appeals to OMB and/or president. Final decisions
1994	
January	Compilation and printing of executive budget
February	President submits budget to Congress no later than first Monday in February
March 15	Congressional committees submit views and estimates on the budget to budget committees
April 15	Deadline for adopting the fiscal year 1995 budget resolution
May 15-July	House action on regular appropriations bills for 1995
July-September	Senate action and conference on regular appropriations; enactment of appropriations
October 1	Fiscal year 1995 starts. Continuing resolutions enacted if all appropriations have not been enacted
October-November	CBO and OMB issue final sequestration reports for the past session of Congress. Reports are due ten and fifteen days respectively after end of session
October 1994-September 1995	Agencies spend resources and carry out activities as authorized by Congress
1995	
January-September	Congress may make supplemental appropriations for fiscal year 1995 in progress
September 30	Fiscal year ends
October 1	Fiscal year 1996 begins
October-December	Agencies, Treasury, and OMB close the books on fiscal year 1995
1996	
February	Actual revenue and expenditure data included in fiscal year 1997 budget
January-December and beyond	Agencies prepare financial statements; postaudits and evaluations are conducted

Authorizing Legislation

Under the rules, before the House or Senate can appropriate funds, the program or agency that is to receive the money must be authorized in law. This requirement contemplates a sequence in which Congress authorizes a program, then appropriates money to it. There are many variations to this sequence, as discussed in chapter 7. Sometimes the authorization is permanent and Congress need only act on appropriations for the particular program or agency to continue in operation; other times the authorization is annual and Congress must pass both it and the appropriations bill. Most authorizations are discretionary: the amount available is determined by annual appropriations. But for some the authorizing legislation provides direct spending.

Most congressional committees are involved in formulating authorizing measures. Each committee goes about the task in its own way. There is no standard structure or style to authorizations

Table 3-8. Budget Functions of Executive Institutions

President	Office of Management and Budget (OMB)	Federal agencies
Establishes executive budget policy and submits annual budget to Congress	Operates executive budget system and advises president on financial and other issues	Submit budget requests to OMB; appeal to president for more funds
Submits supplemental requests, budget amendments, and updates to Congress	Issues procedural and policy guidelines to agencies	Justify president's budget recommendations before congressional committees
Signs (or vetoes) revenue, appropriations,and other budget-related measures passed by Congress	Issues passbacks to agencies and recommends budget levels to the president	Allot funds among subunits
Notifies Congress of proposed rescissions and deferrals	Compiles annual budget submitted to Congress	Maintain accounting systems and systems of internal control
Issues sequestration orders to cancel budget resources	Reviews proposed legislation and testimony and monitors congressional action on appropriations and other measures	Obligate funds and preaudit expenditures
Appoints the director of OMB and other executive officials	Apportions funds and oversees implementation of the budget	Carry out activities for which funds were provided
	Scores revenue and spending legislation, as provided by BEA	Prepare annual financial statements in accord with accounting standards
	Conducts management activities to improve efficiency of federal operations	Measure performance and develop performance-based budgets

and no prescribed volume of this type of legislation. In some sessions the authorizing committees are active and produce much new legislation; in others, they are relatively dormant and authorizing activity is depressed.

Appropriations Bills

Annual appropriations are provided in thirteen regular appropriations bills, each of which is in the jurisdiction of parallel House and Senate subcommittees. Shortly after the president submits his budget to Congress, the various appropriations subcommittees hold hearings at which agency officials justify the amounts requested. Although the thirteen sets of subcommittees act independently, each is limited by the amount of appropriations allowed by the discretionary spending caps. Before any of the subcommittees marks up its bill, the House Appropriations Committee divides the total discretionary funds among them. (A parallel procedure is used by the Senate Appropriations Committee.) When an appropriations bill is considered by the House or Senate, the spending provided in it is compared to the amount allocated to the relevant subcommittee. In some circumstances floor consideration of an appropriations bill may be barred if the sub-

Table 3-9. Budget Functions of Congressional Committees

Authorizing committees	Appropriations committees	Revenue committees	Budget committees
Report authorizing and direct spending legislation	Report regular and supplemental appropriations bills	Report revenue legislation	Report budget resolution
Oversee executive agencies	Review proposed rescissions and deferrals	Report legislation social security, and certain other entitlements	Draft reconciliation instructions and compile reconciliation bill
Recommend changes in laws pursuant to reconciliation instructions	Submit views and estimates to budget committees	Submit views and estimates to budget committees	Allocate new budget authority, outlays, and other aggregates to committees
Submit views and estimates to budget committees on matters in their jurisdiction	Subdivide budget authority and outlays among their subcommittees	Recommend changes in laws pursuant to reconciliation instructions	Monitor budget and advise Congress on budget impact of legislation
Include CBO cost estimates in reports on their legislation	Establish account structure for federal agencies		
	Establish rules for reprogramming		
	Provide guidance to agencies on expenditure of funds		

committee allocation has been exceeded. This rarely occurs, however, because appropriations subcommittees take care to stay within their allocations.

The House takes up the appropriations bills one at a time, usually beginning in June and continuing through July. The Senate also acts on appropriations one by one, after which a conference committee irons out differences between the House and Senate versions. If the process operates on schedule, the thirteen regular appropriations bills should be enacted by October 1, the start of the new fiscal year. When Congress fails to enact all of these bills on time, it provides interim funding in a *continuing resolution*. Congress also enacts supplemental appropria-

tions measures to provide additional funds during the fiscal year.

Budget Implementation

Agencies cannot spend appropriations until the funds have been apportioned by OMB among the time periods (usually quarters) or projects. Most federal agencies have an allotment process that distributes their apportioned funds among administrative units. Agencies generally are not permitted to spend in excess of their apportionments or allotments.

Although agencies must spend funds according to the terms and conditions set by Congress, they sometimes reprogram funds (shift them

Table 3-10. Budget Functions of Congressional Support Agencies

Congressional Budget Office (CBO)	General Accounting Office (GAO)	Congressional Research Service (CRS)
Issues reports with five-year projections on the budget and the economy	Issues accounting guidelines and reviews agency accounting systems	Analyzes legislative issues and proposals affecting agencies and programs
Estimates five-year cost of reported bills; prepares baseline budget projections and maintains database for scorekeeping	Audits operations of certain federal agencies; evaluates programs and recommends improvements	Assists committees and members by providing data and analyses relevant to their legislative responsibilities
Assists the budget, tax, appropriations, and other committees	Issues legal opinions concerning the use of funds	Compiles legislative histories of particular legislation and programs
Issues reports on options for deficit reduction	Reviews deferrals and rescissions to determine whether they have been properly reported and funds released as required	Issues report on the status of legislation
Reviews the president's budget and other proposals		Analyzes proposals to change federal budget practices
	Investigates expenditures and agency operations as requested by congressional committees	
	Settles certain claims and debt collection issues or disputes	

from one use to another in the same account) to meet unanticipated needs or changing conditions. Deviation from spending plans also occurs when funds are impounded–withheld from obligation of expenditure. Special procedures, described in chapter 9, are brought into play when this happens.

Review and audit constitute the final phase of the budget cycle. Agencies have the primary responsibility for ensuring the propriety and efficiency of their expenditures, and most audits are conducted by them or under their auspices. A number of changes have been made recently in the financial management practices of federal agencies. These have been spurred by legislative develop-

ments, in particular the Chief Financial Officers Act of 1990 and the Government Performance and Results Act of 1993. These and other developments have impelled agencies to give increased attention to the manner in which they implement the budget.

Conclusion

One of the frequent complaints about federal budgeting is that the process has grown too complicated and labyrinthine. There are so many rules and requirements, so many opportunities for obstruction and delay, so many deals that have to be made and interests that have to be harmonized, so much confusion and frustration. Just about every committee and member of Congress has a piece of the budgetary action, but nobody has all of it. The same issues come up again and again; they never are finally resolved, nor is there any sure means of bringing them to closure. Fragmentation of responsibility is pervasive, as is duplication of effort. In federal budgeting, it seems, timetables and deadlines are established to be ignored and violated.

The developments described in this chapter have encrusted budgeting with many procedures. Each can be justified on its own, but the cumulative effect is to overload the process with more than it can handle in the time that is available. Clearly, budgeting is far more complex than it was before there were congressional budget resolutions, reconciliation bills, PAYGO rules, discretionary spending caps, impound-

ment procedures, and so on. Isn't it time, the complainers ask, to divest the process of much of the baggage accumulated over the years? This is a question I will return to in chapter 10. For the present, it should be noted that the complexities and conflicts of budgeting have more to do with the size and sprawl of the budget and the difficulties of grappling with the deficit than with the multiplicity of processes that have to be completed each year. The only way to simplify budgeting and get it to operate as clockwork would be to cut back the size of the budget and eliminate or significantly reduce the deficit. Since neither action is likely to occur soon, the many processes and rules introduced in this chapter and detailed in the next six will continue to vex federal budgeting.

Chapter 4

The President's Budget

The Constitution does not require the president to make recommendations concerning the revenues and expenditures of the government. Nevertheless, the budget has become one of the president's most important policy tools, a means of setting forth legislative and program objectives and of charting the nation's economic course. Early in each legislative session–no later than the first Monday in February–the president submits an annual budget to Congress. This executive budget estimates spending, revenues, borrowing, and debt for the next fiscal year; contains policy and legislative recommendations consistent with those estimates; presents data on the actual and projected performance of the economy; and provides detailed information on the finances of federal agencies and programs.

The Budget and Accounting Act of 1921 provides the legal basis for the presidential budget system that has been in operation for the past seventy years. Before that law was enacted, the federal government did not have a comprehensive presidential budget process. Agencies submitted estimates to the secretary of the Treasury, who compiled them into an annual *Book of Estimates*. Presidents were not formally involved in the process, although some actively intervened to shape financial policy. The 1921 act made presidents responsible for the national budget by requiring them to prepare and submit revenue and spending estimates to Congress each year. The act established the Bureau of the Budget (now the Office of Management and Budget) to assist them in formulating and implementing the executive budget. Although it has been amended many times, this statute is still the principal legal source of the president's budget power. It prescribes much of the budget's form and content and defines the role of the president and spending agencies in the process.

The president's budget is only a request to Congress. Congress is not required to adopt the recommendations, and it typically makes hundreds of changes in the course of appropriating funds and acting on legislation. Still, the president's proposals are often the starting point for congressional revenue and spending actions. The extent of presidential influence varies, however, from year to year and depends more on political and economic conditions than on the legal status of the budget.

Presidential Roles and Styles

The formal role assigned to the president by the Budget and Accounting Act does not tell the full story of presidential involvement in the budget process. Each president brings to the office various personal characteristics, along with political skills and weaknesses. Some presidents are interested in financial matters and welcome the opportunity to make expenditure policy; others distance themselves from the budget and its myriad details. Some have robust program ambitions that can be realized only by shaping the budget to their liking; others have more limited agendas that can be served with status quo budgets. Some seek to avoid friction in the annual budget and appropriations cycle; others see conflict as a necessary means of advancing their program. A comparison of Bill Clinton and other recent presidents reveals significant differences in their budgetary roles.

Clinton did not run for president to serve as the chief budget officer of the United States. During the campaign that led to his election in November 1992, he concentrated on domestic issues: jobs, the economy, education, health care. Once elected, he knew that action on his agenda depended on his skill in putting together and winning adoption of a budget that would change federal revenue and spending policies. Even before his inauguration, he made the federal budget his most important legislative concern for 1993.

Clinton's involvement was more a matter of personal temperament and political choice than a legal requirement. George Bush, his immediate predecessor, was largely disengaged from the budget. Bush left the task of formulating and negotiating major budget policies to Richard Darman, his wily OMB director. But the president paid a political price for distancing himself from the budget. He was on the sidelines when the economy went into recession during the early 1990s, and he was maneuvered into signing tax and spending legislation at variance with his stated policies.

In budgeting, as in other areas of national policy and presidential style, Clinton is very different from Bush. The budget bears Clinton's imprint, not only in name but in substance. He has actively participated in making budget policy and has insisted on being given a full array of revenue and spending options. He has tackled issues concerning the size and direction of the government, its role in steering and stimulating the economy, and its budget commitments and constraints. He has also mastered the details of the budget–reviewing hundreds of programs and deciding the amounts to be spent on each. On taking office, he

confronted the budget deficit with the package of revenue increases and spending cuts discussed in chapter 1.

Clinton is not the first president bent on shaping the budget to his will. Ronald Reagan tried in 1981 when he, like Clinton, won enactment of major revenue and spending legislation. But the two presidents moved in opposite directions: Reagan lowered taxes, Clinton raised them; Reagan increased defense spending and cut social programs, Clinton trimmed defense while adding to social expenditures. Yet these ideologically different presidents took similar approaches to the budget. Both understood that political success depends on changing budget policies, both reshaped the budget soon after taking office, and both got Congress to pass most of what they wanted. Both invested a lot of time and political resources in the budget, and both had to fight for the votes needed to give them a slim margin of victory.

One triumph does not make a presidency, nor does it ensure that early success will last. Reagan's first eight months of budgetary blitzkrieg and legislative accomplishments were followed by seven years of political conflict and budgetary stalemate. And it is highly unlikely that what occurred in 1993 will be repeated every year during Clinton's presidency. Although the president submits a budget each year, he does not try to remake it each year. Clinton's fiscal year 1995 budget (issued in February 1994) sought few significant revenue or spending changes; it purposely avoided contentious budget issues so as to clear the path for legislative action on health care reform.

Many presidents enter office seeing the budget as an opportunity to advance their agendas; quite a few have left perceiving the budget as an impediment to policy innovation. As they age in office, presidents become aware of the budget as the accumulation of past decisions rather than as a forum for making new ones. And so recent presidents have characteristically demanded more of the budget during their first years in office than they have during later years. As the encumbrances of past commitments and the difficulties of change accumulate, they trim their ambitions and hope that a budget that is constrained from doing much good will do little harm.

Even when they have early success, as Reagan and Clinton had, budget victories will probably become increasingly difficult to achieve. Presidents dissipate political capital when they prod members of Congress to go along with spending cuts, as occurred in 1981, or with tax increases, as occurred a dozen years later. They cannot repeatedly demand allegiance from members whose political careers might be damaged by hard budget choices. Barely one month after winning major budget battles in the summer of 1981, Ronald Reagan encountered strong opposition from some previous supporters when he sought another round of spending cuts. It is too early to know whether Bill Clinton will be impeded by congressional recalcitrance, but one should not be surprised if future budgets turn into obstacle courses for some of his program initiatives.

Changes in Presidential Budgeting

Whatever his disposition, no modern president can ignore the budget. The annual budget is one of the few tasks a president must complete each year, no matter how difficult the choices or uncertain the outlook. The president must be mindful of how the budget is faring in Congress and must be prepared to intervene when important issues are at stake. When the budget is released, it is the president's reputation that is on the line: the news media, after all, call the document Reagan's budget, Bush's budget, or Clinton's budget. The president's overall rating depends in some measure on how well his budget is received. Through the budget the president becomes responsible for the performance of the economy. He cannot walk away from this responsibility, even when the problems are not of his own making and the solutions are not readily at hand.

The budget can be a burden, and recent presidents have encountered difficulty in grappling with it. The budget seems to be a less effective tool of presidential legislative leadership today than in the past. During the heyday of presiden-

tial budgeting after World War II, the annual budget served as a platform for the president's legislative program and an authoritative statement of national policy. In some recent years, by contrast, the president's recommendations have been little more than opening bids in a bargaining process. This transformation has resulted from changes in federal budgeting: the growth of entitlements that limit presidents' flexibility; tight budgets that have impelled presidents to ask Congress to cut programs and raise taxes; greater congressional independence arising out of a long spell of divided government; increased activity by the many interest groups that monitor all stages of budgeting and offer in-depth alternatives to a president's budget; and second-guessing of a president's numbers by the Congressional Budget Office, the media, and others.

One of the most telling indications of presidential weakness comes from the extensive use of baselines in making congressional budget decisions. As a projection of future spending, assuming no change in policy, the baseline does not reflect any of the president's recommendations. As noted in chapter 2, the baseline does not move up or down a single dollar if the president asks for more or less. The baseline is used by the budget committees in marking up the budget resolution; by authorizing committees in responding to reconciliation instructions; and by congressional scorekeepers in measuring the impact of proposed or approved legislation and in enforcing current budget rules. Interest groups use baselines to calculate whether their programs are being protected against inflation, and even the president must include baseline information in his budget. It is no overstatement to say that baselines have stolen much of the attention once accorded the president's budget.

The president can compensate for weakness by investing political resources in defense of his budget, as Clinton did in 1993. He fought hard for his fiscal 1994 budget and, despite the close votes and compromises, the final version came close in its main lines to his original proposal. With the Democrats controlling both the legislative and executive branches, the fate of Clinton's budgets rests in their hands. If they are unified, the budget may once again be a potent instrument of presidential leadership; if they are divided, confrontation and impasse over the budget will return.

Formulating the President's Budget

Preparation of the executive budget typically begins in the spring (or earlier) each year, at least nine months before the budget is submitted to Congress, about eighteen months before the start of the fiscal year to which it pertains, and about thirty months before the close of that fiscal year. When agencies begin work on a future budget, they are busy implementing the budget for the fiscal year in progress and awaiting appropriations and other legislative decisions for the year after that. In the spring of 1994, for example, most federal agencies were preparing their fiscal 1996 budgets, months before they had final figures for fiscal 1994 or appropriations for fiscal 1995.

The long lead times and the fact that appropriations have not yet been made for the fiscal year immediately ahead mean that budgets are prepared with a great deal of uncertainty about economic conditions, presidential policies, and congressional actions. During the lengthy preparation cycle, there are likely to be important developments on each of these fronts. Agencies cope with budgetary uncertainty by keeping options open until the last moment and by basing future budgets on past ones. Despite the lead times, few agencies do much long-term budget planning because the same staffs that are preparing future budgets are also working on budgets for the current and next fiscal years. Budget preparation is an extremely busy, deadline-driven period, with many levels of review and enormous demands for data.

The length of the budget preparation cycle is largely due to its bottom-up structure. Agency budgets traditionally have been prepared in a decentralized manner, beginning at the lowest level in an organization that is capable of formulating its own request and progressing to succes-

sively higher levels until all requests are consolidated into an agencywide budget (exhibit 4-1 shows this process in the Department of Health and Human Services). At each stage in this and other federal agencies, the divisions, branches, offices, or other administrative units prepare detailed budgets that list estimated expenditures for personnel, travel, supplies, equipment, and so on. These details are reviewed (and usually revised) as the budget moves up the hierarchy, with the result that budget preparation is a time-consuming and burdensome process that stretches over many months, requires agencies to begin work long before they know how the previous year's budget will turn out, and diverts managerial attention from other agency concerns.

The bottom-up process has several other characteristics that bear noting. It encourages incremental behavior and outcomes, assigns the president a rather limited role in the early stages of budget preparation, and orients the process to inputs rather than performance and results.

Incremental Budgeting

The combination of long lead times but not enough time to look ahead reinforces incremental tendencies in budgeting. Over the years, agency officials have generally taken it for granted that activities funded in the previous budget will be continued in the next and that program initiatives will be financed from incremental resources, not from cutbacks in ongoing programs. They have therefore concentrated on how much more to seek for the year after next than they expect to spend in the next year. Agencies have often produced modest savings in ongoing programs to show that they have lean and efficient operations, but their aim has usually been to get more money than they have received for the current year.

Increments come in all sizes. The size appropriate for an ambitious agency may not suit one that has more modest aspirations; the increase sought when a program is hot or the increments are bountiful may be inappropriate when a program is of low priority or resources are tight.

Exhibit 4-1. Agency Schedule for Budget Preparation

March–April	Development of preliminary budget, including submission of professional judgment budgets from ICDs (institutes, centers, divisions) to the National Institutes of Health (NIH)
May	NIH submits preliminary budget to the Public Health Service (PHS)
May	PHS initial allowances; NIH appeals and PHS final allowances
June	PHS submits departmental budget to the Department of Health and Human Services (DHHS)
July–August	DHHS initial allowances; PHS appeals and secretary's final allowances
September	DHHS submits budget to Office of Management and Budget (OMB)
November	OMB provides initial allowances (passback) to DHHS
November–December	DHHS appeals to OMB and president
December	OMB's and president's final policy decisions and allowances
January	DHHS and constituent units conform their budgets to presidential allowances

Source: Internal NIH memorandum, n.d.

(a) This budget calendar for the National Institutes of Health shows a bottom-up process in which lower administrative units submit requests to successively higher units. Some agencies use a more top-down approach in which policy decisions are made at higher echelons and communicated to subordinate units, which then formulate requests consistent with these policies.

(b) The NIH budget process involves at least six levels: institutes, centers, divisions; the National Institutes of Health; the Public Health Service; the Department of Health and Human Services; the Office of Management and Budget; and the president.

(c) The basic steps at each level entail submission of a preliminary budget, issuance of allowance, appeals, and final decisions. Because of the number of levels and steps at each level, the budget cycle is started eighteen months or more before the beginning of the fiscal year.

(d) At the end of the process, DHHS and its administrative units conform their budgets to OMB and presidential decisions.

And agencies and programs do not, of course, grow uniformly. Many go through periods in which funding is relatively stable, followed by growth spurts, followed by a return to stability. The spurts may be due to the entrepreneurial skills of agency officials or to the opportunities of the moment. An agency that asks for negligible increases may have its budget approved with little change; one that seeks substantial growth may get more but at the price of having its ambitions trimmed back by others.

Incremental budgeting requires incremental resources supplied either by a growing economy, as was the case in the 1950s and 1960s, or deficit financing, as occurred in the 1980s. As long as the economy is growing or the government is willing to borrow large amounts, it is possible to concentrate on the extent to which next year's allocation should vary from this year's and to spend little time reexamining past commitments or ongoing activities. But when neither of these conditions suffices to cover the future cost of existing programs, incremental behavior may not be sustainable. Incremental behavior has become virtually untenable in the discretionary budget because the spending caps (discussed in chapter 2) presage a significant decrease in the real resources available to federal agencies. Many agencies have recently oriented budget preparation to a review of existing programs. Budgetary outcomes in the late 1990s should indicate whether agencies are merely trimming programs at the edges to produce sufficient savings or are reexamining their missions and priorities.

The President's Role in Budget Preparation

Where does the president fit into the agency-centered budget preparation process? Does he have any significant input in the early stages when agencies prepare their estimates, or must he wait until the end when final decisions are made?

The president's role has changed over the years in response both to differences in style and in budgetary conditions. During the boom years of economic and program expansion, OMB had a formal process, known as the spring preview, for developing presidential budget guidelines for the next fiscal year. Pursuant to the preview, OMB would give each agency dollar targets (relatively fixed in some years, elastic in others) as well as indications concerning some of the major program issues to be considered in that year's budget cycle. During the 1980s, however, the formal process withered away, possibly because of OMB and White House preoccupation with congressional budget activity and possibly because they did not want to risk premature leaks of program cuts. Before the Clinton administration, therefore, agencies usually were at work preparing their own budgets before presidential policies were communicated to them.

The lack of robust increments and the withdrawal of the president from the early stages of budget preparation has the potential of weakening presidential influence over the executive budget. When increments were plentiful, the president could intervene at a late stage and still ensure that the additional resources were allocated to his priorities. When the president's principal objective was to cut spending, he could also intervene late and impose the cutbacks at the last minute. The former condition characterized budgets in the postwar years; the latter condition characterized it during the Reagan administration. When the president lacks increments but nevertheless wants to undertake major program initiatives, he cannot wait until the end of the preparation cycle to put his stamp on the budget.

Budget Preparation and Input Orientation

Bottom-up budgeting focuses on the resource needs of operating units, the amounts they must have to pay the salaries of current employees, the cost of equipment and the other things they purchase, and all the other inputs that go into sustaining the activities planned for the next fiscal year. Some federal agencies have elaborate policy planning processes that allow objectives established at the outset to guide budget formulation.

Most agencies that lack a budget planning process nevertheless compile estimates with an eye to what they want to do or accomplish in the next fiscal year. Yet the mass of detail on input often crowds out systematic consideration of plans and performance.

This bias is reinforced by the demands of congressional committees, especially the appropriations committees, for extensive documentation of agency requests. The justification material (discussed in chapter 8) typically contains detailed explanations of the amounts spent on salaries, supplies, and so forth. Eliminating some of the detail is not just a matter of efficiency but touches on the role of the appropriations committees in controlling federal expenditures. The issue here is an old one—the power of the purse. It is not just a matter of the type and volume of information assembled in the course of budget preparation.

The executive budget process has been the target of repeated efforts to orient it to outputs and objectives. The major innovations include performance budgeting in the 1950s, program budgeting and planning-programming-budgeting systems in the 1960s, and management by objective and zero-based budgeting in the 1970s. None of these were successful, though each left some impact on budgetary practices. Few efforts were made to alter federal budgeting during the 1980s, though important developments occurred in deficit control rules, financial management, and congressional procedures.

Renewed efforts to orient the budget process to performance and results have been promoted by the National Performance Review and the Government Performance and Results Act, both of which are discussed in chapter 9. In line with these efforts, OMB has encouraged agencies to include performance output and other performance data in their budget submissions (see exhibit 9-9 for a sample format of performance data prepared in support of an agency's budget request).

Making the Process More Responsive

Recent presidents have had little involvement in the early stages of budget preparation, though they generally have intervened at the end in resolving matters that agencies and OMB did not settle on their own. This late involvement has enabled presidents to hold options open until the last minute, but it has also meant that agencies assembled their requests without much policy guidance from the White House. And it has meant that much of the extensive documentation prepared by agencies had to be revised, and some of it discarded, because of presidential decisions. In fact, much of the detail was irrelevant to the budget choices facing OMB and the president.

The 1993 National Performance Review would alter the president's role, giving him a substantial voice at the start in establishing policies and priorities but a smaller role in reviewing agency requests during the end stages. Its presumption is that if agencies prepare their requests in accordance with presidential instructions, there will be less need to cut them at the end. This revised role is consistent with another NPR recommendation that agencies shorten the budget preparation cycle by drawing up detailed estimates after policy decisions have been made rather than before. Agencies could thus focus on policies and performance rather than on expenditure items.

In preparing the fiscal year 1995 budget, President Clinton followed the logic of the NPR recommendations, though he did not apply some of the procedures the NPR proposed. Early in the budget preparation process, OMB issued austere ceilings on agency requests for the next fiscal year. One objective of these guidelines, some of which were relaxed in the give-and-take of budget negotiations, was to make room within the spending caps for the president's initiatives. Clinton thereby sought to obtain incremental resources for his priorities, even though the overall budget did not allow incremental growth in discretionary spending.

Whatever the advantages of early presidential involvement, it would be naive to assume that matters thought to have been settled by presidential guidelines at the start will remain settled through the rough-and-tumble of budget preparation. Although Clinton intervened in the early stages of the fiscal 1995 process, important matters were reopened in the final stages and the president had an unusually active role at the end (box 4-1). Some issues were reopened by OMB when it tallied the numbers and realized that agency requests had to be trimmed, and some were reopened by agencies that wanted more than OMB had recommended for them. For example, in the spring of 1993 Clinton and defense officials struck a deal on defense spending for the next five years. But months later, when final decisions were being made, the Pentagon appealed for additional money, arguing that earlier inflation projections had been erroneous and that congressional actions had added to its costs.

OMB Review

As agencies formulate their budgets, they maintain ongoing contact with OMB examiners. These contacts should provide the agencies with guidance in preparing their requests and sensitize examiners to agency needs and concerns. Despite their best efforts, however, the relationship is often adversarial because agencies ask for more than OMB can give them and OMB cuts some things that agencies want.

The formal side of budget preparation is based on OMB circular A-11, which contains detailed instructions and schedules for submission of estimates and other material. These technical materials go into the preparation of various documents, but they are too detailed to be the basis for presidential-level decisions.

After agency requests are submitted to OMB in late summer or early fall, they are reviewed by OMB staff and, in many cases, presidential aides as well. The review typically has several distinct stages: *staff review*, during which OMB examiners review the requests, consult with agency officials, and prepare recommendations; *director's review*, at which major issues are discussed, OMB examiners

defend their recommendations, and the OMB director makes budget decisions; *passback*, at which agencies are notified of the director's decisions and have an opportunity to appeal aspects of the review they disagree with; *appeals*, which are first taken to OMB, but if agreement is not reached may be taken to the president or certain aides; and *final decisions*, which are made up to the point that the budget documents are printed. Pursuant to the final decisions, agencies revise their requests to bring them into accord with the president's budget. The budget is then printed and distributed to Congress and the public.

The Budget and Accounting Act of 1921 bars agencies from submitting their budget requests directly to Congress. Moreover, OMB regulations provide for confidentiality in all budget requests and recommendations before the transmittal of the president's budget to Congress. But internal budget documents often are leaked or otherwise become public while the budget is still being formulated.

The format and content of the budget are partly determined by law, but the 1921 act authorizes the president to set forth the budget "in such form and detail" as he may determine. Over the years, there has been an increase in the types of information and explanatory material presented in the budget documents.

The president's budget is not likely to be his last word on the subject, for he is required by law to submit an update (reflecting changes in economic conditions, congressional actions, and other developments) by July 15 each year. Moreover, the president may revise his budget any time during the year. Changes submitted before Congress has acted on the original request are called amendments; requests made for additional funds after Congress has acted on the particular appropriation measures are submitted as supplemental requests.

The President's Budget in Congress

The economy is not the only unknown that the president faces after formulating his budget.

Box 4-1. Role of President Clinton in Fiscal Year 1995 Budget Formulation

"The President yesterday, as Mr. McLarty pointed out, completed the final decision-making process for the fiscal year '95 budget. We had, initially, a two-hour overview meeting with the President on November 29. And then, after that, spent almost 15 hours meeting with every one of the Cabinet secretaries, as well as the key agency heads to discuss their budgets. He met with 21 departments and agency heads to discuss their budgets. The meetings began on December 2 [and] concluded last Friday, December 17.

The meetings with department heads by a President were really unprecedented. Normally what has happened in the past is that Presidents only saw fit to meet with Cabinet members after some of the decisions had been made and only on appeals. President Clinton, however, felt it was essential that each department have the ability to present their case for their budget and then discuss the key issues with him before, not after, any final decisions were made.

[OMB Director Leon Panetta] would make a presentation at the beginning of the meeting that summarized the budget for that department and then addressed the major issues that demanded presidential attention. [T]he secretary was then allowed the opportunity to speak to the budget and to those issues. There was usually a question period that followed and a discussion period that followed. [The] meetings themselves were attended by White House staff, as well as some of the NEC–National Economic Council–representatives.

The President spent a total of about six hours, then, this week [December 20 and 21] to go over the final issues [raised during the department meetings] and then made the final decisions yesterday. OMB basically went over the broad and specific issues with him on both specific departments as well as government-wide issues. And so the formal part of this process involved about 23 hours of meetings with the President.

The process now is basically a technical one because the numbers now are basically presented back to the departments and agencies. They, in turn, translate those decisions into what are literally hundreds of thousands of numbers that feed into our budget. And then we [OMB]ultimately scrub those numbers to make sure that they all fit together when we present the final budget on February 7."

Source: Office of the Press Secretary, White House, "Remarks by OMB Director Leon Panetta," December 22, 1993.

57

He must also deal with a Congress that has become increasingly independent on budget and other policy matters over the past twenty-five years. If the president has a status quo budget, he may not encounter much difficulty getting it through Congress. But if the budget proposes major changes in national policy, the president may have to invest substantial time in monitoring legislative action and wooing members.

OMB tracks the progress of the president's budget through Congress, but its formal role in congressional budgeting is limited. OMB officials and other presidential advisors appear before congressional committees to discuss overall policy and economic issues, but they generally leave discussion of particular programs to the affected agencies. Agencies thus bear the primary responsibility for defending the president's recommendations at appropriations hearings and other congressional actions on the budget. Agency representatives are supposed to speak for the president's request, regardless of how much it differs from their original preferences, and OMB maintains an elaborate legislative clearing process to ensure that budget justifications, testimony, and other submissions to Congress are consistent with presidential policy. But the fragmentation of the appropriations process and informal contacts with congressional staff and members often enable agencies to stake out their own position on particular matters.

To get his way, the president must navigate through congressional budget resolutions, reconciliation bills, annual appropriations, tax legislation, deficit and spending controls, and much more. He must be a good budget counter, mindful of how legislation is scored in enforcing congressional budget rules, and a good vote counter in Congress, willing to twist arms to get a needed majority. He must negotiate with members of Congress at some times and go over their heads at others. He must know when to keep a safe distance and when to intervene. He must not make the mistake of being his own budget director or the mistake of delegating too much to others. The tough decisions and important details must be his call.

Resources

The White House is a budget pulpit. From the Oval Office the president has the capacity to define the terms of budget debate for the next year and possibly longer. He decides which issues will be on the table, whether to seek additional revenue, and whether an attempt will be made to curtail existing entitlements. His budget is the trigger for congressional action on these and other matters. Even when the budget is reputed to be dead on arrival, as it sometimes was in the Reagan and Bush years, the president sets the agenda for the bargaining and legislative actions that follow. The news media give the president's budget wide exposure when it is released, policy analysts and interest groups scour the pages for program implications, and the budget, appropriations, and tax-writing committees spring into action.

Not only does the president have the initiative, he is also sure that Congress will act on many of his proposals. Insofar as appropriations are concerned, Congress does not have the option of doing nothing. There is very high probability that it will produce a budget resolution and act on any prescribed reconciliation bill as well as on other budget-related measures.

Having the initiative does not ensure that the president will get his way. Every budget puts the president at risk that Congress will act at variance with his preferences. To nudge legislative outcomes closer to his budget, the president must cajole the members of Congress whose votes spell the difference between victory and defeat. He must reach out to them even when his party has a majority in both the House and Senate. Reagan in 1981 and Clinton a dozen years later met one-on-one with many members, mostly moderate and conservative Democrats whose support gave them a slim margin of victory. In both cases journalists made much of the deals that had been cut to buy votes. In fact, presidents have to offer relatively little in exchange for votes, especially during the afterglow of their election. A president's most valuable resource is not the grants and dollars he doles out but the predisposition of fence-sitting members to vote his way when he asks for their support. A member who enters the Oval Office before an important vote usually enters predisposed to support the president.

Some presidents have been reluctant to go one-on-one in pursuit of votes. Jimmy Carter was discomfited by this aspect of congressional-presidential relations. George Bush had a comfortable relationship with many members of Congress, but he often stood above the fray and did not exploit the advantages of office when votes were needed. Bill Clinton, however, seems to enjoy this part of the job. Rather than regarding a schedule that sets aside big chunks of time to meet or telephone twenty to thirty members as a chore, he relishes the opportunity to tell them that he needs their vote and appreciates their support.

This is a message that wears thin with repetition, which is why presidents do not build every budgetary (or legislative) disagreement with Congress into a cause célèbre. It also explains why Clinton delayed introduction of health care reform legislation in 1993 until Congress had completed work on his budget plan. A president who asks members for support on more than one controversial issue at a time may come away empty-handed.

In addition to lobbying members of Congress, the president can rally support by defending his budget on prime-time television. Although few viewers are interested in the details of the budget, many see the president's appearance as evidence that he is in charge and doing something about the problems that beset the country. Ronald Reagan used television with considerable effectiveness during his early years in office. He often addressed the American people on the eve of important budget votes. He also broadcast weekend radio talks that were widely disseminated by the media on days when there was normally little solid news.

Clinton has a similar penchant for using his office to project his budget message. He made two back-to-back television appearances in February 1993. The first was a brief talk that field-tested his message and primed Americans for the tax increases that he proposed a few days later; the second was a vigorous presentation of his budget plan to Congress. This concentrated television exposure entailed some political risks, but judging from the final results—enactment of the main features of his plan—Clinton's gamble paid off. Of course, the president cannot go to the country every time a budget issue is pending in Congress. Presidents typically limit their television appearances to occasions when truly important matters are at stake.

Presidential style makes a difference in using the budget as a pulpit. It helps if the president is comfortable in the role and is a gifted communicator. It also helps if the president has an upbeat disposition that enables him to bounce back from bad news and has the staying power that enables him to keep important objectives in focus. Budgeting is a grind. Before one budget is resolved, another is on the way. The problems are never fully or finally decided. Even when they appear to be, unexpected developments often intrude and derail budget plans and hopes.

Bill Clinton is resilient and a willing and agile compromiser. He has not confronted Congress on the budget and demanded that it approve everything he has proposed. In 1993, when his proposed energy tax was defeated, he worked with leading members of Congress to devise an alternative that could pass; when his economic stimulus package ran into trouble, he accepted a scaled-down version. And when Congress appropriated only a portion of the funds he sought for investment, the president hailed it as a significant accomplishment. Some presidents refuse to compromise for fear it will be called a defeat; Clinton compromises and calls it a victory.

The Whole and the Parts

Presidential influence is not spread uniformly across all facets of budgeting. The president sometimes has a stronger voice in setting the totals than in deciding how much specific programs shall grow or shrink. When the president submits the budget, his deficit often becomes the outer limit within which Congress operates (table 4-1). In most years since 1981 the congressional

Table 4-1. Aggregates in the President's Budget and the Congressional Budget Resolution, Fiscal Years 1981-94
Billions of dollars

Fiscal year	Revenues		Budget Authority		Outlays		Deficit	
	President	Congress	President	Congress	President	Congress	President	Congress
1981	600	614	696	697	616	614	16	0
1982	650	658	772	771	695	695	45	38
1983	666	666	802	822	758	770	92	104
1984	660	680	900	920	849	850	189	170
1985	745	751	1,007	1,021	926	932	180	181
1986	794	796	1,060	1,070	974	968	180	172
1987	850	852	1,102	1,093	994	995	144	143
1988	917	933	1,142	1,153	1,024	1,041	108	108
1989	965	964	1,222	1,232	1,094	1,100	130	135
1990	1,059	1,066[a]	1,331	1,351[a]	1,152	1,165[a]	93	100[a]
1991	1,170	1,176[a]	1,396	1,388[a]	1,233	1,239[a]	63	64[a]
1992	1,165	1,169	1,578	1,590	1,446	1,448	281	279
1993	1,165	1,173	1,528	1,516	1,515	1,500	350	327
1994	1,251	1,242	1,517	1,507	1,515	1,496	264	254

Sources: *Budget of the United States Government, Fiscal Year 1986-94; Congressional Quarterly Almanac 1985-1992; Congressional Quarterly Weekly Report* vol. 51, nos. 14-15 (1993).
a. Congressional data for fiscal year 1990-91 refer to the House-passed budget resolutions.

budget resolution has provided for a deficit less than or about the same as the level requested by the president. The president's budget does not legitimize high deficits, but the budget does make it difficult for Congress to set a higher amount. If the president projects the deficit at an unrealistically low level, so will Congress.

The president's influence on the budgeted—in contrast to the actual—deficit generated considerable discomfiture for Congress during the Reagan years, when the budget usually was based on unrealistic economic assumptions and on dead-on-arrival proposals to cut domestic programs deeply. Rather than manifesting impotence, Reagan's budgets skillfully positioned him for negotiations with Congress. In these negotiations and in unilateral actions, Congress saved most of the programs targeted by the president for extinction, but it had to do so within the deficit totals that Reagan had imposed. Within these totals, Congress made big shifts in priorities, taking funds from programs (principally defense) the president wanted to expand and giving them to programs he wanted to shrink.

Congress also saved programs by adding to his spending totals. During the 1980s the congressional budget resolution usually allowed more for total budget authority and outlays than had been requested by the president. Congress made room for the additional expenditures by budgeting more for revenues (see table 4-1).

From the perspective of the White House, Congress made more changes than if the budget had been realistic, but the revenue and spending outcomes were closer to the president's preferences than they would have been if he had sent up a realistic spending plan. By using unrealistic numbers, Reagan put Congress on the defensive; it had to act to save programs, thereby forgoing opportunities to expand them. Moreover, Reagan successfully increased defense spending during 1981-85 even though Congress trimmed the size of the increase. But the president's tactical gains came at a high cost: they made the budget into more of a bargaining chip and less of an authoritative guide to national policy.

In working with his own party in Congress, Clinton's task is to restore the budget to its former stature. He had some success in 1993, when Congress adopted a deficit reduction package that corresponded in its overall dimensions and in many particulars with his proposal. But the new president was somewhat less successful when the budget battle moved to individual appropriations bills. Congress gave the president's initiatives less than he wanted–70 percent of his request by OMB reckoning. Congress's ability to be more responsive was constrained by the fact that the president requested more for appropriated accounts than was allowed by the discretionary spending caps.

Information in the President's Budget

Since the early l990s the structure and content of the budget have been in flux. Until then the practice was to publish the budget in as many as seven separate documents. Beginning with the fiscal year 1991, the budget was consolidated in a single volume. However, the Clinton administration split the fiscal 1995 budget into several volumes.

The budget presents the president's budget message, which highlights major policy recommendations and changes. It provides summary information on receipts, trust and federal funds, credit programs, investment outlays, federal aid to state and local governments, federal borrowing and debt, and other financial matters. It presents expenditure data by functions, agencies, and accounts. For each annually appropriated account, it provides the text of the current appropriation with proposed changes, a narrative explanation of the account's programs and performance, a "program and financing schedule" that classifies the account into its various programs and identifies its financing sources, and a schedule of each account's objects of expenditure. Samples of these presentations are displayed in exhibits 4-2 to 4-6. The budget also has special schedules for credit programs (direct and guaranteed loans) and business-type operations. These are displayed in exhibits 4-7 and 4-8. Finally, the budget contains historical tables that provide financial information for previous years, going back in some cases to 1940.

Although the president's budget is the most detailed source of information on the overall federal budget, it may not have sufficient detail for those interested in particular programs or agencies. Additional information may be obtained from the following documents prepared by federal agencies.

–Briefing material distributed to the media shortly after the president's budget is submitted to Congress. Major federal agencies hold press briefings, usually on the day the budget is released or the next day, at which they provide information on their finances and programs.

–Justification material prepared for appropriations hearings. This material, which is very detailed, usually is published a few months after the hearings are held.

–Internal budgets prepared by agencies for their own use. These are not normally made available to the public. Internal budgets are updated during the year to reflect recent developments, such as presidential or congressional decisions.

Conclusion

For every president, budgeting balances what he wants and what he can get. The published words and numbers attest to what the president says he wants, but are silent about what he will do in pursuit of his objectives or what he will settle for. How much of the budget is presidential ambition and how much is political bluster can be known only after Congress has done its work and agencies are implementing the approved spending plans.

A review of the budgetary record of the three most recent presidents shows that each approached the annual round of revenue and spending decisions in distinctive ways. Ronald Reagan endorsed budgets that, he knew, would come out of Congress much changed from what went in. He asked a lot more for defense so that it could get more even though Congress trimmed the increase. He demanded many of the same domestic cuts year after year so that the growth of these programs was slowed or halted, even though Congress restored all or most of the money. He railed against deficit spending, but he presided over record deficits that led to the Gramm-Rudman-Hollings laws in his second term.

George Bush took a less ideological but more rigid posture than Reagan did. Locking himself into a "read my lips, no new taxes" campaign pledge, Bush started his presidency opposed to relatively modest tax increases, only to be compelled by soaring deficits and the Gramm-Rudman-Hollings rules to accept a very large revenue increase. Perhaps because of his lack of success in keeping his pledge, he distanced himself from the budget. In contrast to all other postwar presidents whose budgets were introduced by messages outlining their policies and objectives, Bush's messages were nothing more than perfunctory letters of transmittal to Congress. The real budget messages were those of Richard Darman, his budget director.

Budgeting during the early Clinton years has been a balancing act in which the president has appealed to disparate wings of his own party. He must satisfy middle-of-the-road and some conservative Democrats without alienating liberal members. He must get legislation through the House, which tends to be a bit more liberal than he is, and through the Senate, which tends to be more centrist. In neither chamber can he count on much Republican support for his budget policies.

Balancing seems to come naturally to Clinton, though it sometimes discomfits supporters and leaves others wondering what his real position is. To Clinton, balancing is not just a matter of compromising on differences or walking a center line; it is harmonizing seemingly clashing views by means of policies that embrace both conservative and liberal values. It means producing budgets that cut some programs while expanding others, doing something about the deficit while undertaking major program initiatives, pruning the size of government programs while extracting more tax dollars to finance those programs. Budgeting by Clinton defies conventional classification and accommodates the constraints and opportunities of the moment. As long as he is president, he will be seeking new syntheses that appeal to those Americans who want smaller government and more from government. How long this will be will depend in some measure on his success in reconciling the antipathetic forces of American politics.

Exhibit 4-2. Appropriations Language

Federal Funds

General and special funds:

OPERATIONS, RESEARCH, AND FACILITIES

(INCLUDING TRANSFER OF FUNDS)

For necessary expenses of activities authorized by law for the National Oceanic and Atmospheric Administration, including acquisition, maintenance, operation, and hire of aircraft; *not to exceed* 439 commissioned officers on the active list; as authorized by 31 U.S.C. 1343 and 1344; construction of facilities, including initial equipment as authorized by 33 U.S.C. 883i; grants, contracts, or other payments to nonprofit organizations for the purposes of conducting activities pursuant to cooperative agreements; and alteration, modernization, and relocation of facilities as authorized by 33 U.S.C. 883i; [$1,521,416,000] *$1,529,258,000*, to remain available until expended[, of which $37,000,000 is available to initiate the procurement of two additional NOAA Advanced Tiros-N polar-orbiting weather satellites from the current contractor, and of which $288,000 shall be availble only for a contract with the National Research Council to conduct an assessment of the status of Columbia River endangered salmon stocks, and of which $576,000 shall be available for operational expenses and cooperative agreements at the Fish Farming Experimental Laboratory at Stuttgart, Arkansas]; and in addition, [$55,000,000] *$61,400,000* shall be derived by transfer from the fund entitled "Promote and Develop Fishery Products and Research Pertaining to American Fisheries": *Provided*, That grants to States pursuant to section 306 and 306(a) of the Coastal Zone Management Act, as amended, shall not exceed $2,000,000 and shall not be less than $500,000[: *Provided further*, That in applying the provisions of section 606 of this Act to the programs, projects, and activities of the National Oceanic and Atmospheric Administration, the notification requirements of section 606 shall apply to the proposed reprogramming of funds in excess of $250,000 or 5 per centum, whichever is less, for each program, project, or activity].

Source: *Budget of the United States Government, Fiscal Year 1994*, pp. A-420–A-421.

(a) This and the next four exhibits display the information provided in the president's budget for each account funded by annual appropriations. All these exhibits pertain to the account for the National Oceanic and Atmospheric Administration. Besides appropriated accounts, the budget sets forth schedules for various types of revolving funds, business-type operations, and credit programs.

(b) For each account funded by annual appropriations, the budget prints the text of the current and proposed appropriations. The material in brackets is current appropriations language proposed for deletion; the material in italics is proposed to be added.

(c) The appropriations language is followed by a citation of the act in which the appropriation for the current fiscal year was provided.

(d) "General provisions" appear at the end of the departmental chapter in the budget (in this case for the Department of Commerce) to which they pertain. "General provisions" pertaining to the entire federal government are enacted in the Treasury-Postal Service Appropriations Act and appear at the beginning of the appendix to the budget.

Exhibit 4-3. Program Description

National Ocean Service.—These programs provide scientific, technical, and management expertise to (1) promote safe and efficient marine and air navigation; (2) assess the health of coastal and marine resources; (3) monitor and predict the coastal ocean and global environments; and (4) protect and manage the Nation's coastal resources. An increase is proposed to maintain traditional geodetic activities and to enhance support for the National Water Level Measurement System, essential for marine navigation and storm surge warnings.

National Marine Fisheries Service.—These programs provide for the management and conservation of the Nation's living marine resources and their environment, including marine mammals and endangered species. An increase is proposed to maintain research facilities and staffing necessary to implement statutory requirements.

Oceanic and Atmospheric Research.—These programs provide: the understanding and technique development necessary to improve NOAA services (weather warnings and forecasts, solar-terrestrial services, climate predictions, and marine services); and the understanding of environmental systems necessary for national policy formulation (e.g., long term climate change, acid rain and ozone issues) and the enhanced use of ocean resources (e.g., fisheries, and water quality). An increase is proposed to improve measurements and research on climate, air quality, and atmospheric and marine processes, and to enhance atmospheric prediction and observation technologies and space weather observations.

Source: *Budget of the United States Government, Fiscal Year 1994,* p. A-421.

(a) For most accounts, the budget describes the programs funded in the account and provides relevant workload or other performance data. These descriptions have been revised in recent budgets to make them briefer and to relate them to the particular year's budget decisions.

(b) Although OMB instructions call for agencies to justify their requests with detailed analyses of workload, unit costs, productivity trends, and performance standards, the amount of such data included in the budget is limited.

(c) More detailed program descriptions and performance data are provided by agencies in the justification material submitted to the Appropriations Committees. The justification material is included in the published Appropriations Committees hearings.

Exhibit 4-4. Program and Financing Schedule: Program by Activities

Program and Financing (in thousands of dollars)

Identification code 13–1450–0–1–306	1992 actual	1993 est.	1994 est.
Program by activities:			
Direct program:			
00.01 National Ocean Service	157,881	184,272	148,826
00.02 National Marine Fisheries Service	218,191	238,081	224,043
00.03 Oceanic and Atmospheric Research	211,386	207,667	188,497
00.04 National Weather Service	453,605	553,798	546,510
00.05 National Environmental Satellite, Data, and Information Service	355,481	358,122	352,973
00.06 Program support	150,174	147,321	145,109
00.91 Total direct program	1,546,718	1,689,261	1,605,958
Reimbursable program:			
01.01 National Ocean Service	57,208	65,834	61,796
01.02 National Marine Fisheries Service	27,634	45,794	36,444
01.03 Oceanic and Atmospheric Research	34,333	75,441	73,393
01.04 National Weather Service	189,546	153,342	193,398
01.05 National Environmental Satellite, Data, and Information Service	22,511	14,763	11,795
01.06 Program support	15,698	13,907	13,559
01.91 Total reimbursable program	346,930	369,081	390,385
10.00 Total obligations	1,893,648	2,058,342	1,996,343

Source: *Budget of the United States Government, Fiscal Year 1994*, p. A-421.

(a) The program and financing schedule for each budget account consists of four parts: program by activities (shown here); financing; relation of obligations to outlays; and adjustments.

(b) Each account has an eleven-digit identification code. The first two digits designate the agency; the next four are the account number; the seventh digit indicates the type of request (such as regular or supplemental); the eighth indicates the type of fund; and the last three refer to the function in which the account is classified.

(c) The first part of the program and financing schedule divides resources among the programs and activities contained in the account. OMB instructions call for agencies to define activities that are based on the accounting structure, are related to the administrative operations of the agency, and are useful for program analysis and evaluation.

(d) The schedule shown here does not distinguish between operating expenses and capital investments. (Unlike state and local governments, the federal government does not budget separately for operating and capital spending.)

Exhibit 4-5. Program and Financing Schedule: Financing

Financing:				
17.00	Recovery of prior year obligations	−22,417	−11,800	−13,800
21.40	Unobligated balance available, start of year	−64,969	−72,214	
24.40	Unobligated balance available, end of year	72,214		
39.00	**Budget authority (gross)**	**1,878,476**	**1,974,328**	**1,982,543**
	Budget authority:			
	Current:			
40.00	Appropriation	1,461,999	1,586,416	1,529,258
40.78	Reduction pursuant to P.L. 102-396		−65,000	
42.00	Transferred from other accounts	63,100	61,225	61,400
43.00	**Appropriation (total)**	**1,525,099**	**1,582,641**	**1,590,658**
	Permanent:			
60.05	Appropriation (indefinite)		5,100	
62.00	Transferred from other accounts	6,447	17,506	1,500
63.00	**Appropriation (total)**	**6,447**	**22,606**	**1,500**
68.00	**Spending authority from offsetting collections**	**346,930**	**369,081**	**390,385**
	Relation of obligations to outlays:			
71.00	Total obligations	1,893,648	2,058,342	1,996,343
72.40	Obligated balance, start of year	919,470	892,275	980,000
74.40	Obligated balance, end of year	−892,275	−980,000	−1,018,631
78.00	Adjustments in unexpired accounts	−22,417	−11,800	−13,800
87.00	**Outlays (gross)**	**1,898,427**	**1,958,817**	**1,943,912**
	Adjustments to budget authority and outlays:			
	Deductions for offsetting collections:			
88.00	Federal funds	−278,405	−332,128	−353,650
88.30	Trust funds	−35,389		
88.40	Non-Federal sources	−33,136	−36,953	−36,735
88.90	**Total, offsetting collections**	**−346,930**	**−369,081**	**−390,385**
89.00	**Budget authority (net)**	**1,531,546**	**1,605,247**	**1,592,158**
90.00	**Outlays (net)**	**1,551,497**	**1,589,736**	**1,553,527**

Source: *Budget of the United States Government, Fiscal Year 1994*, p. A-421.

(a) The financing portion of this schedule (continued from the previous exhibit) shows the source of funds. In the account exhibited here, the bulk of the funds come from annual appropriations, but resources also come from permanent appropriations, offsetting collections, transfers from other accounts, and other sources.

(b) The next section of the schedule relates obligations to outlays. The outlay figure for the budget year (1994 in this case) is only an estimate, not a recommendation or a limit.

(c) The final "adjustments" portion of the schedule relates gross and net amounts of budget authority. The difference can be calculated by comparing lines 39.00 and 89.00 for budget authority and lines 87.00 and 90.00 for outlays. (These code numbers are used for classifying the entries.) Net budget authority and outlays are derived by deducting offsetting collections from gross budget authority and outlays.

Exhibit 4-6. Object Classification

Object Classification (in thousands of dollars)

Identification code 13–1450–0–1–306	1992 actual	1993 est.	1994 est.
Direct obligations:			
Personnel compensation:			
11.1 Full-time permanent	433,917	510,508	534,123
11.3 Other than full-time permanent	22,688	12,613	17,643
11.5 Other personnel compensation	24,082	24,700	24,902
11.9 Total personnel compensation	480,687	547,821	576,668
12.1 Civilian personnel benefits	93,804	106,112	116,345
13.0 Benefits for former personnel	6,402	11,026	7,873
21.0 Travel and transportation of persons	23,992	18,710	18,707
22.0 Transportation of things	8,644	7,963	8,028
23.1 Rental payments to GSA	31,494	52,348	61,996
23.2 Rental payments to others	13,005	9,320	9,580
23.3 Communications, utilities, and miscellaneous charges	37,907	29,828	14,990
24.0 Printing and reproduction	8,108	5,194	5,447
25.1 Consulting services	644	532	527
25.2 Other services	526,891	616,161	545,997
26.0 Supplies and materials	61,793	37,291	38,821
31.0 Equipment	72,106	44,638	36,406
32.0 Land and structures	4,483	1,816	11
41.0 Grants, subsidies, and contributions	176,639	200,486	164,547
42.0 Insurance claims and indemnities	42	14	14
43.0 Interest and dividends	77	1	1
99.0 Subtotal, direct obligations	1,546,718	1,689,261	1,605,958
99.0 Reimbursable obligations	346,930	369,081	390,385
99.9 Total obligations	1,893,648	2,058,342	1,996,343

Personnel Summary

Identification code 13–1450–0–1–306	1992 actual	1993 est.	1994 est.
Direct: Total compensable workyears:			
1001 Full-time equivalent employment	11,541	11,809	11,904
1005 Full-time equivalent of overtime and holiday hours	381	391	391
Reimbursable: Total compensable workyears:			
2001 Full-time equivalent employment	2,211	1,213	1,213
2005 Full-time equivalent of overtime and holiday hours	73	64	64

Source: *Budget of the United States Government, Fiscal Year 1994*, p. A-422.

(a) This schedule, which accompanies every appropriations account, classifies obligations among the major objects of expenditure. The same object codes are used for all federal agencies.

(b) Some objects are divided into subclasses to provide more detailed information on expenditures. Note, however, the substantial resources classified as "other services."

(c) For each account with personnel compensation, the budget presents summary data on the number of full-time equivalent (FTE) work years.

(d) Agencies usually have some flexibility in shifting funds among object classes. However, most have ceilings or floors on the number of FTEs, and many are expected by their appropriations subcommittees to implement their budgets, to the maximum extent practicable, in accord with the object schedules. In 1993 the National Performance Review proposed that agencies be given substantial discretion in spending appropriated funds, including the determination of staffing levels.

Exhibit 4-7. Direct Loans: Program Account Data

Summary of Loan Levels, Subsidy Budget Authority and Outlays by Program

(in thousands of dollars)

Identification code 12–2081–0–1–371		1992 actual	1993 est.	1993 est.
Direct loan levels supportable by subsidy budget authority:				
1150	Single family housing	1,253,800	1,295,000	1,574,575
1150	Multi-family housing	573,900	573,900	546,878
1150	Housing repair	11,330	14,651	11,959
1150	Farm labor housing	15,942	16,300	16,012
1150	Site development	371	600	616
1150	Credit sales of acquired property	183,802	185,200	168,955
1159	Total direct loan levels	2,039,145	2,085,651	2,318,995
Direct loan subsidy (in percent):				
1320	Single family housing	22.64	20.96	20.02
1320	Multi-family housing	43.30	52.73	57.39
1320	Housing repair	42.92	39.90	39.06
1320	Farm labor housing	55.21	48.29	51.50
1320	Site development	0.27	−3.89	−2.83
1320	Credit sales of acquired property	14.69	13.52	15.22
1329	Weighted average subsidy rate	28.10	31.22	28.79
Direct loan subsidy:				
1330	Single family housing	283,860	306,943	315,230
1330	Multi-family housing	248,499	305,602	313,853
1330	Housing repair	4,863	5,948	4,671

Source: *Budget of the United States Government, Fiscal Year 1994*, pp. A-337-A-338.

(a) The president's budget presents a series of schedules for each account that has direct loans or loan guarantees. As explained in chapter 2, direct and guaranteed loans have program accounts that receive appropriations to cover subsidy costs and financing accounts that handle all the cash flows of the loan program. Only the program account is exhibited here.

(b) This loan account (for the Rural Housing Insurance Fund) comprises five separate programs administered by the same federal agency. Although the various programs are consolidated in a single account, separate subsidy rates are calculated for each.

(c) The loan level that can be supported by a particular amount of budget authority depends on the subsidy rate. In this case, single-family loans budgeted for fiscal year 1994 (last column) have a subsidy rate of 20.02 percent and therefore require a subsidy of $315 million (which is appropriated as subsidy budget authority) to support $1,574 million in direct loans.

(d) The terms "subsidy budget authority" and "subsidy loans" distinguish these entries from budget authority and outlays for nonloan programs. However, all budget authority and outlay entries, regardless of type, are added together to calculate the budget totals.

Exhibit 4-8. Business-Type Statements

Financial Condition (in thousands of dollars)

Identification code 12–4215–0–3–371	1991 actual	1992 actual	1993 est.	1994 est.
Assets:				
1000 Fund balance with Treasury and cash: Fund balance with Treasury	....	23,607	23,607	23,607
1100 Accounts receivable: Federal agencies	....	260,277	368,336	417,278
1800 Loans receivable, gross	....	1,365,903	3,252,655	5,461,641
1805 Allowances for subsidy cost	....	−313,277	−894,651	−1,513,841
1809 Loans receivable, net present value	....	1,052,626	2,358,004	3,947,800
1999 Total assets	....	1,336,510	2,749,947	4,388,685
Liabilities:				
2615 Intragovernmental debt: debt to Treasury	....	1,052,626	2,358,004	3,947,800
2999 Total liabilities	....	1,052,626	2,358,004	3,947,800
Equity:				
3200 Appropriated fund equity: Appropriated capital	....	283,884	391,943	440,885
3299 Subtotal, revolving fund balances	....	283,884	391,943	440,885
3999 Total equity	....	283,884	391,943	440,885

Source: *Budget of the United States Government, Fiscal Year 1994*, p. A-339.

(a) Business-type statements are prepared for government corporations and various revolving funds. For some, the budget presents a statement of revenue and expense (not shown here) on an accrual basis—with revenue recorded when earned and expenses recorded when incurred.

(b) This statement, for the Rural Housing Insurance Fund, gives some indication of the size of federal corporations. The assets of this fund exceed $4 billion, largely in the form of loan receivables; the liabilities, approaching $4 billion, are monies borrowed from the Treasury.

(c) The statement of financial condition shows assets, liabilities, and equity at the end of each fiscal year. This statement is similar to a commercial balance sheet and generally relies on private sector accounting principles.

Chapter 5

The Congressional Budget Resolution and Reconciliation

The budget resolution is the means by which Congress establishes budget policies and priorities and coordinates the various budget-related actions (such as consideration of revenue and spending measures) it takes each year. Revenue and spending amounts set in the annual budget resolution provide the basis for enforcing congressional budget policies when the House and Senate consider financial legislation. It initiates the reconciliation process for conforming revenue and spending laws to current budget policies. The budget resolution must be consistent with the rules of the Budget Enforcement Act, discussed in chapter 3. These rules include deficit targets, limits on discretionary spending, and pay-as-you-go (PAYGO) constraints on revenue and spending legislation.

Why Congress Has a Budget Resolution

The budget resolution is a concurrent resolution, a measure that is approved by both the House and the Senate but is not submitted to the president for his signature or veto. Because the budget resolution is not a law, no money can be raised or spent pursuant to it. Congress still must enact revenue and spending legislation to give its budget decisions legal effect.

Why does Congress go through the motions of adopting a budget resolution each year when it still must pass separate bills that enable the government to impose taxes and spend public funds? In fact, Congress operated for almost 200 years–from its first session in 1789 until 1975–without a budget resolution. During that period it made numerous budget decisions each year, acting on revenue and spending bills one at a time. Congress did not vote on the total budget, nor did it expressly decide to give higher priority to some programs than to others. The total was simply the sum of its many separate decisions; priorities emerged only by comparing the various actions taken during the year. However, now that Congress adopts a budget resolution, it votes on both the totals and spending priorities, in addition to voting on legislation affecting the budget.

To understand why Congress devised a budget resolution, one must consider three questions. How did Congress operate without a budget resolution in the past? Why did Congress change course in the 1970s and establish its own budget process? What purpose is served by having a budget resolution in the 1990s?

As to how it operated without a budget resolution, Congress is a decentralized institution that must, because of its representative character, give many members and committees a voice in making budget decisions. Since many committees and subcommittees are responsible for revenue, appropriations, and authorizations, most members of Congress have some influence on the budget. Congress's habit of operating in a piecemeal fashion, taking up the many budget-related measures one at a time, is a political imperative, not an institutional defect. To understand why it must decentralize budgetary power, consider what might happen if a single committee in the House and one in the Senate had jurisdiction over all budget matters. Given the size and importance of the budget, those committees would be able to use their budgetary power to control virtually all legislative activity. Members of Congress who served on these committees would have sufficient clout to influence substantive legislation not directly related to the budget. Most other members would be without a significant legislative role or influence. This concentration of budgetary power would be neither acceptable nor durable. Sooner or later, the majority who lacked budgetary influence would wrest control from the few who had it.

In the past the fragmentation of the budget process--no one in charge, most members and committees having some budget-making power--worked. That is, it produced satisfactory results, at least as measured by the modest size of the deficit. Except for wartime and periods of economic upheaval, the federal budget was at or near balance. Even though revenue and spending decisions were uncoordinated, Congress achieved seemingly coordinated results. It did not need a budget resolution to determine the totals.

By the 1970s, however, this system had broken down, and Congress could no longer balance revenues and expenditures without voting on the budget's totals and priorities. Evidence of breakdown could be readily found in escalating budget deficits, which were very high by past standards. The breakdown had various causes, two of which have a direct bearing on Congress's decision to establish its own budget process. One was conflict with the president over the budget and other matters; the other was the rapid rise in spending

on entitlements.

In the past, although Congress acted on the budget in piecemeal fashion, it was guided by the president's recommendations. Every step of the way, especially in making appropriations and writing tax legislation, members tried to keep their actions in line with the president's proposals. Congress made many spending changes, but they were typically small and incremental, with the result that even though it did not explicitly decide what the totals should be, the sum of all its actions usually was close to the president's budget. In this way decentralization still led to coordinated budget decisions. But in the late 1960s and early 1970s the Vietnam War, the Watergate scandal, and conflict between the White House and Capitol Hill over spending policies eroded Congress's willingness to follow the president's lead on budget matters as well as other policies. In establishing its own coordinated budget process, Congress was able to stake out a position independent of the president's on fiscal policy and budget priorities.

Congress also was provoked to act by the growing costs of mandatory entitlements such as medicare, most of which were in the jurisdiction of the authorizing committees. These expenditures grow automatically, as required by law, without any new congressional decision and regardless of the condition of the budget. Entitlements could not be controlled through the annual appropriations process. Congress needed a broader process that would cover all expenditures, regardless of the committees that have jurisdiction, and that would coordinate revenue and spending decisions.

In establishing a comprehensive budget process, Congress still had to disperse budgetary power broadly. It did so by layering the budget resolution on top of existing authorizations, appropriations, and revenue-raising processes--all of which have been continued with only minor changes. It sought to have the best of both worlds: an integrated budget process and decentralized revenue and spending processes. This combination has made for complicated, ever changing relationships between Congress's budget process and its other budget-related activities.

The arrangement has now been in effect for twenty years. During this period the congressional budget process has reinvented itself almost every year, depending on the circumstances and opportunities of the moment. In some years, such as from 1987 through 1990, major budget policies have been made in summit negotiations between presidential aides and congressional leaders, and the budget resolution has rubber-stamped these decisions. In other years, especially 1982 through 1986, Congress has ventured on its own, and the budget resolution has been crucial in determining legislative policies.

Currently, the budget resolution serves three important legislative purposes: it facilitates major changes in budget policy; it is the source of allocation of budget resources to congressional committees; and it triggers reconciliation legislation.

The role of the budget resolution depends on the extent to which it redirects budget policy or merely reflects the policies already in place. In 1981 Ronald Reagan exploited the congressional budget process to enact far-reaching changes in tax and spending policy; Bill Clinton did the same thing in 1993. These presidential triumphs, a dozen years apart and for very different purposes, have been the biggest events in the short history of budget resolutions. In most years the resolution has had a more modest role; it has been more a means of organizing congressional action than of changing national policy. The budget resolution was devised to be an instrument of congressional independence, but in some years it has been an instrument of presidential power.

Another function of the budget resolution is to allocate budget authority and outlays among congressional committees, which in turn subdivide their share of the budget among their subcommittees. This "section 602" procedure, which is described later in this chapter, sets the financial boundaries within which the appropriations committees operate. For the budget resolution to serve this purpose, it must be adopted in a timely manner, before the House and Senate take up the appropriations bills. As we shall see, this has not always been the case.

Finally, the budget resolution may contain directives that initiate the reconciliation process and lead in some years to significant changes in revenue and spending legislation. Congress did not activate reconciliation in 1991 and 1992, two years during which the budget resolution merely continued along the path marked out by the Budget Enforcement Act of 1990. But in 1981, 1982, 1984, 1990, and 1993 major budget changes were enacted through reconciliation procedures.

Structure and Content of the Budget Resolution

Each budget resolution covers five fiscal years: the next fiscal year, for which appropriations and other budget actions are pending in Congress, and four out-years. The aggregate amounts set for the next year are binding; Congress must adhere to them in making revenue and spending decisions. Those for the out-years are targets that are likely to be revised when future budget resolutions are formulated. However, the out-years may be enforced by points of order pursuant to the Budget Enforcement Act.

Each resolution is organized into two or three main sections: budget aggregates, functional allocations, and sometimes reconciliation directives. Congressional rules allow certain other budget-related matters such as "sense of the Congress" statements and special procedures to be included in the resolution.

Budget Aggregates

Exhibits 5-1 and 5-2 display the aggregates set for fiscal year 1994; the form is common to each resolution. The main aggregates are

–total revenue and the amount by which the total should be increased or decreased;

–total new budget authority and total outlays;

–total direct loan obligations and primary loan guarantee commitments;

72

–the deficit or surplus; and
–the public debt.
Except for the public debt, the aggregates do not include the social security trust funds, which are by law off budget.

The budget resolution requires members of Congress to vote on, and in a sense to take responsibility for, total spending and the size of the deficit. If there were no resolution, these totals would simply be the arithmetic sum of the many different actions taken during the year, the impact of past decisions (such as the 1965 law establishing medicare and medicaid) on current budgets, and the impact of economic conditions on revenues and expenditures. Voting on total outlays and the deficit are among the most onerous tasks facing members, who are put in a position of endorsing deficits they do not want and over which they have little control. In view of the size of recent deficits, many members try to avoid blame by voting against the budget resolution or vote for it only under intense pressure from party leaders.

The limit on public debt is another hard vote. The limit is not an effective means of controlling the budget; the size of the debt is determined by past deficits and the deficits expected to be incurred in the years immediately ahead. Nevertheless, because the size of the debt is limited by law, Congress must periodically pass legislation raising the limit. The House has a special procedure whereby passage of the budget resolution is also deemed to pass the debt limit legislation. The Senate does not have a comparable procedure; therefore, senators often must vote twice on the public debt: once on the budget resolution and again on the statutory debt limit.

Functional Allocations

The resolution allocates total new budget authority, outlays, direct loans, and loan guarantees among the twenty functions listed in exhibit 5-3. These functions include national defense, agriculture, medicare, veterans, benefits, interest, and other major areas of federal spending. The

functional allocations must add up to the corresponding budget aggregates. For example, the sum of the outlays allocated to the twenty functions must equal total outlays.

The requirement of arithmetic consistency is so fundamental to budgeting that it is taken for granted. After all, how can something be a budget if the parts do not add up to the whole? But in the political arena, consistency is not always easy to achieve. Public opinion polls generally show that Americans want bigger programs and a smaller budget. They favor reductions in total federal spending, but oppose reductions in particular programs. Arithmetic consistency means that elected politicians are barred from behaving the way voters profess to want them to behave. The House and Senate may not increase spending for any function without offsetting the amount in another function or increasing total expenditures. Some members of Congress grandstand: they vote to raise some functional allocations but then oppose the budget resolution on the ground that the deficit is too big. But to pass the resolution, a majority in the House and Senate must behave consistently by casting their lot with large deficits or risk the wrath of voters by voting to cut program expenditures. Putting together this majority has not been an easy task.

The budget resolution does not allocate funds to specific programs or accounts: any attempt to do so would run afoul of the jurisdictions of the appropriations committees, which vigilantly guard their control of line items. The lack of detail in the budget resolution makes it difficult for members to take credit for earmarking funds for particular programs. Thus the rules of congressional budgeting call for members to vote for spending without getting political credit for favored expenditures and often without knowing exactly how much each program will get.

Nevertheless, members and committees seek to influence spending for favored programs by specifying program assumptions in the House and Senate Budget Committee reports that accompany each budget resolution. Exhibit 5-4 provides an excerpt of the assumptions made by the House

Exhibit 5-1. Budget Aggregates: Revenues and Budget Authority

(i) The recommended levels of Federal revenues are as follows:

  Fiscal year 1994: $905,500,000,000.
  Fiscal year 1995: $973,800,000,000.
  Fiscal year 1996: $1,037,600,000,000.
  Fiscal year 1997: $1,093,300,000,000.
  Fiscal year 1998: $1,143,200,000,000.

(ii) The amounts by which the aggregate levels of Federal revenues should be increased are as follows:

  Fiscal year 1994: $27,400,000,000.
  Fiscal year 1995: $40,400,000,000.
  Fiscal year 1996: $58,000,000,000.
  Fiscal year 1997: $73,600,000,000.
  Fiscal year 1998: $73,200,000,000.

(2) NEW BUDGET AUTHORITY.—(A) For purposes of comparison with the maximum deficit amount under sections 601(a)(1) and 606 of the Congressional Budget Act of 1974 and for purposes of the enforcement of this resolution, the appropriate levels of total new budget authority are as follows:

  Fiscal year 1994: $1,223,400,000,000.
  Fiscal year 1995: $1,289,600,000,000.
  Fiscal year 1996: $1,347,500,000,000.
  Fiscal year 1997: $1,409,900,000,000.
  Fiscal year 1998: $1,474,500,000,000.

Source: *Conference Report on the Fiscal 1994 Budget Resolution*, H. rept. 103-48, 103 Cong. 1 sess (1993).

(a) The first part of each budget resolution sets forth total revenues, new budget authority, outlays, and other aggregates. The revenue and budget authority aggregates are displayed here; other aggregates are shown in the next exhibit.

(b) Each budget resolution covers five fiscal years, in this case the years 1994 through 1998. The fiscal 1994 budget resolution reflected congressional policy, portions of which were enacted in the reconciliation act, for a five-year period. Some facets of that policy are likely to be changed before the five years are completed.

(c) The totals do not include receipts and expenditures of the social security trust funds. In comparing budget data from different sources, one should ascertain whether social security is included. The totals shown in the president's budget usually include social security; hence direct comparison with the aggregates in the budget resolution may not be appropriate.

(d) The amounts set forth for revenue increases cover only amounts to be obtained through new legislation, not increases resulting from the level of economic activity. The budgeted increases were enacted in the 1993 reconciliation act.

Exhibit 5-2. Budget Aggregates: Outlays, Deficit, and Debt Limit

(3) BUDGET OUTLAYS.—(A) For purposes of comparison with the maximum deficit amount under sections 601(a)(1) and 606 of the Congressional Budget Act of 1974 and for purposes of the enforcement of this resolution, the appropriate levels of total budget outlays are as follows:

Fiscal year 1994: $1,218,300,000,000.
Fiscal year 1995: $1,280,600,000,000.
Fiscal year 1996: $1,323,200,000,000.
Fiscal year 1997: $1,371,300,000,000.
Fiscal year 1998: $1,435,900,000,000.

(4) DEFICITS.—(A) For purposes of comparison with the maximum deficit amount under sections 601(a)(1) and 606 of the Congressional Budget Act of 1974 and for purposes of the enforcement of this resolution, the amounts of the deficits are as follows:

Fiscal year 1994: $312,800,000,000.
Fiscal year 1995: $306,800,000,000.
Fiscal year 1996: $285,600,000,000.
Fiscal year 1997: $278,000,000,000.
Fiscal year 1998: $292,700,000,000.

(5) PUBLIC DEBT.—The appropriate levels of the public debt are as follows:

Fiscal year 1994: $4,731,900,000,000.
Fiscal year 1995: $5,097,900,000,000.
Fiscal year 1996: $5,453,700,000,000.
Fiscal year 1997: $5,812,700,000,000.
Fiscal year 1998: $6,182,400,000,000.

Source: See exhibit 5-1.

(a) The "maximum deficit amount" referred to for outlays and the deficit (and, in exhibit 5-1, for budget authority) is the deficit target established in accordance with the Budget Enforcement Act. The totals in the budget resolution may not exceed the maximum deficit amounts.

(b) The outlay amounts in the budget resolution are estimates; the actual outlays depend on the rate at which budget authority and other budget resources are spent. However, the Budget Enforcement Act imposes limits on discretionary outlays and imposes other spending controls, as explained in chapter 3.

(c) Each year's increase in the public debt is greater than that year's deficit. The main reason for this discrepancy is that the public debt includes amounts borrowed from trust funds, including social security funds. Amounts borrowed from trust funds increase the public debt but (with the exception of social security) reduce the deficit set forth in the budget resolution.

Exhibit 5-3. Functional Budget Categories

(050)	National Defense
(150)	International Affairs
(250)	General Science, Space, and Technology
(270)	Energy
(300)	Natural Resources and Environment
(350)	Agriculture
(370)	Commerce and Housing Credit
(400)	Transportation
(450)	Community and Regional Development
(500)	Education, Training, Employment, and Social Services
(550)	Health
(570)	Medicare
(600)	Income Security
(650)	Social Security
(700)	Veterans Benefits and Services
(750)	Administration of Justice
(800)	General Government
(900)	Net Interest
(920)	Allowances
(950)	Undistributed Offsetting Receipts

(a) The functional categories group together related programs. A single category may cover programs funded in several appropriations acts and carried out by various federal agencies. The functional categories are the basis for allocating budget authority and outlays in the budget resolution.

(b) Each function is divided into a number of subfunctions, and each budget account is assigned to a single subfunction. The last three digits in an account's identification code represent its functional classification (see exhibit 4-6).

(c) Although the functional allocations express Congress's budget priorities, the appropriations committees are not bound by them in dividing funds among their subcommittees or in recommending funds for federal programs and agencies.

(d) Interest is budgeted on a net basis, that is, interest paid by the federal government minus the interest received by it.

(e) Allowances are estimates of future civilian pay increases and funds set aside for contingencies; undistributed offsetting receipts are budgeted as offsets to total spending, not as revenues. These receipts are explained in chapter 2.

Budget Committee in its report on the fiscal year 1994 budget resolution. Although these assumptions are not binding, they often reflect understandings negotiated during formulation of the resolution, and they thereby influence spending decisions later in the year when Congress turns to the appropriations process. But it is rare that the appropriations committees, which value their independence, implement all the budget resolution's assumptions. In the competition for scarce funds, these committees may favor existing programs, even if it means shortchanging some of the initiatives assumed in the budget resolution. This happened in the fiscal 1994 appropriations cycle when there was not enough money to support ongoing programs and fully finance the program initiatives advocated by President Clinton and endorsed in the budget assumptions.

Formulating the Budget Resolution

Although it is a brief document, the budget resolution covers the entire $1.5 trillion budget and touches the interests of virtually all House and Senate committees. The budget committees cannot mark up the resolution in the normal legislative manner, relying on hearings to become expert in their subject. Their subject--the budget--happens to be the business of the revenue committees, the appropriations committees, and most authorizing committees. Although the budget committees must comprehend the budget, it is equally important for them to know what other committees care about. The budget committees hold hearings before formulating the resolution, but they also rely on data from the Congressional Budget Office and the so-called views and estimates reports from other committees to gain a broad understanding of budget issues and congressional sentiment.

CBO issues a stream of reports on the president's budget, economic conditions, federal programs, and, in most years, options for reducing the deficit. The agency maintains an extensive (mostly unpublished) database that it and the budget committees use to make baseline projections for the budget as a whole as well as for many programs and accounts. The baseline estimates, which were discussed in chapter 2, project future revenues and expenditures under assumed economic and program conditions and assuming no change in policy. By providing a neutral starting point, which is not influenced by the president's recommendations, the baseline enables the budget committees to concentrate on the policy changes sought or opposed by other congressional committees.

These changes are often highlighted in the views and estimates reports submitted by House and Senate committees approximately six weeks after the president issues his budget. The reports sometimes provide specific information on the preferences and legislative plans of committees regarding the budgetary matters in their jurisdiction. But because the views and estimates are prepared early in the session, many committees avoid committing themselves to specific proposals. Instead, they practice defensive budgeting, seeking to head off presidential recommendations they oppose and to keep options open for taking advantage of legislative opportunities that may emerge later in the year. The budget committees supplement these reports with extensive behind-the-scenes consultations involving both members and staff of other committees. The consultations serve to build support for the budget resolution and flesh out the program assumptions underlying the functional allocations.

This fleshing out continues during markup of the resolution by the budget committees. Although the resolution does not itself mention programs, much of the discussion at markup concerns particular programs. In committee, members often try to amend the resolution to encourage increased funds for the programs they favor. These amendments establish a legislative history that might make the difference later in the year when appropriations are decided.

The markup often divides the budget committees along party lines. This has been particularly so in the House, where Democratic members of the committee usually review the chairman's recommendations before the full committee takes up

Exhibit 5-4. Budget Committee Assumptions Underlying the Budget Resolution

The Committee assumes that the Administration's mandatory initiative to purchase vaccines for childhood immunizations will be authorized and that the legislation will be budget neutral and in compliance with pay-as-you-go provisions of the Budget Enforcement Act.

The Committee assumes that the mandatory Vaccine Injury Compensation Act will be reauthorized in a budget-neutral manner, consistent with the pay-as-you-go requirements of the Budget Enforcement Act.

The Committee recommendation supports additional initiatives, including several other components vital to insure that all children are protected against preventable diseases. There is a pressing need to invest in rebuilding the nation's public health infrastructure in order to make immunization services available in medically underserved communities. More nurses and new clinics to immunize children in rural communities and low-income neighborhoods are needed.

The Committee supports the creation of a national tracking system to follow the immunization status of individual children. The system will remind parents when their children are due for immunization and identify communities with very low immunization levels. The tracking system will allow public health agencies to focus resources to reach out to the most at-risk communities. Research and development of new and safer vaccines should be a priority.

Source: *Concurrent Resolution on the Budget—Fiscal Year 1994*, H. rept. 103-31, 103 Cong. 1 sess. (1993).

(a) This report pertains to the health function. Similar report language was inserted for other budget functions. The Senate Budget Committee also issued a report accompanying the budget resolution. When the two committees resolve differences in conference, they must agree on the numbers in the resolution; they do not always agree on the underlying assumptions.

(b) Although these (and many other) program assumptions are quite detailed, they do not specify amounts of money. The failure to assume funding levels differs from past practice and may be due to the budget committee's unwillingness to differ expressly with President Clinton's budget proposals.

(c) Although these assumptions do not bind the appropriations committees, they may represent a consensus and thereby influence actual funding levels. However, because the discretionary caps on fiscal 1994 spending could not accommodate all proposed spending, the appropriations committees only partly funded some of the program initiatives assumed here.

the resolution. Once the Democrats agree among themselves, they have sufficient votes in the committee to report the resolution. Over the years there has tended to be somewhat less partisanship on the Senate Budget Committee, but there, too, Democrats and Republicans have recently parted company on budget policy. Partisan conflict was especially pronounced in 1993 when all Republicans on the House and Senate Budget Committees voted against the resolution formulated by the Democratic majority.

Party lines are sharply drawn in the House, where Democrats and Republicans have usually taken opposing positions on the budget resolution (table 5-1). As the majority party in the House, the Democrats have had to supply most of the votes for adopting the resolution; doing so has required sensitive allowance for the wide differences on budget policy between the liberal and conservative wings of the party. The most important variable in determining the ease with which the resolution navigates the House has been the number of Democratic defectors. Early in 1993 the winning margin was relatively wide because Bill Clinton's popularity enabled him to hold most Democrats in line. Later in the year, however, when Congress had to deal with the specifics of the Clinton program, the number of defections escalated and his margin almost vanished.

The situation has been somewhat different in the Senate, where bipartisanship facilitated adoption of the budget resolution in the 1970s (table 5-2). Partisanship emerged when the Republicans gained control of the Senate from 1981 to 1986 and persisted when the Democrats recaptured it in 1987. Partisanship was extreme in 1993, when all Senate Republicans voted against the resolution produced by the Democratic majority.

One does not have to look far to explain why the budget resolution invites partisan strife. The aggregates split the two parties on critical issues such as the size of government and tax increases versus spending decreases to achieve deficit reduction. The functional allocations divide Republicans and Democrats on how much to support defense versus domestic programs and other spending priorities. When they vote on specific expenditures, Republicans and Democrats often join ranks; when they grapple with budget policy, they usually go their separate ways.

Floor consideration of the budget resolution is guided by House and Senate rules and practices. The two chambers have very different traditions, but both employ special procedures to ease passage of the resolution. In the House the Rules Committee (which currently serves as an arm of the Democratic leadership) devises a special rule in the form of a simple resolution that, once approved, establishes the terms and conditions under which the budget resolution will be considered. This special rule typically specifies which amendments may be considered and the sequence in which they are to be voted on. Recent practice has been to permit only a few amendments that substitute for the entire resolution and present broad policy choices. Amendments targeting particular functional areas are usually ruled out. This tactic compels the House to treat the budget resolution as a package, and it thereby thwarts efforts by Republicans to offer piecemeal amendments that may attract Democratic votes. Republicans often complain that the special rules deprive them of an effective role in the legislative process. The Democrats, however, reply that the rules are responsible for getting the resolution adopted.

In the Senate the amendment process is less structured and generally relies on agreements reached by party leaders through broad consultation. Budget rules in the Senate limit floor debate on the resolution to fifty hours, thus precluding filibusters and other dilatory tactics. In both House and Senate, amendments must preserve the arithmetic consistency of the budget resolution. An amendment changing any of the functional allocations must make offsetting or reciprocal changes in other parts of the resolution. As a practical matter, this rule, in combination with PAYGO rules, the BEA cap on dis-

Table 5-1. House Votes on Adoption of the Budget Resolution, by Party, 1976-94[a]

Fiscal year	Total		Democrats		Republicans	
	Yes	No	Yes	No	Yes	No
1976	200	196	197	68	3	128
1977	221	155	208	44	13	111
1978	213	179	206	58	7	121
1979	201	197	198	61	3	136
1980	220	184	211	50	9	134
1981	225	193	203	62	22	131
1982	270	154	84	153	186	1
1983	219	206	63	174	156	32
1984	229	196	225	36	4	160
1985	250	168	229	29	21	139
1986	258	170	234	15	24	155
1987	245	179	228	19	17	166
1988	215	201	212	34	3	167
1989	319	102	227	24	92	78
1990	263	157	157	96	106	61
1991	218	208	218	34	0	174
1992	261	163	243	17	18	145
1993	224	191	219	39	5	151
1994	243	183	242	11	0	172

Sources: *Congressional Quarterly Almanacs, 1975-92*, vols. 32-49 (Washington: CQ Press); *Congressional Quarterly Weekly Report*, March 30, 1993, p. 653.
a. Votes are on adoption of the budget resolution in the House, not on the conference report. For fiscal years 1976-82 Congress adopted two or more resolutions; for those years the votes shown here are on the first resolution.

cretionary spending, and the deficit, makes it difficult to adopt floor amendments increasing expenditures or cutting revenues.

Delay in Adopting the Budget Resolution

In the final stage of the budget resolution process, a conference committee resolves differences between the House and Senate versions and Congress approves the conference report. These actions often occur long after the deadline for adoption of the budget resolution (table 5-3). The original deadline was May 15; the Gramm-Rudman-Hollings Act moved it one month earlier, but to little avail.

Deadlines are missed because members often have more reasons to vote against the budget resolution than for it. It is easier to vote against big deficits than for them, easier to favor less spending than more, but it is not easy to vote for spending cuts. Deadlines are missed because nothing stops if the budget resolution is behind schedule. Federal agencies do not

Table 5-2. Senate Votes on Adoption of the Budget Resolution, by Party, 1976-94[a]

Fiscal year	Total		Democrats		Republicans	
	Yes	No	Yes	No	Yes	No
1976	69	22	50	4	19	18
1977	62	22	45	6	17	16
1978	56	31	41	14	15	17
1979	64	27	48	8	16	19
1980	64	20	44	5	20	15
1981	68	28	49	6	19	22
1982	78	20	28	18	50	2
1983	49	43	3	41	46	2
1984	50	49	29	17	21	32
1985	41	34	1	31	40	3
1986	50	49	1	45	48	4
1987	70	25	38	6	32	19
1988	53	46	50	3	3	43
1989	69	26	44	6	25	20
1990	68	31	38	17	30	14
1991	n.a.	n.a.	n.a.	n.a.	n.a.	n.a.
1992	n.a.	n.a.	n.a.	n.a.	n.a.	n.a.
1993	54	35	36	15	18	20
1994	54	45	54	2	0	43

Source: See table 5-1.
n.a. Not available.

a. Votes are on adoption of the budget resolution in the Senate, not on the conference report. For fiscal years 1976-82 , Congress adopted two or more resolutions; for those years, the votes shown here are on the first resolution. The budget resolutions for the 1991 and 1992 fiscal years were passed by voice vote. Voice votes are often used to expedite passage of minor or noncontroversial measures. The voice vote for the 1991 fiscal year was probably due to weariness. Many senators were sick and tired of the stalemated budget process. The voice vote for fiscal 1992 reflected the relative lack of controversy because of the summit agreement that established budget policy for the year.

shut down, programs continue, the work of Congress goes on.

The budget has been the political battle of our times. Republicans have one plan for dealing with the deficit, Democrats another. The president presents one set of priorities, Congress another. Debate on the budget has set one wing of each party against the other, the House against the Senate, the parts against the whole, the prefer-ence for smaller government against the prefer-ence for bigger programs. The budget resolution is not a law, but it may have spawned more strife than if it were. It is a symbol of what divides the parties, of what Americans think is wrong with government, of the frustrations and pains of weak economic performance, and of the failures of will and of leadership. If it were a law the resolution would have to be enacted in a more timely man-

Table 5-3. Adoption Dates for the Budget Resolution, Fiscal Years 1977-94[a]

Fiscal year	Date of adoption	Days after deadline	Fiscal year	Date of adoption	Days after deadline
1977	May 13	0	1986	August 1	78
1978	May 17	2	1987	June 27	73
1979	May 17	2	1988	June 24	70
1980	May 24	9	1989	June 6	52
1981	June 12	28	1990	May 18	33
1982	May 21	6	1991	October 8	176
1983	June 23	39	1992	May 22	37
1984	June 23	39	1993	May 21	36
1985	October 1	139	1994	April 1	0

Sources: *Congressional Quarterly Almanacs, 1975-92*, vols. 32-49 (Washington: CQ Press); *Congressional Quarterly Weekly Report*, April 3, 1993, p. 821.

a. The dates pertain to the first budget resolution for the 1977-82 fiscal years and to the annual resolution for subsequent years. Before fiscal year 1987, Congress was supposed to adopt the resolution by May 15; since then, the scheduled adoption date has been April 15.

ner, because missing legal deadlines matters in ways that missing symbolic ones does not.

Yet the budget is conflict that has a resolution. One way or another Congress has always managed to produce a budget resolution. The actual adoption dates suggest a patternless process, budgeting without routine. One year the deadline is missed by a few days, the next by a few months. The budget resolution makes it through because enough members of Congress want it to. But missing deadlines is powerful evidence that the process does not work as intended; and failure to adopt the resolution would be powerful evidence of institutional breakdown.

Is the reverse true--that meeting the deadline with time to spare exemplifies institutional efficiency? Bill Clinton and congressional Democrats thought so in 1993, as Ronald Reagan and congressional Republicans thought in 1981 when they accelerated the process and adopted the resolution ahead of schedule. But each year is another story, and the successes of 1981 had long faded by 1984 when the resolution was not adopted until October 1, the first day of the fiscal year. One cannot know yet whether budget politics in

Clinton's presidency will end the way his administration started, with resounding triumphs, or the way Reagan's ended, with protracted stalemate. But the budget resolution will be an important marker of how well Clinton is doing.

The Reconciliation Process

Reconciliation is the process used by Congress to bring revenue and spending under existing laws into conformity with the levels set in the budget resolution. As applied in recent years, it has been the principal means by which Congress has enacted legislation reducing the deficit. The process has two stages: issuance of reconciliation instructions in the budget resolution and enactment of a reconciliation bill that changes revenue or spending laws. The need for two distinct operations arises because the budget resolution is not a statute and cannot alter existing law.

Reconciliation is an optional process; it is not activated every year. It is likely to be used if the president's budget recommends revenue increases or spending cutbacks and if Congress wants to take active steps to reduce the deficit. These conditions have been present in most years since 1980, the first year reconciliation was used. They tend not to be present during the middle years of a multiyear budget agreement.

Reconciliation begins with a directive in a budget resolution instructing designated committees to report legislation that changes existing law (or pending legislation). Exhibit 5-5, taken from the budget resolution for the 1994 fiscal year, shows the kind of language found in these instructions. The instructions have three main components: they name the committees directed to report legislation; they specify the revenue or expenditure amounts by which existing laws are to be changed; and they set a deadline by which the designated committees are to recommend the changes in law. The Senate and the House issue separate instructions to their committees, allowing each chamber to fine-tune the language to its own circumstances and to select deadlines that suit its schedule. The instructions cover the same fiscal years covered by the budget resolution, with separate amounts specified for each of the years or for a period of years.

By law, reconciliation instructions may not direct changes in the social security program. By practice, the instructions are not currently applied to discretionary authorizations (which are funded by annual appropriations). Thus reconciliation instructions are given only to committees that have jurisdiction over revenues or direct (mandatory) spending programs. They are not issued to the appropriations committees, though reconciliation decisions may affect the annual spending bills, or to authorizing committees whose jurisdiction is limited to discretionary programs. The House Ways and Means and the Senate Finance Committees, which have jurisdiction over revenue legislation and some major entitlement programs, always participate. The extent to which other committees are drawn in depends on the scope of the year's reconciliation process or on the amount of deficit reduction sought. In the eventful years of 1981, 1990, and 1993 most House and Senate committees were given reconciliation instructions.

The dollar amounts in the instructions are computed with reference to the CBO baseline. Thus a change represents the amount by which revenues or spending would increase or decrease from baseline levels as a result of changes made in existing law. This computation is itself based on assumptions about the future level of revenues under current law or policy and about the dollar changes that would ensue from the new legislation. Thus the savings associated with the reconciliation instructions always are assumed savings. The actual changes in revenues or spending may differ from those estimated when the reconciliation instructions are formulated.

The instructions do not specify how the dollar changes are to be made or which laws or programs are to be altered. Mentioning programs at this stage of the process would violate the political division of labor between the budget committees and other congressional committees. This division gives the budget committees control of money and the other committees control of programs. Reconciliation would surely be swamped by antagonism or even outright subversion if the budget committees used it to dictate which programs would shrink.

But although the instructions do not mention programs, they are based on assumptions as to the savings or deficit reduction that would accrue from particular changes in revenue provisions or spending programs. These program assumptions are sometimes printed in the reports on the budget resolution. Even when they are not published, committees and members usually have a good idea of the legislation contemplated by the instructions.

The reconciliation instructions are not self-implementing. To achieve the savings, Congress must enact a reconciliation bill that incorporates the legislation recommended by the committees responding to the instructions. Although there are no sanctions against committees that fail to produce the required savings, committees usually do what is expected of them. When a budget resolution has been approved by Congress, the reconciliation instructions have the status of orders by the House and Senate to designated commit-

Exhibit 5-5. Reconciliation Instructions in Budget Resolution

Senate committees

> *(2) COMMITTEE ON ARMED SERVICES.—The Senate Committee on Armed Services shall report changes in laws within its jurisdiction to reduce the deficit $128,000,000 in fiscal year 1994 and $2,361,000,000 for the period of fiscal years 1994 through 1998.*
>
> *(3) COMMITTEE ON BANKING, HOUSING, AND URBAN AFFAIRS.—The Senate Committee on Banking, Housing, and Urban Affairs shall report changes in laws within its jurisdiction to reduce the deficit $401,000,000 in fiscal year 1994 and $3,131,000,000 for the period of fiscal years 1994 through 1998.*

House committees

> *(4) COMMITTEE ON EDUCATION AND LABOR.—The House Committee on Education and Labor shall report changes in laws within its jurisdiction that provide direct spending sufficient to increase outlays by $118,000,000 in fiscal year 1994, and to reduce outlays as follows: $72,000,000 in fiscal year 1995, $792,000,000 in fiscal year 1996, $2,173,000,000 in fiscal year 1997, and $2,898,000,000 in fiscal year 1998.*
>
> *(5) COMMITTEE ON ENERGY AND COMMERCE.—The House Committee on Energy and Commerce shall report changes in laws within its jurisdiction that provide direct spending sufficient to reduce outlays, as follows: $4,342,000,000 in fiscal year 1994, $7,491,000,000 in fiscal year 1995, $13,422,000,000 in fiscal year 1996, $17,518,000,000 in fiscal year 1997, and $21,744,000,000 in fiscal year 1998.*

Source: See exhibit 5-1.

(a) Separate instructions, with differences in wording, are issued for House and Senate committees. These instructions cover five fiscal years (1994-98), but unlike the House, which specified dollar amounts for each of the years, the Senate provided dollar instructions only for the first year (1994) and the total of the five years.

(b) The House and Senate had different deadlines (not shown here) for committees to report reconciliation legislation. The House deadline was May 14, 1993; the Senate deadline was June 18, 1993. These deadlines were staggered to enable the Senate to take up the reconciliation bill after the House had completed work on the measure.

(c) The Senate instructions direct each named committee to "report changes in laws within its jurisdiction to reduce the deficit." This wording does not dictate which laws should be changed. Because only the first year and the sum of all five years were specified, Senate committees were given discretion to decide what portion of the deficit reduction would be achieved in each year.

tees. It is expected that committees will carry out the will of their parent chamber, and they normally do so.

In responding to the reconciliation instructions, a committee can decide on the legislative changes to be recommended. It is not bound by the program changes assumed by the budget committees. But a committee's recommended legislation should produce estimated dollar changes equal to the amounts it has been instructed to achieve. It has to meet both the budget authority and outlay targets for each fiscal year.

When more than one committee of the House or Senate is instructed, the reconciliation legislation is consolidated by the budget committees into an omnibus bill. The role of the budget committee is limited at this stage; it must include what has been recommended by the committees of jurisdiction, without substantive revisions. This restriction pertains even when the budget committees estimate that the proposed legislation will fall short of the dollar changes called for in the instructions. Sometimes the budget committees, working with the leadership, develop alternatives to the committee recommendations, which are then offered as floor amendments.

Omnibus reconciliation bills are considered by the House and Senate under procedures and conditions that severely constrain the time available for debate and the opportunity to amend the measure. Although the House Rules Committee has the option of writing an open rule (that would allow any amendment members wish to offer), it invariably prescribes a restrictive rule that, despite the extraordinary scope of some recent reconciliation bills, permits few amendments. The rule is usually crafted to keep the package intact and to enable the House to come to closure on these massive bills. Of course, the restrictive rule also assists the Democratic majority in warding off Republican attacks on the reconciliation bill.

The Senate allows only twenty hours of debate on the reconciliation bill, which works out to just twelve minutes a member and, in some years, barely one minute a page. This time limit is incorporated in the standing rules of the Senate; it does not have to be voted on whenever a reconciliation bill is up for consideration.

Restrictive rules in the House and time limits in the Senate combine with two other features of reconciliation to make floor amendment very difficult. One is a requirement that amendments be deficit neutral. To meet this requirement, an amendment reducing revenues or increasing spending must itself contain equivalent revenue increases or spending cuts. The second feature is the free ride given committees to include matters not related to the budget in their recommended legislation. This practice has been particularly troubling to the Senate because of its twenty-hour limit on debate.

In response to this problem, the Senate has adopted the "Byrd rule" to restrict the inclusion of extraneous matter in a reconciliation bill. The Byrd rule specifies that a provision is considered extraneous if it (a) does not change revenue or outlays, (b) increases outlays or decreases revenue for a committee not in compliance with its reconciliation instructions, (c) is outside the jurisdiction of the committee that inserted the provision in the reconciliation bill, (d) would increase future deficits, (e) has revenue or outlay provisions that are merely incidental to nonbudgetary components, or (f) would change social security. Any senator may raise a point of order claiming that certain provisions are extraneous. The Byrd rule may be waived only by a three-fifths vote of the Senate.

In 1993 the rule was used to strike three provisions of the reconciliation bill prepared by Senate committees and to bar floor consideration of three amendments. It was also used in conference to drop provisions in the House-passed reconciliation bill. Because of the complexity of the rule, its application depends on parliamentary interpretations. Provisions that some people may deem relevant to deficit reduction have been blocked, while others that have little bearing on it have been retained. In 1993, House-passed provisions establishing a new procedure for reviewing entitlement expenditures were deleted in the

Senate on grounds that they were not germane to deficit reduction.

Whenever the budget resolution has contained reconciliation instructions, Congress has enacted a reconciliation bill. Sometimes enactment has occurred well beyond the deadline set in the instructions. Nevertheless, this cumbersome process works. Why? How is it that Congress, which seemingly stubs its toes on simple tasks, manages to complete a reconciliation process that not only requires the orchestration of so many committees and actions, but also has the unpleasant chore of cutting expenditures and raising taxes? Part of the answer is that concern over the deficit has impelled Congress to act; another part is that reconciliation's cumbersome procedures are fine-tuned to produce wanted results.

What budget experts label the reconciliation bill is routinely called the deficit reduction bill by the news media. The fact that a reconciliation bill packages so many different provisions from so many committees in a single measure transforms the vote from cutting programs or raising taxes to cutting the deficit. The procedures are cumbersome because they balance the interests of budgeting and legislating. The budget resolution targets the savings; the reconciliation legislation selects the programs. These tasks are in the jurisdiction of different committees. Reconciliation would be a lot simpler if the budget committees could do the whole job. But such a procedure would not survive long.

Balance comes at some cost. Reconciliation is a leaky process in which not all the deficit reduction promised at the start is achieved at the end. It allows both dollars and programs to be saved, that is, for the deficit reduction targets to be met without serious retrenchment. Since its inauguration in 1980, reconciliation has claimed more than $1.5 trillion in deficit reduction, almost $1 trillion (over five years) in 1990 and 1993 alone. But since 1980 it has coexisted with the largest deficits in U.S. history. Huge deficits are not reconciliation's fault, but they do point to its limitations.

Enforcing Congressional Budget Decisions

The budget resolution is a statement of congressional policy whose achievement depends on legislative actions, the performance of the economy, and the operation of federal programs. Some critical variables lie beyond Congress's direct control. If economic growth, employment, inflation, interest rates, or other conditions vary significantly from projected levels, so too will actual revenues and expenditures. Budget results will also diverge from projections if program assumptions, such as the rate at which agencies spend appropriated funds or the number of participants in entitlement programs, prove faulty.

The budget resolution is enforced by means of the only variable that is directly controlled by Congress: new legislation. Congress has tightened enforcement of budget policies in recent years. Table 5-4 compares actual and budgeted deficits for fiscal years 1980-93. CBO classifications distinguish between variances due to policy initiatives, economic conditions, and estimation errors. In every year until 1993 the actual deficit was higher than the level set in the budget resolution. More than half of the total variance has been due to differences between projected and actual economic performance, and a small portion has been the result of faulty estimates. The remainder has been attributed to policy changes, including truly unforeseen events such as Operation Desert Storm in 1991.

Despite the recession that began just about the time the 1990 budget deal was hatched, Congress resisted most demands for new fiscal legislation. Recent congressional adherence to its adopted budget policies has been partly the result of BEA rules, but various enforcement mechanisms have also promoted legislative compliance. These include revenue floors and spending ceilings, the allocation of budget shares to congressional committees and subcommittees, cost estimates and scorekeeping reports on the budget impact of legislation, and various points of order to block legislation that violates budget rules.

Table 5-4. CBO Computation of Variance between Budgeted and Actual Deficits, by Cause, Fiscal Years 1980-92[a]
Billions of dollars

Fiscal year	Policy changes	Economic conditions	Estimation errors[b]	Total change in deficit
1980	13	4	19	37
1981	28	1	29	58
1982	-12	76	9	73
1983	22	59	11	91
1984	15	3	-14	4
1985	23	15	-16	22
1986	16	11	22	49
1987	-15	15	6	6
1988	9	8	29	46
1989	17	-20	20	17
1990	20	49	50	119
1991	-19	32	2	15
1992	12	25	-26	11
1993	12	9	-93	-72
Average difference	10	21	3	34

Source: Congressional Budget Office, *The Economic and Budget Outlook: Fiscal Years 1995-1999* (January 1994), table B-3.
a. The budgeted deficit is the deficit set forth in the first or only budget resolution adopted for a fiscal year.
b. CBO designates estimation errors as technical differences.

Revenue Floors and Spending Ceilings

During the two decades of congressional budgeting, enforcement rules have been tightened and new points of order have been added. The original budget resolution process enforced ceilings on total budget authority and outlays and a floor under total revenue. Section 311 of the Congressional Budget Act bars consideration of any measure that would cause the revenue or spending aggregates to be violated. This prohibition applies only to the totals; there is no ban on measures that would cause a functional allocation to be exceeded.

It did not take long for the shortcomings of this arrangement to become apparent. If only the totals are enforced, legislation can proceed as long as there still is room in the budget, even if the inevitable effect would be to cause problems later on. Once the totals were violated, however, nothing could proceed, not even legislation that had been assumed in the budget resolution. Of course, if major or coveted legislation was in the pipeline, Congress would not allow it to be blocked merely because some total in a budget resolution had been exceeded. At times, Congress has stopped minor measures, but it has rarely applied the rules against important bills such as supplemental appropriations.

In budgeting, the totals are not effective enforcement tools. This lesson, which was learned when congressional budgeting was inaugurated, was relearned when the Gramm-Rudman-Hollings Act sought to control the deficit in the 1980s. The totals do not provide a sufficient basis for control because there is a tension between them and the various parts of the budget. Most Americans want the totals to be smaller and the parts to be larger; they want, as has already been observed, more programs and less government. Unless the parts are directly controlled, they determine budget outcomes, even when laws such as the Budget Enforcement Act and the Gramm-Rudman-Hollings Act purport to cap the totals. They win because claimants for funds are stronger in Congress than are guardians of the budget. It does not take much daring for claimants to disable or outmaneuver the controls. They can ignore the rules, waive the rules, play fast and loose with the numbers, or sequence congressional actions so that popular measures are trapped by the rules and will cause the greatest outcry for passage.

Committee and Subcommittee Allocations

Although revenue and spending totals are still controlled, the enforcement of congressional budget decisions relies principally on allocations to committees and subcommittees. These section 302 and 602 allocations recognize that Congress operates through its committee system. (Sections 302 and 602 are virtually identical provisions of the Congressional Budget Act. Section 302 was part of the original act; section 602 was added in 1990. Both are referred to here as section 602.) To control spending, it is necessary, therefore, that committees be held accountable for their legislative actions. The basic rule is that committees cannot spend more by way of legislation than has been allocated to them in the budget.

Section 602 mandates a two-step procedure: the spending totals in each budget resolution are allocated among House and Senate Appropriations Committees, then each committee divides the amount allocated to it among its subcommittees. This procedure forms a chain of control that links budget totals to specific spending measures. The

amounts allocated to committees cannot exceed the budget authority and outlay totals in the budget resolution; the amounts distributed to subcommittees may not exceed the total available to the parent committee; and the cost of legislation may not exceed the amount available to the subcommittee.

The first step, known as section 602(a), is usually taken by the House and Senate Budget Committees in the statement of managers accompanying the conference report on the budget resolution. Allocations are made only to the appropriations committees; no allocation is made for discretionary authorizations whose funding is determined in annual appropriations. Although these allocations are made by the budget committees, they are based on assumptions and understandings developed in the course of writing the budget resolution. By the time members vote on the resolution, they have a pretty firm idea of how the funds will be parceled.

The House and Senate have different practices for allocating budget shares among committees. The House distinguishes between *current level* of spending, which reflects mandatory spending under existing law and *discretionary action*, which represents spending changes resulting from appropriations (exhibit 5-6). This distinction permits it to consider spending legislation as long as the committee of jurisdiction is within its discretionary level, even if total spending has been exceeded. In the House, therefore, committees are held accountable only for expenditures resulting from legislative action. The Senate, however, gives a single allocation to each committee and does not distinguish between spending resulting from new or old legislation (exhibit 5-7). In the Senate, appropriation bills can be blocked when spending levels have been exceeded because of general economic changes and other factors beyond the control of the Appropriations Committee. This is one of several enforcement rules that are tougher in the Senate than in the House.

Each appropriations committee subdivides its budget share among its thirteen subcommittees, as provided by section 602(b) (exhibit 5-8).

Exhibit 5-6. Section 602(a) Allocations to House Committees

ALLOCATION OF SPENDING RESPONSIBILITY TO HOUSE COMMITTEES PURSUANT TO SEC. 602(a) OF THE CONGRESSIONAL BUDGET ACT—FISCAL YEAR 1994—Continued

	Budget authority	Outlays	Entitlement authority
FOREIGN AFFAIRS COMMITTEE			
Current level (enacted law):			
150 International affairs	13,263	13,720	0
600 Income security	453	444	434
800 General government	6	6	0
Subtotal	13,721	14,170	434
Committee total	13,721	14,170	434
Discretionary action (assumed legislation):			
600 Income security	−2	−2	−2
Subtotal	−2	−2	−2
Committee total	13,719	14,168	432
GOVERNMENT OPERATIONS COMMITTEE			
Current level (enacted law):			
800 General government	15	13	0
Subtotal	15	13	0
Committee total	15	13	0
HOUSE ADMINISTRATION COMMITTEE			
Current (level enacted law):			
500 Education, training, employment, and social services	20	16	0
800 General government	29	0	92
Subtotal	49	16	92
Committee Total	49	16	92

Source: See exhibit 5-4.

(a) The House and Senate Budget Committees make separate allocations to the committees of their respective chambers. The two committees use different approaches in making allocations. (See exhibit 5-7 for allocations made by the Senate Budget Committee.)

(b) The House Budget Committee allocates entitlement authority, in addition to new budget authority and outlays, to the authorizing committees that have legislative jurisdiction. These allocations include entitlements funded by permanent or current appropriations.

(c) "Current level" refers to spending under existing law, such as previously enacted entitlements; "discretionary action" refers to legislation changing entitlements and new appropriations. The distinction between "current level" and "discretionary action" enables a committee to use its full discretionary amount, even when the total spending allocation has been exceeded. (The term "discretionary spending" has a somewhat different meaning in the Budget Enforcement Act procedures discussed in chapter 3.)

Exhibit 5-7. Section 602(a) Allocations to Senate Committees

SENATE COMMITTEE BUDGET AUTHORITY AND OUTLAY ALLOCATIONS PURSUANT TO SECTION 302 OF THE CONGRESSIONAL BUDGET ACT BUDGET YEAR TOTAL: 1994

[Dollars in millions]

Committee	Direct spending jurisdiction		Entitlements funded in annual appropriations	
	Budget authority	Outlays	Budget authority	Outlays
Appropriations	$773,585	$802,521		
Agriculture, Nutrition, and Forestry	11,649	9,769	$16,527	$6,973
Armed Services	39,990	39,901		
Banking, Housing, and Urban Affairs	15,872	4,688		
Commerce, Science, and Transportation	2,543	(1,536)	537	535
Energy and Natural Resources	1,434	1,243	37	37
Environment and Public Works	23,818	1,680		
Finance	529,934	527,947	139,738	139,422
Foreign Relations	13,716	14,161		
Governmental Affairs	50,498	49,116	100	100
Judiciary	2,899	2,639	180	179
Labor and Human Resources	5,160	5,095	5,175	4,705
Rules and Administration	50	16		
Veterans Affairs	1,315	1,198	17,516	18,839
Select Indian Affairs	587	574		
Small Business	187	(292)		
Not Allocated to Committees	(249,923)	(240,415)		
Total	1,223,314	1,218,305	179,810	170,790

Source: See exhibit 5-1.

(a) As required by section 602 of the Budget Act, the Senate Budget Committee allocates spending to committees for the next fiscal year and (not shown here) the sum of the next five fiscal years.

(b) "Direct spending" includes both discretionary appropriations and mandatory entitlements. It thus differs from the use of this term in the pay-as-you-go (PAYGO) process discussed in chapter 3.

(c) "Entitlements funded in annual appropriations" are displayed for informational purposes. The amounts shown in this column are allocated as direct spending.

(d) Senate allocations do not distinguish between "current level" and "discretionary action" (see exhibit 5-6), nor are they divided among functional categories.

(e) The amounts "not allocated to committees" refer to offsetting receipts, which are subtracted from the committee allocations in computing the totals.

(f) In the Senate, legislation exceeding either the budget authority or outlay allocations to committees is subject to a point of order that may be waived only by a three-fifths vote of the membership.

Because the total distributed to subcommittees may not exceed the total available to the full committee, appropriations subcommittees must compete against one another for scarce funds. This rule also forces programs and accounts funded by the same appropriations bill into a zero-sum competition. These two levels of competition–among subcommittees and among programs–are discussed in chapter 8.

The subcommittee allocations are similar to bank accounts. Whenever a subcommittee produces spending legislation, its account is charged the estimated cost. Subcommittees are not permitted to overdraw their accounts. They must spend within budget.

Scorekeeping and Points of Order

Enforcing committee and subcommittee allocations depends on two types of scorekeeping information: estimates of the cost of pending legislation and reports on the status of the budget. Scorekeeping (or scoring) is the term used in Congress for measuring the budgetary effects of pending and enacted legislation in the light of the congressional budget resolution and the committee allocations made pursuant to it. Scorekeeping reports inform members of Congress and the public about the budgetary consequences of legislation--for example, whether a pending amendment or bill would be consistent with BEA rules or with the adopted budget resolution. Scorekeeping also enables members to assess what must be done in upcoming legislation to achieve the year's budgetary goals. Exhibit 5-9 shows one type of scorekeeping report issued by CBO.

Congress's principal scorekeepers are the House and Senate Budget Committees. They provide the official estimates that determine whether legislation is within the budget resolution totals or subcommittee allocations. The committees issue summary scorekeeping reports on a frequent but irregular basis, as required by the pace of legislative activity. CBO assists the monitoring of effects on the budget by preparing cost estimates of legislation reported by House and Senate committees (exhibit 5-10). These estimates are especially valuable in assessing the budgetary impact of entitlement legislation that establishes eligibility criteria and payment formulas but rarely stipulates the total to be spent. These cost estimates are based on projections of the number of people who will participate in the entitlement program and the payments to be made to them.

Scorekeeping is not just an informational exercise. Its most important use is in sustaining or rejecting points of order against pending legislation. The congressional budget process provides for both substantive and procedural points of order. The enforcement of budget resolution totals–the revenue floor and spending ceilings–is somewhat more relaxed in the House than in the Senate. The House may take up any spending measure within a committee's discretionary action allocation, even if it would cause total spending to be exceeded. The Senate does not exempt this situation from points of order. Neither chamber bars spending legislation that would cause functional allocations in the budget resolution to be exceeded.

Section 602 of the Congressional Budget Act bars both the House and Senate from considering any measure that would cause a subcommittee's allocation of new budget authority to be exceeded. But the Senate enforces some points of order that are not operative in the House. These include points of order for violating allocations to committees or subcommittees, BEA's discretionary spending limit and deficit target, and the budget resolution's revenue and spending levels for social security. The Senate has toughened some of these points of order by requiring a three-fifths vote of its membership to waive them. Some of these points are listed in box 5-1. In fact, the Senate has imposed a sixty-vote minimum on almost two dozen budget rules. In view of the party lineup in the Senate, neither Democrats nor Republicans can unilaterally waive budget violations. The House, however, never requires a super majority to waive

Exhibit 5-8. Section 602(b) Allocations to Appropriations Subcommittees

Exhibit 5-8. Section 602(b) Allocations to House Appropriations Subcommittees, Fiscal Year 1994
Million of dollars

Subcommittees	Discretionary		Mandatory		Total	
	Budget authority	Outlays	Budget authority	Outlays	Budget authority	Outlays
Agriculture	14,629	14,340	44,482	34,822	59,111	49,162
Commerce, Justice, State, Judiciary	22,969	23,156	561	547	23,530	23,703
Defense	240,746	255,615	180	180	240,926	255,795
District of Columbia	700	698	n.a.	n.a.	700	698
Energy and water development	22,017	21,702	n.a.	n.a.	22,017	21,702
Foreign operations	13,783	13,918	44	44	13,827	13,962
Interior and related agencies	13,736	13,731	96	96	13,832	13,827
Labor, HHS, and Education	66,983	68,290	195,981	195,183	262,964	263,473
Legislative branch	2,300	2,289	92	92	2,392	2,381
Military construction	10,337	8,784	n.a.	n.a.	10,337	8,784
Transportation	13,134	34,739	589	592	13,723	35,331
Treasury	11,319	11,522	11,483	11,482	22,802	23,004
VA, HUD, and independent agencies	68,311	69,973	18,642	20,266	86,953	90,239
Total	500,964	538,757	272,150	263,304	773,114	802,061

Source: *Report on the Subdivision of Budget Totals for Fiscal Year 1994*, H rept., 103-113, 103 Cong. 1 sess. (GPO, 1993), pp. 2-3.
n.a. Not available.

(a) It is not in order to consider appropriations measures in the House or Senate until the Appropriations Committee has filed a report setting forth its allocations to subcommittees. Each Appropriations Committee may revise its allocations at any time by filing a new report.

(b) The amounts allocated to subcommittees may not exceed the total amount allocated under section 602(a) to the Appropriations Committee.

(c) The distinction here between "discretionary" and "mandatory" corresponds to the definitions used in the Budget Enforcement Act. "Discretionary" refers to amounts determined by annual appropriations; "mandatory" refers to amounts determined by other legislation even if (as indicated here) funded in annual appropriations. Most of these mandatory amounts are appropriated entitlements.

Exhibit 5-9. Scorekeeping Report

CONGRESSIONAL BUDGET OFFICE,
Washington, DC, August 2, 1993.
Hon. JIM SASSER,
Chairman, Committee on the Budget,
U.S. Senate, Washington, DC.

DEAR MR. CHAIRMAN: The attached report shows the effects of Congressional action on the budget for fiscal year 1993 and is current through July 30, 1993. The estimates of budget authority, outlays, and revenues are consistent with the technical and economic assumptions of the Concurrent Resolution on the Budget (H. Con. Res. 287). This report is submitted under section 308(b) and in aid of section 311 of the Congressional Budget Act, as amended, and meets the requirements for Senate scorekeeping of section 5 of S. Con. Res. 32, the 1986 First Concurrent Resolution on the Budget.

Since my last report, dated July 27, 1993, there has been no action that affects the current level of budget authority, outlays, or revenues.

Sincerely,
ROBERT D. REISCHAUER,
Director.

THE CURRENT LEVEL REPORT FOR THE U.S. SENATE, 103D CONG., 1ST SESS., AS OF CLOSE OF BUSINESS JULY 30, 1993

[In billions of dollars]

	Budget resolution (H. Con. Res. 287)	Current level [1]	Current level over/under resolution
On-budget:			
Budget authority	1,250.0	1,248.4	– 1.6
Outlays	1,242.3	1,242.9	.6
Revenues:			
1993	848.9	849.4	.5
1993–97	4,818.6	4,820.0	1.4
Maximum deficit amount	420.8	392.4	– 28.4
Debt subject to limit	4,461.2	4,255.6	– 205.6
Off-budget:			
Social Security outlays:			
1993	260.0	260.0	....
1993–97	1,415.0	1,415.0	....
Social Security revenues:			
1993	328.1	328.1	[2]
1993–97	1,865.0	1,865.0	[2]

[1] Current level represents the estimated revenue and direct spending effects of all legislation that Congress has enacted or sent to the President for his approval. In addition, full-year funding estimates under current law are included for entitlement and mandatory programs requiring annual appropriations even if the appropriations have not been made. The current level of debt subject to limit reflects the latest U.S. Treasury information on public debt transactions.

[2] Less than $50,000,000.

Note.—Detail may not add due to rounding.

Source: *Congressional Record*, daily edition, August 3, 1993, S10223.

(a) The Congressional Budget Act requires the House and Senate Budget Committees to issue scorekeeping reports on the status of the congressional budget. These committees insert CBO reports into the *Congressional Record* as frequently as the pace of legislative activity requires. The CBO report takes the form of a letter, with accompanying tables, addressed to each budget committee chairman.

(b) Scorekeeping reports are used principally in determining whether a pending measure would violate section 311 of the Congressional Budget Act by causing total budget authority or outlays to exceed, or total revenues to fall below, the levels set in the budget resolution.

(c) As used here, "current level" includes both new legislation enacted during the session and revenue or spending resulting from existing law. The scorekeeping reports take account only of legislation passed by Congress; they do not take account of pending measures, not even those whose enactment is expected.

(d) These scorekeeping reports deal only with budget totals, not with functional or committee allocations. But see exhibit 8-5 for a report pertaining to the section 602 committee allocations.

Exhibit 5-10. CBO Cost Estimates

CONGRESSIONAL BUDGET OFFICE COST ESTIMATE

1. Bill number: H.R. 2010.
2. Bill title: National Service Trust Act of 1993.
3. Bill status: As ordered reported by the House Committee on Education and Labor on June 16, 1993.
4. Bill purpose: To amend the National and Community Service Act of 1990 to establish a Corporation for National Service, to enhance opportunities for national service, to provide national service educational awards to persons participating in such service, and for other purposes.
5. Estimated cost to the Federal Government:

Federal Government Costs
[By fiscal year, in millions of dollars]

	1994	1995	1996	1997	1998
AUTHORIZATIONS OF APPROPRIATIONS					
National Service Act Programs					
School-Based and Community-Based Service-Learning Programs:					
Authorization	45	46	47	....	....
Estimated outlays	11	61	47	20	0
National Service Trust Programs:					
Authorization	389	399	409	....	....
Estimated outlays	97	523	405	172	0
Corporation for National Service:					
Estimated authorization	20	21	21	....	....
Estimated outlays	20	21	21	0	0
Points of Light Foundation:					
Authorization	5	5	5	....	....
Estimated outlays	5	5	5	0	0
Subtotal, National Service Act Programs:					
Estimated authorization	459	471	482	....	....
Estimated outlays	133	610	478	192	0

Source: *National Service Trust Act of 1993*, H. rept. 103-155, 103 Cong. 1 sess. (GPO, 1993), p. 134.

(a) Section 403 of the Congressional Budget Act requires that CBO prepare five-year cost estimates of all public bills (other than appropriation bills) reported by House or Senate committees. These estimates are usually published in the reports accompanying the relevant measure. The cost estimate exhibited here pertains to a bill that affects direct spending, revenues, and discretionary spending. Only the discretionary spending estimate is displayed here.

(b) In estimating the cost of discretionary authorizations, whose funds are provided in annual appropriations, CBO assumes that the authorization will be fully funded. The outlay estimates are based on past spendout rates.

(c) In estimating the cost of entitlement legislation, CBO must project participation rates, price changes, and other relevant financial and demographic factors. This type of legislation usually is open ended; it does not specify or limit the amount to be spent. Hence the CBO cost estimate may be critical in determining compliance with PAYGO rules.

(d) CBO cost estimates for revenues reflect information provided by the Joint Committee on Taxation.

Box 5-1. Selected Senate Budget Prohibitions Requiring Sixty Votes to Waive a Point of Order[a]

Consideration of spending legislation from a committee that has not made required section 302(b) allocations to its subcommittees.

Legislation that would cause outlays, budget authority, or entitlement spending to exceed the amount allocated to the relevant committee or subcommittee.

An amendment that is not germane to a budget resolution.

An amendment that would reduce revenue increases or outlay reductions in a reconciliation bill below the amount specified in the reconciliation instructions.

Inclusion of social security legislation in a reconciliation bill.

Any measure causing total revenues to be lower than, or total outlays or budget authority to be higher than, the aggregates set forth in the budget resolution.

Extraneous matter in a reconciliation bill.

A budget resolution that would exceed the discretionary spending limits established by the Budget Enforcement Act.

A budget resolution that exceeds the mandatory deficit amounts established by the Gramm-Rudman-Hollings Act.

Source: Senate Committee on the Budget, *Budget Process Law Annotated*, S. Prt. 103-49, October 1993, sec. 904, p. 364.

a. The sixty-vote requirement to waive certain points of order is provided by section 904 of the Congressional Budget Act. Section 904 requires three-fifths of the Senate membership, not of the members actually voting. There is no comparable requirement in the House. This is a partial list of the sixty-vote waiver requirements. A super majority is also provided to waive various provisions of the Gramm-Rudman-Hollings law not listed here.

points of order. It often waives budget requirements by adopting a special rule.

The two chambers have moved in different directions on budget matters as well as on other procedural issues. Many of the Senate's three-fifths requirements to waive budget rules were imposed by Gramm-Rudman-Hollings, which was enacted when Republicans had a majority. Even though the Democrats recaptured the Senate in the 1986 elections, the Senate has continued to be stricter than the House on budget issues.

The Senate Budget Committee is also stronger than the House Budget Committee. Senators have permanent appointments to their committee; House members serve limited terms on theirs, as does the chair. The House Budget Committee

is inclined to accommodate other committees; the Senate Budget Committee is more likely to fight for institutional power. The plethora of points of order and super-majority rules gives the Senate Budget Committee a decisive voice in determining whether pending legislation is consistent with budget rules. The relative laxity of House budget rules and the ease with which they can be swept aside by a majority reflects the weakness of its Budget Committee.

The differences between the House and Senate on budget matters are also rooted in more general institutional developments. The rules in the House are designed to facilitate the passage of legislation produced by committees. The Senate's are designed to constrain the spending ambitions of committees and members. A House majority–which almost always means the Democrats–can remove any barrier to floor action on a bill while also preventing members from offering their own amendments. In dealing with the budget the House apparently distinguishes between procedural and substantive violations, often waiving the former but not the latter, except when they are deemed to be minor or technical. The Senate, however, has to be more guarded in the budget proposals it considers. Because it does not restrict floor amendments, it is more vulnerable than the House to proposals that would violate budget policy. The Senate protects itself by strictly enforcing budget policy, but it does permit a super majority to override the rules.

Conclusion

During its two decades, the congressional budget process has been frequently remade, either through formal changes in the rules or informal adaptation. At the outset, there were two budget resolutions a year, at least one too many for those who did not want to face repeated votes on the deficit and other difficult matters. By the early 1980s the second resolution was discarded and the surviving resolution was transformed from a target into a constraint. Congress also shifted reconciliation from the end of the annual congressional budget cycle to the beginning. It stretched the periods covered by the resolution from one year to three and then to five. It tinkered with the calendar, accelerating action on the budget resolution and permitting House consideration of appropriations bills after May 15, even if the resolution had not been adopted. The budget resolution has played many roles. In some years it has merely rubber-stamped decisions made previously; in others it has taken the lead in recasting budget policy. Most times the resolution has accommodated the demands of revenue and spending committees; sometimes, however, it has challenged them. Occasionally the resolution has been adopted on schedule; most often it has been more than one month late.

The variability of the budget resolution reflects instability and weakness in the process. Even after twenty years the process has not earned a secure niche among legislative practices. Each year it is only as important as Congress wants it to be, only as effective as the budget committees are. The budget resolution is a strange breed, more than a symbolic statement but less than a law. Nothing has to stop if the resolution is delayed; nothing has to be changed if its numbers prove faulty or if they are overtaken by economic circumstance. The resolution cannot be ignored, but neither must it be followed.

In this unsure environment, the congressional budget process has attracted contradictory reform proposals. Some would weaken or do away with the budget resolution, others would strengthen it. Abolishing it, along with its associated committees and procedures, would return Congress to the pre-1974 situation when the totals were added up without anyone having voted on them. The argument for terminating the budget process rests on the fact that some of its key objectives, such as deficit control, have not been achieved and on complaints that it has spawned confusion and delay in Congress. Some critics have even argued that the process has weakened presidential responsibility and spurred increased spending.

The problem with abolishing the congressional budget process is that it would not return the budget to what it was before 1974. The deficit is much higher than it was then, the appropriations committees control a much smaller share of federal spending, and entitlements take a much larger share. Without a budget process, there would be no reconciliation bill, which has been, at least thus far, the only means Congress has devised to curb entitlements and impel revenue increases. Perhaps the budget committees could survive as monitors of fiscal behavior, but it is doubtful that they would be effective without a more active role. Perhaps party leaders could maintain budgetary discipline, a task they have gravitated to over the years, but they would not be likely to enforce budget policy with the same single-mindedness that the House and Senate

Budget Committees have.

Short of abolishing these committees, the resolution could be limited to aggregates, without the functional allocations that are now made in it. The functions are after all not binding and are often ignored when the more important subcommittee allocations are made. Nevertheless, the functions give the totals meaning and the resolution some arithmetic consistency. Eliminating them would encourage members to make cheap shot cuts in budget totals without much awareness as to how the parts would be affected.

Changes in congressional budget rules would influence the authorizations and appropriations processes but in ways that could be neither predictable nor welcome. These processes have been in operation since the First Congress two centuries ago, but they have experienced considerable stress in recent years and may also be ripe for reform. Chapters 7 and 8 explain how they function.

Chapter 6

Revenue Legislation

Attention to the revenue side of the budget depends on the extent to which the president proposes and Congress considers changes in tax legislation. In some years the budget merely estimates the yield from existing taxes and proposes no significant changes. In others, revenues are the controversial feature of the budget. When deficit reduction is a priority, as it has been in many recent years, legislation to increase revenues has usually been a prominent part of the reconciliation package. Even when tax policy is quiescent, Congress takes up some revenue measures during the session, either tinkering with the tax code or extending some expiring provisions.

Congress rarely considers major tax or other revenue issues on its own initiative. Typically, it swings into action after the president has proposed changes in revenue legislation. But once Congress gets involved, it usually exercises considerable independence, altering the mix or burden of taxes to suit its preferences. Even when it meets the president's revenue target, it does so in its own way.

Congressional independence is propelled by two enduring features of tax legislation: it affects many Americans and it is controversial. Tax legislation invariably attracts intensive lobbying by the interests affected. Members of the tax-writing committees (the House Ways and Means and the Senate Finance Committees) often receive more campaign money from political action committees than do the members of any other congressional committees. In the wake of the money comes pressure to modify some presidential proposals or to give taxpayers a break.

Two centuries ago Americans did not like taxation without representation; today, many do not even like taxation with representation. Getting tax legislation through Congress has become a difficult chore, but one that big deficits have impelled members to tackle repeatedly in recent years. The task is eased somewhat by treating revenue legislation as an opportunity to benefit some households or businesses. Legislating taxes is almost always a redistributive activity in which some gain and others lose. The winners and losers are decided through a legislative process that often produces an act whose complexity rivals its size.

Revenue Legislation in Congress

The Constitution gives Congress the power to levy taxes, but it says little about how this power is to be exercised. One of its few provisions on this subject is that revenue legislation must originate in the House. This sequence—the House first and then the Senate—has given rise to significant differences in the way the two chambers handle revenue measures. Although the annual budget resolution, which sets forth total revenue for the next five years, sometimes originates in the Senate, this sequence does not violate the Constitution because the resolution itself does not raise revenue. Moreover, this sequence and other rules affecting revenue legislation are not always followed in handling user charges and other offsetting collections discussed later.

Almost all revenue measures begin their legislative journey in the House Ways and Means Committee, whose jurisdiction also reaches to social security, unemployment benefits, trade legislation, and health programs (some of which are shared with the Energy and Commerce Committee). Revenue legislation is tackled by the full Ways and Means Committee, though minor matters may be handled by subcommittees. At one time the committee shielded itself from lobbyists by operating behind closed doors, but House rules now require open sessions unless the committee expressly votes to meet in executive session. Sometimes, therefore, the chair convenes the full committee only after bargains have been struck, at least among its Democratic members. The committee once prided itself on bipartisan cooperation, but given the polarization of the two parties on tax policy, that no longer is common.

Consultation among committee Democrats facilitates producing legislation that can pass the House, as does the practice of considering revenue measures in the House under a *closed* or *limited* rule that either bars any floor amendments or severely restricts those that may be offered. The House rarely acts on such measures under an *open* rule that would allow any floor amendment to be offered. Doing so would inevitably encourage representatives, for whom the next election is always less than two years away, to offer amendments that would lower taxes. A closed or limited rule protects the Treasury against floor raids on its revenues while giving Ways and Means tighter control vis-à-vis rank-and-file members that other committees may not have. But the tax

writers have a reciprocal obligation to produce legislation that is acceptable to the full House.

Senate work on revenue measures begins in the Finance Committee, whose legislative jurisdiction is even broader than that of its House counterpart. Although the Senate is supposed to wait until a revenue measure has passed the House, the Finance Committee sometimes strips a minor House-passed measure of all text except for the enacting clause and then inserts its own provisions. Until the mid-1980s marking up tax bills in the Finance Committee was an unrestricted process in which members vied to add provisions reducing federal revenues. The process was fondly known as Christmas treeing the bill. This activity continued in the full Senate, aided by the lack of restrictions on floor amendments. It was not uncommon for the Senate to turn a House-passed bill that raised revenue into one that reduced revenue.

This behavior has been constrained by strict budget rules that can block revenue legislation or floor amendments that would cause the deficit to increase. The Senate still handles many more floor amendments to revenue bills than the House does, but far fewer than it did as recently as a decade ago.

Because the House and Senate versions of revenue measures often are so different, the conference committee has a significant role in determining what is enacted. It is commonly said on Capitol Hill that tax bills are written in conference. Conferees sometimes go so far as to add provisions that were not in either the House or the Senate measures or substantially revise some that were. Sometimes the gap between the House and Senate bills is so wide and the need for action so urgent that hammering out the final version is entrusted to the chairs of the Ways and Means and Finance Committees. After these negotiators have reached an agreement, they convene the conferees to ratify what they have done.

Pay-As-You-Go Rules

The 1990 Budget Enforcement Act established pay-as-you-go (PAYGO) rules to govern the consideration of revenue and direct spending legislation in Congress. The basic rule is that congressional action on revenue and direct spending legislation should not add to the budget deficit. Legislation reducing federal revenues must be offset by measures increasing revenues or decreasing direct spending. If Congress fails to fully offset the net revenue loss, funds are to be sequestered from certain direct spending programs.

In enforcing PAYGO, congressional scorers must distinguish between baseline revenues deriving from existing laws and changes in revenues resulting from new legislation. Congress is not required to offset a drop in revenues resulting from changing economic conditions or reestimates of the yield of existing tax laws. It would, however, be required to act if the projected decrease in revenues results from new legislation.

PAYGO is a multiyear control enforced one year at a time. The revenue impact of legislation is computed separately for each fiscal year covered by PAYGO. Moreover, PAYGO is enforced against all revenue and direct spending legislation affecting a fiscal year, not against individual measures. The rules do not bar Congress from considering a measure that would reduce revenues; the enforcement mechanism is triggered only if all such legislation enacted for a fiscal year would push the deficit higher than the baseline estimate.

The North American Free Trade Agreement approved by Congress in 1993 provides a recent example of how PAYGO works. At the time it was considered, NAFTA was estimated to result in tariff losses and certain expenses that would have cost $2.7 billion over five years. Although PAYGO did not require that the NAFTA legislation itself offset the $2.7 billion loss, Congress could not muster a majority to pass the measure unless it came up with an equivalent amount of revenue. The administration first proposed to double customs fees on passengers arriving in the United States and to generate additional revenue through other fee adjustments. House Republicans, whose votes were needed to pass NAFTA, labeled the proposal a tax increase and threatened to vote against it. The administration then worked out a compromise in which most of the additional revenue would come from bookkeeping changes in several taxes plus a small increase in customs fees. Once an agreement was reached on meeting PAYGO requirements, a sufficient number of Republicans voted for NAFTA to pass it in the House.

Operation of PAYGO depends on the estimated revenue effects of legislation. Early in each session the Congressional Budget Office issues revenue estimates, developed in consultation with the Joint Committee on Taxation, of the revenue impact of the president's budget proposals. During the Reagan and Bush presidencies, these estimates often differed significantly from those presented by the president. In the late 1980s, for example, George Bush asked for a reduction in the capital gains tax rate, arguing that this move would generate additional revenues. Using its own assumptions and models, however, CBO advised Congress that a lower capital gains rate would reduce revenue over a five-year period. At one level this was simply a technical argument between experts who knew what the past behavior of taxpayers was but could not agree on what it would be in the future. At another level it was a dispute between the president and many congressional Democrats over tax policy.

Estimating the revenue impact of tax legislation is exceedingly difficult because possible changes in the behavior of taxpayers must be taken into account. In the case of capital gains, well-informed analysts disagreed on the extent to which a lower rate would unlock long-held assets or spur additional investment. But this was also a political fight between two branches of government pursuing different tax policies. In an age of big deficits, proposals projected to reduce revenue have a difficult time in Congress. Opponents of the capital gains proposal used the CBO estimates to defeat the measure.

But this was not the end of the story. When the Budget Enforcement Act was written in 1990, the Office of Management and Budget insisted that its estimates be determinative in enforcing PAYGO and related budget controls. Congress still uses CBO estimates in considering legislation, but once a tax measure has been enacted, OMB decides whether the impact on revenues and the deficit is neutral.

Tax Expenditures

Congress regards tax legislation as an opportunity to benefit certain households or businesses. These benefits usually appear in the budget as *tax expenditures*, which are defined in law as revenue losses resulting from deductions, exemptions, credits, and other exceptions to the normal tax structure. Tax expenditures are the breaks and loopholes that reduce the tax liability of some taxpayers.

Tax expenditures are a means by which the federal government pursues certain public objectives and, as the term denotes, may be regarded as alternatives to direct spending and other policy instruments. A preferential rate on capital gains may be a means of stimulating investment; deduction of mortgage interest payments may foster home ownership; credits for child care expenses may encourage parents to work. But the government can also promote some of these objectives through grants rather than tax breaks. It can encourage home ownership by providing cash grants to buyers, and it can assist parents working outside the home by operating day care centers. To facilitate comparisons to direct spending programs, the budget classifies tax expenditures by functional category. The budget presents two measures of tax expenditures: revenue losses and outlay equivalents. Revenue loss is a measure of the revenue that the government forgoes. Outlay equivalents is a measure of the direct spending

that would be required to provide taxpayers with the same after-tax income. The budget lists ninety tax expenditures with revenues forgone of $50 million or more (the largest are listed in table 6-1). Most of the major tax expenditures have been in effect since the early years of the federal income tax, but some, notably accelerated depreciation and exceptions from passive loss rules, are of relatively recent vintage.

Despite the budgetary treatment of tax expenditures, there is little explicit trading off between them and direct expenditures. Members of Congress sometimes compare the two types of transactions, but they do not have a formal mechanism for substituting one for the other. Moreover, the two types are likely to be in the jurisdiction of different committees and are almost always considered in different types of legislation. Trade-offs between annual appropriations and tax expenditures are blocked by BEA rules, which subject appropriations to discretionary spending caps and tax expenditures to PAYGO requirements.

Although tax expenditures are rarely traded off with spending, they have come under intense scrutiny. Virtually every deficit reduction package enacted since 1980 (the major exception was 1981) has curtailed some tax expenditures. Congress recognizes that there is a trade-off between breaks and tax rates: the more breaks in the tax code, the higher the rates will have to be to meet revenue targets. This relationship shaped the Tax Reform Act of 1986, which significantly reduced marginal income tax rates in exchange for eliminating or curtailing some important tax expenditures. It should be noted, however, that the 1993 tax legislation moved in the opposite direction, raising marginal tax rates on upper-income earners while expanding some tax expenditures.

Although Congress has cut tax expenditures back significantly, the amount of revenue lost has continued to increase. The most costly tax expenditures tend to be among the oldest in the tax code; their revenue loss rises automatically without action by Congress. Some analysts have

Table 6-1. Major Tax Expenditures and Estimated Revenue Losses, Fiscal Year 1994

Millions of dollars

Tax expenditure	Revenue forgone
Exclusion of employer plans pension contributions and earnings	52,600
Employer contributions for medical insurance and care	50,820
Mortgage interest on owner-occupied homes	48,145
Accelerated depreciation	28,775
Deduction of state and local taxes	27,195
Rebasing of capital gains at death	26,820
Exclusion of social security payments to retired workers	19,025
Charitable contributions	16,825
Deferral of capital gains on home sales	14,620
State and local property taxes	14,015
Employer share of medicare hospital insurance tax	12,230
Interest on state and local debt	12,030
Interest on life insurance savings	8,200
Exception from certain passive loss rules	6,245

Source: *Budget of the United States Government, Fiscal Year 1993, Historical Tables*, p. 561.

a. Table displays tax expenditures with an estimated revenue loss in excess of $5 billion; the fourteen tax expenditures listed here account for well over 75 percent of estimated revenue losses.

Because of interactions among various tax expenditures, it is not appropriate to add them; if one tax expenditure were curtailed, tax-payers might avail themselves of others instead.

suggested that, to the extent practicable, tax expenditures be treated the same as direct expenditures. If funds were sequestered to reduce the deficit, for instance, there might be across-the-board cuts in tax expenditures, just as there would be in the case of ordinary expenditures. But in view of the ingrained American dislike of taxes, having increased taxes go into effect without the express vote of Congress might draw strong protest.

Trends in Federal Revenues

Federal revenues crossed the $100 billion-a-year mark for the first time in 1963; thirty years later, they were more than $1 trillion a year. This increase has been driven more by the growth of the U.S. economy than by revenue legislation. Revenues are elastic; they grow automatically as the economy expands and personal and corporate incomes rise. Thus despite their increase, federal revenues have been remarkably stable as a share of gross domestic product. Budget receipts totaled 18.3 percent of GDP in 1960 and 18.8 percent in 1990 (table 6-2). During this long period, there was much less variability in revenues than in outlays. The gap between the highest and lowest ratios of revenue to GDP was 1.3 percentage points; on the expenditure side of the budget, the gap was 6.8 points.

The stability in federal revenues has been due to public policy, not happenstance. Although few Americans know how much the government collects, their sensitivity to taxes tends to increase when the total exceeds historical trends. This happened during 1976-81 when budget receipts soared from 17.7 percent of GDP to 20.2 percent. The culprit was high inflation, which pushed millions of households into higher marginal tax brackets. In response, legislation in 1981 cut tax rates and indexed individual income tax brackets to the rate of inflation. Before indexation, Congress periodically corrected higher tax burdens by reducing tax rates. This arrangement enabled the president and Congress to take credit for reducing taxes while also favoring some taxpayers with bigger reductions. But high inflation during the 1970s exposed politicians to blame for allowing tax burdens to float upward. Since the legislative response always lagged behind, there was a period during which tax burdens were above the trend line.

Indexation, which did not take effect until 1985, enables the president and Congress to avoid blame for raising taxes. The adjustment

Table 6-2. Federal Revenues, by Type, as Share of Total Receipts and GDP, Selected Years, 1960-95[a]

Revenue category	1960	1970	1980	1990	1995[b]
	Percentage of total receipts				
Individual income taxes	44.0	46.9	47.2	45.3	44.0
Corporate income taxes	23.2	17.0	12.5	9.1	10.4
Social insurance taxes	15.9	23.0	30.5	36.9	36.2
Excise taxes	12.6	8.1	4.7	3.4	5.3
All other receipts	4.2	4.9	5.1	5.4	4.1
	Percentage of GDP				
Individual income taxes	8.1	9.2	9.2	8.5	8.5
Corporate income taxes	4.3	3.3	2.4	1.7	2.0
Social insurance taxes	2.9	4.5	6.0	6.9	7.0
Excise taxes	2.3	1.6	0.9	0.6	1.0
All other receipts	0.8	1.0	1.0	1.0	0.8
Total receipts	18.3	19.6	19.6	18.8	19.3

Source: *Budget of the United States Government, Fiscal Year 1995, Historical Tables*, tables 2.2 and 2.3.
a. Revenues do not include offsetting collections, which are counted as negative expenditures.
b. Estimated.

for inflation is automatic–although not complete because not all relevant features of the tax system are indexed–and the lag is relatively brief. Indexation also means that politicians no longer have the easy option of reducing nominal tax rates to compensate for inflation. Instead, their role often is to raise taxes or other revenues to curtail the budget deficit. In fact, since indexation was enacted, Congress has passed more than a dozen major revenue-raising measures. Significant income tax increases were enacted in 1982, 1990, and 1993; smaller "revenue enhancements" were enacted in 1984, 1986, and 1987. No significant tax reductions have been enacted since indexation took effect, though Congress has occasionally redistributed the tax burden, as it did in the Tax Reform Act of 1986.

Indexation fundamentally changed the focus of tax legislation from stabilizing tax burdens to producing additional revenue that reduces budget deficits. Once politicians were blamed for doing nothing about hidden tax increases; today, they are blamed for doing something about taxes. This shift in attitude has made tax legislation an unpleasant chore on Capitol Hill and has greatly added to the difficulty of reducing the deficit. But the fact that Congress has frequently raised taxes attests to its willingness to act despite the political costs.

Types of Federal Tax Revenue

Over the years there have been some significant changes in the composition of federal revenues. Individual income taxes have been a stable source of revenue, accounting for about 45 percent of total receipts since 1960, as well as a stable percentage of GDP (see table 6-2). But the portion of federal revenue derived from corporate income taxes is now less than half of what it was after World War II, though it has begun to rise again because of tax legislation enacted in the 1990s. The portion coming from social insurance taxes has quadrupled since the war. The share of revenues coming from excise taxes has dropped sharply because many of the excise taxes enacted during World War II or the early cold war years have expired.

The drop in corporate taxes has been partly caused by reductions in marginal tax rates, but weak profits have been an even more prominent factor. In 1960 corporate profits amounted to 10 percent of GDP; by 1990 they had slipped to 6 percent. Greater reliance on debt financing and more aggressive tax avoidance may also have contributed to the decline in corporate tax revenues. Whatever the reasons, corporations paid more than 40 percent of their profits as taxes in 1960, but only 30 percent in 1990.

The increase in social insurance taxes, which has been accompanied by an increase in social expenditures, has had far-reaching implications for tax policy and the budget. Social insurance taxes are less progressive than personal income taxes, especially when the employers' share is reckoned as a tax on employees. The rise in these taxes was a main reason why the overall federal tax burden became less progressive during the 1980s. Congress took two steps in 1993 to make social insurance taxes more progressive. It applied the medicare tax to all earned income, not just a portion; and it raised the taxable portion of social security payments for higher-income persons from 50 percent to 85 percent. The overall progressivity of social insurance taxes depends on the distribution of benefits linked to it. To the extent that social security payments replace a higher portion of low-income wages, they mitigate the regressivity of social security taxes.

Social insurance taxes are earmarked to particular uses and are not available for the general purposes of government. Earmarking has increased the portion of revenues channeled into trust funds and has correspondingly decreased the portion that goes into federal funds (almost all of which are general funds). Although total receipts have been a stable share of GDP for the past thirty years, federal funds revenues have dropped sharply from 15 percent of GDP in 1960 to less than 12 percent today (table 6-3).

Moreover, federal funds now account for 62 percent of total receipts, compared to 82 percent three decades ago. These receipts financed almost all federal outlays in the 1960s, but now cover only three-quarters; the remainder is financed with borrowed funds. During the same period, net interest charges soared from less than 10 percent of federal funds receipts to 25 percent. This share is even greater when computed in terms of gross interest, almost all of which is paid out of federal funds.

These trends point to the conclusion that the deficit problem is concentrated in the federal funds. This portion of the budget finances interest payments, national defense, the operating expenses of virtually all federal agencies, and the hundreds of programs that do not have dedicated sources of revenue. General fund expenditures add up to more than $1 trillion a year, but the general revenues that finance them are $300 billion less. This shortfall is greater than the budget deficit because the trust funds run surpluses in excess of $100 billion a year. In fact, if federal funds revenues were the same share of GDP that they were thirty years ago–before food stamps, medicaid, and other multi-billion-dollar programs were established–the federal budget would be close to balance.

The sharply different financial condition of federal funds and trust funds has its roots in Americans' dislike of being taxed for the general purposes of government. But they have a somewhat greater willingness to be taxed when the revenues are earmarked for specific purposes. Although opposition to general taxes certainly is not new–until recently, major increases in these taxes usually occurred only in wartime–the recent deterioration in the condition of federal funds suggests that generating revenues to pay the expenses of government has become more difficult. Factors that may have contributed to this problem include decreasing confidence in government, protracted conflict between a Republican president and a Democratic Congress over revenue policy, the increased attentiveness of affected groups to tax legislation, and the indexation of individual income taxes.

The 1993 budget actions attempted to reverse

Table 6-3. Federal Funds Revenues as Share of GDP, Total Receipts, and Federal Funds Outlays, Selected Years, 1960-95

Item	1960	1970	1980	1990	1995[a]
Federal funds receipts as percent of GDP	15.0	14.6	13.3	11.6	11.9
Federal funds receipts as percent of total receipts	81.8	74.2	67.8	61.6	62.0
Federal funds receipts as percent of federal funds outlays	101.1	91.6	80.9	65.0	75.8
Net interest as percent of federal funds receipts[b]	9.2	10.0	15.0	29.0	25.4
Total interest on the public debt as percent of federal funds receipts	n.a.	13.5	21.3	41.7	37.1

Source: *Budget of the United States Government, Fiscal Year 1995, Historical Tables*, tables 1.2, 1.4, 3.2.
n.a. Not available.
a. Estimated.
b. Net interest is total interest paid by the government minus the interest earned by trust funds and other federal entities. Total interest is about $100 billion higher than net interest.

this trend. Most of the new revenues are not earmarked for particular purposes. Even the increased revenues from gasoline taxes are deposited in the general fund instead of the Highway Trust Fund. General fund revenues have also been augmented by increases in corporate and individual income tax rates. The 1993 revenue legislation should improve the condition of the general fund in the years ahead, although this portion of the budget will continue to experience sizable deficits.

The Growing Importance of Trust Funds

In contrast to federal funds, which are available for the general purposes of government, trust funds contain revenues set aside for particular purposes or programs. The more than 160 trust funds in the budget take in $700 billion a year (including money transferred between funds) and account for almost 50 percent of total receipts, up from less than 20 percent in 1960. Most of the trust funds are small; the 8 largest account for 97 percent of these revenues. Social security, highways, and other large trust funds were established by

laws that designated them as trust funds. Many of the small funds were established pursuant to a trust agreement between a government agency and a donor. The budget also has various special funds that are earmarked by law for specific purposes. Although special funds are accounted for in the federal funds portion of the budget, there are few substantive differences between them and trust funds. The main difference is that trust funds earn interest on fund balances borrowed by the Treasury; special funds do not.

The trust funds established by the federal government differ significantly from those maintained in the private sector. In the private sector, trustees have a fiduciary responsibility to use the fund only for the purposes allowed by the trust. But the federal government can abolish its trust funds, change the rules for determining what is deposited into them or paid out, or transfer them to other uses. The revenue sharing trust fund (financed out of general revenues) was terminated during the 1980s, some Highway Trust Fund money has been diverted to mass transit, and the Airports and Airways Trust Fund has paid operating expenses of the Federal Aviation Administration.

Despite these and other invasions, it is not accurate to say, as some have, that establishing a trust fund has no bearing on how money is spent. A trust fund is somewhat less than an ironclad commitment but much more than an empty gesture. Almost all trust fund money is spent only on the purposes for which the trust was established. Even when funds are diverted, they tend to be used for related purposes, as in the case of the highway and airports trust funds.

Even though trust funds are not inviolable, earmarking taxes to them influences budget outcomes. Trust funds establish a strong expectation, bordering in some cases on an entitlement, that the money will be used only for the prescribed purposes. Moreover, when revenues are set aside in a trust fund, any groups that are affected can easily monitor the budget to ensure that money is not diverted. But a trust fund is only as influential as its clientele. When the clientele is powerful, the government is not likely to risk the political costs of diverting funds; when it is weak, there may be little risk. With more than 40 million Americans drawing monthly benefits from social security and most current workers expecting to be paid from it in the future, this fund is virtually inviolable. But the Revenue Sharing Fund, which lacked its own revenue source and made payments to state and local governments rather than to households, was not strong enough to withstand the budget pressures of the 1980s.

Proposals have been made to prevent the diversion of trust fund revenues by removing them from the budget. But although giving these funds off-budget status might diminish the inclination of politicians to raid them, the budget's effectiveness as an instrument of economic policy would be impaired. Besides, diversion of earmarked revenue has been rare. Channeling increases in gasoline taxes to the general fund is not diversion but a legislative decision concerning the future use of federal revenues; providing for airports and airways money to pay a portion of the considerable expense of operating the Federal Aviation Administration is not a diversion but a defensible shift of costs of the airports and air-

ways system to users. In these and other cases, keeping the trust funds in the budget broadens the policy options available to the government.

User Charges

The federal government collects more than $120 billion a year in user charges. These charges differ from taxes in that they are levied on those who receive particular benefits of services or whose actions impose costs on society.

The Congressional Budget Office has identified four types of user charges (table 6-4). First, fees paid by individuals or businesses for goods and services provided by the government and obtained voluntarily account for three-quarters of all user charges. These fees typically resemble business transactions in that the payer freely decides to buy the goods or services. Familiar user fees include highway and waterway tolls, charges for use of federal lands or facilities, and postal services.

Second, regulatory charges are paid by those subject to regulation of their businesses or activities. Typically, users can escape payment only by not engaging in the regulated activities. These charges include copyright and patent fees and licenses required as a condition for conducting certain activities.

Third, benefit-based charges are similar to user fees in that they are levied on consumers of federally provided goods and services. But unlike user fees, there is a weaker link between the benefit received and the amount paid. In the CBO scheme, highway tolls are user fees; taxes on tires and trucks are benefit charges.

Finally, liability-based charges are imposed for various activities to compensate for damage to the environment or other interests. These charges, which typically resemble taxes, are dedicated to trust funds set up to eliminate the damage or compensate those injured by it. Taxes on coal mining compensate miners suf-fering from black lung disease (or their survivors); taxes on vaccines compensate those injured by measles shots or other prescribed vaccinations; taxes on crude oil

Table 6-4. Federal User Charges, by Source, 1981, 1986, 1991

Millions of dollars

Source	1981	1986	1991
Fees for benefits and services			
Postal services	18,373	29,099	42,592
Deposit insurance	829	3,624	6,586
Medicare premiums	3,340	5,740	12,174
Other insurance charges	3,239	4,889	7,094
Other user fees	3,354	4,454	6,613
Outer continental shelf	10,138	4,716	3,150
Other rents and royalties	1,658	2,640	1,094
Sales of products	7,076	10,067	11,507
Regulatory fees[a]	834	1,534	4,056
Benefit-based taxes[a]			
Highway	6,305	13,363	16,979
Airports and airways	21	2,736	4,910
Other benefit-based taxes	51	209	723
Liability-based taxes[a]	365	562	2,510
Total	55,583	83,633	119,988

Source: Congressional Budget Office, *The Growth of Federal User Charges* (1993).

a. All revenues from benefit- and liability-based taxes and a portion of revenue from regulatory fees ($1 billion in fiscal 1991) are budgeted as receipts. All other amounts are accounted for in the budget as offsetting collections. If the offsetting collections are credited to a particular expenditure account, they are budgeted as a reimbursement to appropriations. The classification determines which budget rules are applied.

finance the cleanup of oil spills and provide compensation for damages resulting from them.

Beginning in the mid-1980s and continuing into the 1990s, Congress has broadened the applicability of certain user charges to generate additional revenue. Before the 1980s the prevailing policy was to charge beneficiaries for the cost of providing goods or services. This policy was incorporated into a 1952 statute that expressed the sense of Congress that benefits and services provided by federal agencies "shall be self-sustaining to the full extent possible." But the law also provided that fees should be fair and equitable and should take into account (among other considerations) the public policy or interest served. The implementing guidelines issued by OMB provided for user charges to be imposed only for special benefits available to identifiable recipients, not imposed on the general population.

The Consolidated Omnibus Budget Reconciliation Act of 1985 expanded the reach of user charges to cover not only the costs of providing services but also to recover some or all of the operating expenses of an agency. For example, the law directed the Nuclear Regulatory Commission to recover one-third of its annual operating expenses; the 1990 reconciliation legislation raised the target to all operating expenses. These mandated charges boosted NRC collections from $46 million in 1986 to $439 million in 1991. Other federal agencies that have recently been directed to recover all or a portion of operating costs include the Customs Service, the Patent Office, and the Federal Energy Regulatory Commission.

This expansion of user charges has been propelled by efforts to curtail the budget deficit and by budget scorekeeping rules. The budget enforcement rules now in effect may permit increased spending by an amount equal to the additional revenue. If a user charge is imposed in an appropriation act, it may free up an equivalent amount within the discretionary spending caps; if it is imposed in authorizing legislation, it may offset an equivalent amount of revenue reduction or mandatory spending increase. These rules are complex and are affected by scorekeeping procedures and budget classifications. But they have given congressional committees an incentive to generate additional revenue through user charges.

107

Offsetting Collections

User charges not only affect the reported amounts of revenue or spending but also affect revenue legislation in Congress. Certain user charges and other collections are classified for budgetary purposes as offsetting collections; that is, they are counted as reductions in expenditures, not as revenue. These collections offset budget authority or outlays by an equivalent amount. For example, $50 million of offsetting collections credited to an account would reduce budget outlays in that account by $50 million. Many user charges are scored as offsetting collections, as are income from the sale of assets, other business or market-type operations, interest earned by federal entities, and certain flows of money between federal accounts or funds.

When is a receipt scored as revenue and when is it budgeted as an offsetting collection? The basic rule, laid down by the President's Commission on Budget Concepts in 1967, is that activities "essentially governmental in character, involving regulation or compulsion, should be reported as receipts," but that "business-type enterprises" or "market-oriented" activities should be offset against expenditures. Under this rule, charges levied by the government in the exercise of its sovereign power are treated as revenues. In practice, however, the statute authorizing the user charge often specifies that regulatory fees be offset against appropriations. Moreover, the treatment of certain receipts has been changed to serve the budgetary interests of either the executive or legislative branch. Until 1983, premiums paid by medicare participants were recorded as receipts; since then, they have been offsetting collections. These premiums, which amount to more than $15 billion a year, are still recorded as receipts in the national income and product accounts.

Although classifying income as an offsetting collection rather than as a receipt does not affect the size of the deficit, it can affect the fate of legislation under the rules of the 1990 Budget Enforcement Act. When mandatory income is classified as a receipt, it is included in the PAYGO part of the budget. But when it is recorded as an offsetting collection, it must be classified as discretionary, which may affect the amount that can be spent via the appropriations process.

Conclusion

As one of the most basic powers of Congress, the way taxes are levied today strongly resembles procedures used before Wold War II, when annual revenues were less than one-hundredth of their current level. Revenue measures still originate in the House, and the House Ways and Means and Senate Finance Committees still have virtually exclusive jurisdiction. But there have been important changes, some impelled by the growth in earmarked and trust fund revenue, some by the proliferation of budget rules. Revenue legislation is now formulated in the context of a congressional budget resolution and often rides to enactment in a reconciliation bill. Revenue measures must abide by the budget enforcement rules discussed earlier. Indexation and chronic deficits have changed the characteristic congressional tax action from reducing taxes to raising them. Behavioral differences between the House and Senate have been narrowed. In fact, the Senate is sometimes the more constrained chamber in considering tax legislation.

Additional changes in the revenue process are likely in the years ahead, especially if big deficits persist. Developing clear rules for the budgetary treatment of revenues is one possible means of reform. The line between taxes and fees is sometimes blurred, as is the distinction between receipts and offsetting collections. If a balanced budget were mandated by the Constitution, it would undoubtedly give impetus to standards for revenues and other budgetary transactions.

If the future is like the recent past, revenue legislation will be a recurring concern on

Capitol Hill. Although tax specialists habitually urge Congress to refrain from making frequent changes in the rules, pressure to do something about the deficit and to favor certain taxpayers has led to a surfeit of tax legislation. Congress indexed individual income tax rates in 1981 to avoid blame for inflation-induced increases in tax burdens that had been taking effect without its vote. Today it faces blame for deficit-induced increases in tax burdens that take effect by its vote. This is not a felicitous situation for politicians, who get blamed for the deficit if they fail to vote tax increases and for tax increases if they do something about the deficit.

Chapter 7

Authorizing Legislation

Congress has two distinct processes for establishing and funding federal programs and agencies. One is the enactment of *authorizing legislation*, which establishes the legal foundation for the operation of federal agencies and programs; the other is the *appropriation of money*, which enables agencies to incur obligations and expenditures. These steps are often taken in separate measures, but they are sometimes combined in direct spending legislation. The distinct actions are contemplated by House and Senate rules, which bar unauthorized appropriations and legislation in appropriation bills. Although the rules allow certain exceptions and are sometimes waived or disregarded, they delineate the different functions of authorizing legislation and appropriations measures.

The distinction between the two types of measures was incorporated into House rules in the 1830s and into Senate rules two decades later, and is now codified in House rule XXI and Senate rule XVI (exhibits 7-1 and 7-2). The practice, however, predates the establishment of Congress. The First Congress, which met in 1789, took it for granted that substantive legislation should not be commingled with appropriations. It thus passed one law establishing the War Department and another appropriating funds to the department and the other newly established agencies. The separation of authorizations and appropriations was placed into the rules decades later in response to the frequent insertion of riders and other substantive provisions into appropriations bills.

Early debates in the House and Senate suggest two reasons for separating these measures. One was concern that conflict over legislation would impede the supply of funds to federal agencies; the other was that the urgent need to finance ongoing operations would impel Congress to enact ill-considered legislation

included in appropriations bills. Both concerns have contemporary relevance for Congress. Protracted delay in legislation is usually caused by conflict over legislation, not money. Moreover, many provisions that probably would not have been enacted on their own have been enacted in appropriations bills.

The two-step, authorizations-appropriations sequence is embedded in legislative practice, but it is not the only form of congressional action. This chapter discusses both conventional authorizations, in which the two steps are separated, and direct spending, in which they are combined. The appropriations process is discussed in chapter 8.

Types of Authorizing Legislation

Authorizations represent the exercise by Congress of the legislative power accorded to it by the Constitution. (At one time, what is now termed as authorization was referred to simply as legislation.) In the exercise of its legislative power, Congress can place just about any kind

Exhibit 7-1. Prior Authorization: House Rules

2. (a) No appropriation shall be reported in any general appropriation bill, or shall be in order as an amendment thereto, for any expenditure not previously authorized by law, except to continue appropriations for public works and objects which are already in progress.

§ 834. Unauthorized appropriations and legislation on general appropriation bills.

(b) No provision changing existing law shall be reported in any general appropriation bill except germane provisions which retrench expenditures by the reduction of amounts of money covered by the bill, which may include those recommended to the Committee on Appropriations by direction of any legislative committee having jurisdiction over the subject matter thereof, and except rescissions of appropriations contained in appropriations Acts.

Source: House rule XXI, clause 2.

(a) House rules do not expressly require authorization; they bar unauthorized appropriations. Under the rules, before the House can consider most appropriations measures, the expenditure must be authorized in law. The House sometimes waives the rule against unauthorized appropriations by adopting a "special rule" before taking up the appropriations bill.

(b) The rule against unauthorized appropriations applies only to general appropriations bills. Under the precedents of the House, a continuing resolution (providing interim funding for agencies that have not yet received regular appropria-

tions) is not deemed to be a general appropriations bill. Hence unauthorized programs may be funded in it.

(c) A change in existing law constitutes legislation and cannot, under the rules, be made in an appropriations bill. Clause 2 (c), not shown here, bars floor amendments changing existing law.

(d) The authority to include provisions that retrench expenditures in appropriations bills is known as the Holman rule. This rule was devised in the 1870s and is rarely used anymore. During the 1980s rule XXI was modified to permit legislation rescinding funds in appropriations acts.

Exhibit 7-2. Prior Authorization: Senate Rules

1. On a point of order made by any Senator, no amendments shall be received to any general appropriation bill the effect of which will be to increase an appropriation already contained in the bill, or to add a new item of appropriation, unless it be made to carry out the provisions of some existing law, or treaty stipulation, or act or resolution previously passed by the Senate during that session; or unless the same be moved by direction of the Committee on Appropriations or of a committee of the Senate having legislative jurisdiction of the subject matter, or proposed in pursuance of an estimate submitted in accordance with law.

2. The Committee on Appropriations shall not report an appropriation bill containing amendments to such bill proposing new or general legislation or any restriction on the expenditure of the funds appropriated which proposes a limitation not authorized by law if such restriction is to take effect or cease to be effective upon the happening of a contingency, and if an appropriation bill is reported to the Senate containing amendments to such bill proposing new or general legislation or any such restriction, a point of order may be made against the bill, and if the point is sustained, the bill shall be recommitted to the Committee on Appropriations.

Source: Senate rule XVI.

(a) Paragraph 1 bars unauthorized appropriations; paragraph 2 bars the appropriations committee from adding legislation to appropriations bills; paragraph 4 (not shown here) bars floor amendments that add legislation to appropriations bills. Unlike House rules, Senate rules do not bar appropriations in authorizing legislation.

(b) The word *amendments* in these paragraphs refers to any change made by the Senate–in committee or on the floor–to a House-passed appropriations bill. When the House and Senate conferees meet on appropriations bills, they act on Senate amendments that are numbered sequentially, as shown in exhibit 8-7.

(c) Senate rules allow several exceptions, listed in paragraph 1, to the bar against unauthorized appropriations. Thus enforcement of this rule is more lenient in the Senate than in the House.

(d) When a point of order is made that a provision is legislation on an appropriations bill, the Senate usually votes on whether the matter is germane. If the Senate decides that the provision is germane, the point of order fails.

of provision in an authorizing measure. It can prescribe what an agency must do or may not do in the performance of assigned responsibilities. It can spell out the agency's organizational structure and operating procedures. It can give an agency a broad grant of authority or it can legislate in great detail. These measures do not have a uniform structure. Some are divided into titles or chapters, others have only sections. Some are only one or two pages long, a few run into hundreds of pages. Some enable agencies to obligate money, most do not.

The broad scope and variety of authorizing measures has sown considerable confusion about them. The term *authorization* does not help, for it has several meanings in budgeting. To sort out the different types of measures, it is necessary to draw distinctions between discretionary authorizations and direct spending, substantive legislation and the authorization of appropriations, and temporary and permanent authorizations of appropriations. Each distinction affects both the legal status of authorizing legislation and the manner in which it is handled by Congress (see figure 7-1 for a diagram of the various types of authorizations).

Discretionary Authorizations and Direct Spending Legislation

At the outset a distinction must be drawn between *discretionary authorizations*, which provide only a license under the House and Senate rules to obtain appropriations, and *direct spending legislation*, which actually provides budgetary resources or enables an agency to obligate funds. The Budget Enforcement Act of 1990 defines discretionary and direct spending programs. The basic difference is that discretionary authorizations can be spent only to the extent provided by appropriations, but direct spending legislation either provides budget authority or mandates certain expenditures. Throughout this book, the term *authorizing legislation* generally refers to discretionary programs. Although direct spending also is a form of authorizing legislation, the application of budget rules and procedures requires that it be labeled separately.

Substantive Legislation and Authorization of Appropriations

Authorizing legislation generally has two main components, corresponding to the two basic functions of such measures. An authorization typically contains substantive legislation, which establishes a program and prescribes the terms and conditions under which it operates, and the authorization of appropriations, which provides authority under the House and Senate rules for Congress to appropriate funds. The first of these features looks outward to federal agencies and establishes the basis for congressional control of their policies and operations; the second looks inward to Congress and establishes the basis for subsequent appropriations. The two components are usually combined in the same measure as, for example, when the same bill both establishes a program and authorizes appropriations to be made for it (exhibit 7-3). For reasons that will soon become clear, Congress sometimes makes an unauthorized appropriation when the "authorized to be appropriated" language has expired but the agency is still governed by substantive provisions; it does not make unauthorized appropriations for programs lacking substantive provisions.

Temporary and Permanent Authorizations

An authorization law–substantive legislation as well as the "authorized to be appropriated" language–is permanent unless the language expressly limits its duration. (Provisions in appropriations acts, however, are operative for only a single fiscal year unless the law expressly gives them a longer period of effectiveness.) The permanent provisions continue in effect year after year until such time as they are terminated or superseded by new authorizing legislation. In many areas of federal activity, the

113

Figure 7-1. Authorizing Legislation

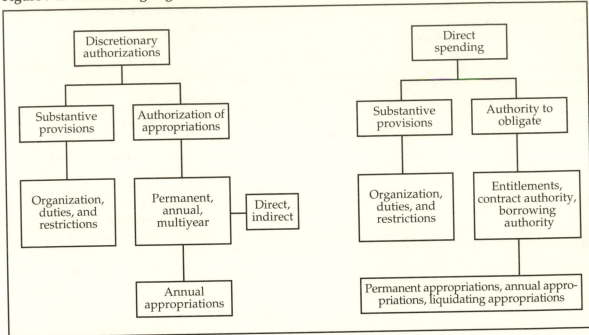

permanence of authorizing law frees Congress from considering new legislation each year. Of course, even when authorizations are permanent, Congress has the option of producing new laws on the subject.

Although the substantive provisions are almost always permanent, the "authorized to be appropriated" provisions often pertain to specific fiscal years. These authorizations of appropriations fall into three categories, depending on their duration. Permanent authorizations do not mention time limits and continue in effect until they are changed by Congress. *Permanent authorizations* usually are for "such sums as may be necessary" and do not mention amounts of money. An agency having a permanent authorization need only obtain annual appropriations to continue in operation. *Annual authorizations* are for a single year and usually for a fixed amount of money. Under the rules, these authorizations have to be renewed each year before appropriations are made. Strictly speaking, all Congress has

to do is to extend the "authorized to be appropriated" language for another fiscal year, but in the course of doing so it often makes other changes in authorizing law. *Multiyear authorizations* are typically in effect for two to five years and have to be renewed when they expire (exhibit 7-4 provides examples of the three types of authorizations).

Until the 1950s virtually all authorizations of appropriations were permanent. But most programs established over the past thirty years have annual or multiyear authorizations, and many older programs have been converted from permanent to temporary status. This change can be mandated either by requiring new authorizations before appropriation or by barring agencies from obligating funds unless the program affected is reauthorized.

There are two main reasons for the trend to temporary authorizations, corresponding to the two functions of authorizing legislation as substantive policy and as a license to obtain appropriations. A temporary authorization

Exhibit 7-3. Basic Features of Authorization Acts

Establishment of agency

> **"SEC. 2351. ESTABLISHMENT OF OFFICE.**
>
> "(a) IN GENERAL.—There is established within the National Institutes of Health an office to be known as the Office of AIDS Research. The Office shall be headed by a director, who shall be appointed by the Secretary.

Duties and functions

> "(b) DUTIES.—
>
> "(1) INTERAGENCY COORDINATION OF AIDS ACTIVITIES.—With respect to acquired immune deficiency syndrome, the Director of the Office shall plan, coordinate, and evaluate research and other activities conducted or supported by the agencies of the National Institutes of Health. In carrying out the preceding sentence, the Director of the Office shall evaluate the AIDS activities of each of such agencies and shall provide for the periodic reevaluation of such activities.

Authorization of appropriations

> "(d) FUNDING.—
>
> "(1) AUTHORIZATION OF APPROPRIATIONS.—For the purpose of carrying out AIDS activities under the Plan, there are authorized to be appropriated such sums as may be necessary for each of the fiscal years *1994 through 1996.*

Source: *National Institutes of Health Revitalization Act of 1993*, P.L. 103-43, 107 Stat. 192, 194-95.

(a) These excerpts from recent legislation illustrate the basic elements of authorizations: establishment of federal agencies or programs, specification of the agency's duties and functions (including any restrictions), and authorization of appropriations. The first two of these are referred to in the text as substantive legislation.

(b) Authorizing legislation does not always prescribe how an agency should be organized. But the trend has been to specify major organizational units in law, as shown here for the National Institutes of Health.

(c) There also has been a trend to spell out the agency's functions in detail. Only a small portion of the duties assigned to the Office of AIDS Research is displayed here.

(d) The office was given temporary (three-year) indefinite authorization of "such sums as may be necessary." Typically, temporary authorizations are for definite amounts.

Exhibit 7-4. Duration of Authorization to Appropriate

Permanent

> **(d) AUTHORIZATIONS.—For fiscal year 1990, and each fiscal year thereafter, there are authorized to be appropriated such sums as may be necessary to carry out the provisions of this section.**

Annual

> (c) OCEAN AND COASTAL MANAGEMENT.—There are authorized to be appropriated to the Department of Commerce for carrying out ocean and coastal management activities of the National Oceanic and Atmospheric Administration under title III of the Marine Protection, Research, and Sanctuaries Act of 1972 (16 U.S.C. 1431 et seq.), the Coastal Zone Management Act of 1972 (16 U.S.C. 1451 et seq.), the Deep Seabed Hard Mineral Resources Act (30 U.S.C. 1401 et seq.), and any other law involving those activities, not more than $57,752,000 for fiscal year 1990.

Multiyear

> (a) SUPPORTIVE SERVICES AND SENIOR CENTERS.—Section 303(a) of the Older Americans Act of 1965 (42 U.S.C. 3023(a)) is amended to read as follows:
>
> "(a) There are authorized to be appropriated $379,575,000 for the fiscal year 1988, $398,554,000 for the fiscal year 1989, $418,481,000 for the fiscal year 1990, and $439,406,000 for the fiscal year 1991, for the purpose of making grants under part B of this title (relating to supportive services and senior centers).".

Sources: *Permanent*: sec. 222(d), S. 1610 (101 Cong.), as printed in *Congressional Record*, vol. 135, November 21, 1989; *Annual*: sec. 2(c), P.L. 101-224, 103 Stat. 1905; and *Multiyear*: sec. 122(a), P.L. 100-175, 101 Stat. 933.

(a) The three examples shown here are of discretionary authorizations. For each the amounts available for obligation are determined in annual appropriations.

(b) A permanent authorization has no time limit. It is usually indefinite (no dollar limit) and authorizes "such sums as may be necessary."

(c) Annual authorizations are renewed each year (unless Congress terminates the program or makes unauthorized appropriations). They usually specify the amounts authorized for the fiscal year.

(d) Multiyear authorizations are typically for two to five years, with amounts specified for each year. These amounts often escalate, with higher amounts authorized each year than for the previous year.

gives Congress, especially the committees of jurisdiction, frequent opportunities to review an agency's activities and to make such changes in law as they deem appropriate. Temporary authorizations are a short leash that Congress can pull to compel changes in an agency's policies or actions. Congress is likely to seek additional control when it lacks confidence in the agency, as happened after the Watergate scandals, when Congress shifted the Justice Department and intelligence agencies from permanent to temporary authorization.

Temporary authorizations are also sought by authorizing committees to increase their legislative influence, especially with respect to the amounts subsequently appropriated to a particular agency. This influence arises out of a feature of temporary authorizations that generally distinguishes them from permanent ones. Permanent authorizations rarely specify amounts of money; temporary authorizations almost always do. In fact, some temporary authorizations are very detailed in specifying the amounts authorized to be appropriated for particular projects or activities. Although the amount appropriated does not have to equal the authorized level–under the rules the appropriation can be as much as or less than the authorized amount–there often is a close correspondence between the two. This is particularly so in annually authorized programs, in which the appropriation typically exceeds 90 percent of the authorized level. Inasmuch as the two measures are annually enacted back to back in the same session and under the same political and fiscal conditions, the annual authorization strongly influences the subsequent appropriation. The annual defense authorizations and appropriations acts best exemplify this pattern.

The link tends to be considerably weaker in multiyear authorizations, if only because these typically specify escalating amounts for each fiscal year. Since appropriations for these programs are made one year at a time, there is likely to be a widening gap between the authorized and appropriated amounts. Moreover, committees that specialize in multiyear authorizations, such as the House Education and Labor Committee, tend to become strong advocates of their programs, leading them to give less weight to fiscal conditions than to program needs. The gap between authorized and appropriated levels has induced some interest groups to demand full funding for their programs, by which they mean that Congress should appropriate the amounts promised in authorizations.

Congress often sets aside its rules and makes appropriations for programs whose "authorized to be appropriated" language has expired without being renewed. Table 7-1 lists some programs whose authorization had expired at least five years earlier but still received appropriations for the 1993 fiscal year. (An appropriation in excess of the authorized amount also is deemed to be unauthorized.) In most such cases the full appropriation is available for expenditure, except when there is a statutory prohibition against the obligation or use of unauthorized funds (exhibit 7-5). When Congress appropriates funds for programs whose "authorized to be appropriated" provision has expired, the funds are spent according to the permanent substantive provisions of law in effect. Congress, however, rarely makes appropriations for programs that lack substantive authorization. Doing so would infringe on the authorization process and would leave the agency without statutory guidance on how the funds should be spent.

Authorizing Legislation in Congress

There is no prescribed legislative path for authorizations. Some originate in the House, others in the Senate. Many are considered by only one committee in each chamber, but some are jointly or sequentially referred to two or more committees.

Authorizing legislation demarks the jurisdiction of most House and Senate committees. Most of the work of congressional committees involves their authorizing responsibilities; for

Table 7-1. Appropriations for Programs Lacking Authorization for Five Fiscal Years or More, Fiscal Year 1993

Millions of dollars

Program	Last fiscal year authorized	Fiscal year 1993 appropriation
Naval petroleum reserve	1984	236
Nuclear Regulatory Commission	1985	535
Family planning and related activities	1985	181
EPA toxic substance control	1983	n.a.
Federal Energy Regulatory Commission and Energy Department administration	1984	564
Energy supply and R and D activities	1984	1,300
Strategic petroleum reserve	1982	175
Federal Trade Commission	1982	70
Foreign assistance	1987	855
Department of Justice	1980	8,631
Legal Services Corporation	1979	357
Economic Development Administration	1982	217
Power Marketing Administration	1984	391
Appalachian Regional Commission	1982	190

Source: Congresional Budget Office, *Unauthorized Appropriations and Expiring Appropriations* (1993). CBO is required by law to submit an annual report to Congress listing all programs funded to the current year that lack authorization of appropriations and all programs for which the authorization of appropriations for the next fiscal year will expire.

most members of Congress, legislative influence derives from their service on these committees (table 7-2 shows the authorizing committee jurisdiction of selected programs). These committees vary greatly in legislative productivity. Some have robust agendas and produce significant legislation every year; others are inactive and go through long stretches without much output. The active committees are those that have strong leadership and jurisdiction over matters of current interest.

The authorization process flourishes when the White House takes the lead in proposing new programs and funds are available to pay for them. Neither of these conditions prevailed during the 1980s, a decade in which President Reagan sought to curtail many domestic programs and chronic deficits ruled out major initiatives. Although some significant program legislation was enacted, the decade was a period of relatively low authorizing activity. With the start of the Clinton presidency in 1993 there was a surge of new legislation.

The Relationship of Authorizations and Appropriations

It is a basic rule of federal law that funds provided in appropriations acts are to be spent according to the terms set in the authorizing legislation. Thus the contemplated relationship of these enactments is for appropriations to determine the amounts available for expenditure and for authorization acts to determine how the funds are to be spent. In practice, however, the relationship is not always clear-cut and there is considerable friction between the two legislative processes. Some authorizations provide budget authority, and most appropriations acts contain substantive law. The relationship is sometimes complicated by differences between the reports filed by the relevant authorizing and appropriations committees. Today, the best course of action is to look everywhere before drawing conclusions on how federal money may be spent.

The relationship of appropriations and authorizations has been affected by the insertion of legislative provisions in appropriations acts, extensive earmarking of funds, the growth in direct spending legislation, and the insertion of appropriation-forcing language in authorizing legislation. Legislating in appropriations bills is discussed in chapter 8; the

Exhibit 7-5. Reauthorization Requirements in Law

Restriction on appropriation

> (b) No funds may be appropriated after December 31, 1960, to or for the use of any armed force of the United States for the procurement of aircraft, missiles, or naval vessels unless the appropriation of such funds has been authorized by legislation enacted after such date.

Restriction on obligation

> (a)(1) Notwithstanding any provision of law enacted before the date of enactment of the State Department/USIA Authorization Act, Fiscal Year 1975 [enacted Oct. 26, 1974], no money appropriated to the Department of State under any law shall be available for obligation or expenditure with respect to any fiscal year commencing on or after July 1, 1972—
>
> > (A) unless the appropriation thereof has been authorized by law enacted on or after February 7, 1972; or
> >
> > (B) in excess of an amount prescribed by law enacted on or after such date.

Restriction on appropriation for unauthorized projects

> Notwithstanding any other provision of this Act—
> > (1) no amount appropriated pursuant to this Act may be used for any program deleted by Congress from requests as originally made to either the Committee on Commerce, Science, and Transportation of the Senate or the Committee on Science, Space, and Technology of the House of Representatives;
> >
> > (2) no amount appropriated pursuant to this Act may be used for any program in excess of the amount actually authorized for that particular program by section 4 (a), (b), and (d); and

Sources: *Military Construction Authorization Act of 1959*, section 412(b), P.L. 86-149, 73 Stat. 322; 22 U.S.C. 2680(a); and *NASA Authorization Act, Fiscal Year 1992*, P.L. 102-195, 105 Stat. 1611.

(a) The first of the three excerpts shown here was the genesis of annual authorization of the Defense Department. Before then, the department had a permanent authorization. Annual authorization was initially applied to certain procurement expenditures; since then, it has been extended to the entire department. Inasmuch as the bar is only against appropriations, the funds would be available for expenditure if appropriations were made for unauthorized programs.

(b) The second example is the provision of law that converted the State Department from permanent to temporary authorization. In this case, unauthorized appropriations may not be used, because the bar is against obligation, unless the appropriations act expressly waives the prohibition.

(c) The final example is from an annual authorization act for the National Aeronautics and Space Administration. Once again, there is a bar against using unauthorized appropriations, but in this instance (unlike the previous example) it pertains only to that year's appropriations.

Table 7-2. House and Senate Authorizing Committee Jurisdictions for Selected Programs[a]

Program	House Committee	Senate Committee
Aid to families with dependent children	Education and Labor	Labor and Human Resources
Food stamps	Agriculture	Agriculture
School lunch	Education and Labor	Agriculture
Civil service	Post Office and Civil Service	Governmental Affairs
Social security	Ways and Means	Finance
Veterans' pensions	Veterans' Affairs	Veterans' Affairs
Medicaid	Energy and Commerce	Finance
Medicare-part A	Ways and Means	Finance
Medicare-part B	Energy and Commerce	Finance
NASA	Science, Space, and Technology	Commerce, Science, and Transportation
National Institutes of Health	Energy and Commerce	Labor and Human Resources
National Science Foundation	Science, Space, and Technology	Labor and Human Resources
Highways	Public Works and Transportation	Commerce, Science, and Transportation
Maritime Administration	Merchant Marine and Fisheries	Commerce, Science, and Transportation
National parks	Natural Resources	Energy and Natural Resources

a. The authorizing jurisdictions of House and Senate committees are not parallel. Thus a House committee may be paired with a Senate committee on some matters but not on others. (The jurisdictions of House and Senate appropriations subcommittees are identical.) On major legislation, two or more House or Senate committees may claim jurisdiction. For example, medicare jurisdiction is shared by the House Energy and Commerce Committee and the House Ways and Means Committee. Because the House has more committees than the Senate, it has more overlapping jurisdictions.

When two or more committees have jurisdiction over portions of the same bill, the measure may be assigned to them concurrently (multiple referral) or sequentially. In the case of sequential referral, after the first committee has completed its work, the remaining committees usually are given a deadline by which to report the bill.

other practices affecting the relationship of authorizations and appropriations are considered next.

Earmarks in Legislation and Reports

Authorizing legislation can be as general or as detailed as Congress wants. If it is general, as was once the usual practice, affected agencies may have considerable scope in spending appropriated funds. If it is specific, the basic rule that appropriations must be spent according to the provisions of authorizing legislation will limit agency discretion. During the 1970s and 1980s, conflict with the executive branch impelled Congress to write more detailed authorizing legislation. Earmarking an amount for each autho-

rized project or activity, as displayed in exhibit 7-6, became common. Funds also are earmarked in reports from authorizing committees.

Authorizing committees are not the only earmarkers; the appropriations committees also get into the act. Appropriations acts generally have few earmarks, though some have many more than was customary one or two decades ago. But, as chapter 8 shows, the appropriations committees often write earmarks and other detailed instructions into the reports that accompany their bills. Earmarking has resulted in increased conflict between the two sets of committees. Conflict can occur when appropriations are earmarked to unauthorized projects or when the two laws (or the reports on them) earmark funds to different purposes. In 1993, for example, fighting broke

Exhibit 7-6. Earmarked Authorizations

SEC. 104. NATIONAL INSTITUTE OF STANDARDS AND TECHNOLOGY.

(a) FISCAL YEAR 1992.—(1) There are authorized to be appropriated to the Secretary, to carry out the intramural scientific and technical research and services activities of the Institute, $210,000,000 for fiscal year 1992, which shall be available for the following line items:

    (A) Electronics and Electrical Measurements, $33,700,000.

    (B) Manufacturing Engineering, $13,500,000.

    (C) Chemical Science and Technology, $22,000,000.

    (D) Physics, $27,000,000.

    (E) Materials Science and Engineering, $30,000,000.

    (F) Building and Fire Research, $12,300,000.

    (G) Computer Systems, $16,000,000.

    (H) Applied Mathematics and Scientific Computing, $6,500,000.

    (I) Technology Assistance, $11,000,000.

    (J) Research Support Activities, $38,000,000.

(2)(A) Of the total of the amounts authorized under paragraph (1), $2,000,000 are authorized only for steel technology.

    (B) Of the amount authorized under paragraph (1)(I)—

        (i) $500,000 are authorized only for the evaluation of non-energy-related inventions and related technology extension activities;

(c) TRANSFERS.—(1) Funds may be transferred among the line items listed in subsection (a)(1) and among the line items listed in subsection (b)(1), so long as the net funds transferred to or from any line item do not exceed 10 percent of the amount authorized for that line item in such subsection and the Committee on Commerce, Science, and Transportation of the Senate and the Committee on Science, Space, and Technology of the House of Representatives are notified in advance of any such transfer.

Source: *American Technology Preeminence Act of 1991*, P.L. 102-245, 106 Stat. 9-10.

(a) Some authorizing measures, such as the one excerpted here, earmark amounts for specific programs and activities. Extensive earmarking increases the likelihood of conflict between the amounts authorized and the amounts appropriated for particular programs.

(b) An appropriation in excess of an earmarked amount is an unauthorized appropriation. When this occurs, the appropriated funds may be used unless there is a legal bar, such as the one shown in the second part of exhibit 8-3, on doing so.

(c) Authorizing legislation sometimes provides flexibility to shift funds among earmarked programs. This discretion usually has a percentage limitation and a requirement that relevant congressional committees be informed of the action. Although the law shown here labels the shifts as "transfers," they are similar to "reprogrammings" in that the affected funds are in a single appropriations account.

out into the open when the House Transportation Appropriations Subcommittee earmarked more than $300 million to fifty-eight highway projects that had not been authorized in legislation passed two years earlier. The authorization had more than 600 earmarks, some of which would have lost funding under the 1993 appropriations bill. The dispute clearly was over control of earmarked projects. The authorizers wanted final say over which projects would be funded, while the appropriators insisted on their right to fund projects that had not been authorized. After months of bickering and delay, the House voted 257-163 to delete most of the unauthorized projects from the appropriations bill.

Appropriation-Forcing Language

Discretionary authorizations do not enable agencies to incur obligations or spend money; the authorized funds are available only to the extent provided in appropriations acts. Authorizing committees sometimes expand their budgetary influence by inserting appropriation-forcing language in legislation. In these instances the funds are provided in appropriations acts but pursuant to conditions that leave the appropriations committees little discretion or induce them to provide the amounts sought by the authorizing committees. In some instances the authorizing legislation stipulates an amount that "shall be available"; in others it bars the use of funds for certain purposes unless a minimum amount is appropriated for other purposes. The appropriations committees do not have to provide the minimum amount, but if they do not, other funds provided by them may remain unavailable.

Conflict between Authorizations and Appropriations

Appropriation-forcing language is a manifestation of conflict between the authorizing and appropriating committees over spending priorities. Conflict also flares up when the two sets of committees have different earmarks,

when unauthorized appropriations are made, or when there is a clash between substantive provisions in the two types of measures.

Several principles guide the adjudication of conflicts between authorizations and appropriations, but application of the principles may turn on the precise wording of the statutes in question. One principle is that legislation in an appropriations act, even when enacted in violation of House or Senate rules, is valid law. Substantive provisions enacted in appropriations acts generally have the same legal effect as authorizing legislation. One major difference, however, is that provisions in appropriations acts are effective for only a single fiscal year unless the text of the law gives them a longer duration. In fact, these provisions usually are reenacted again and again in appropriations acts.

A second principle is that appropriations law can repeal or amend authorizing legislation, but only if it is done so expressly or in a manner that makes the intent of Congress to supersede the earlier law manifest. Whenever possible, the two laws should be applied so as to reconcile their intent. Suppose, for example, that Congress appropriates funds to an agency that is barred by law from spending or obligating unauthorized funds. Although one might assume that Congress intended that the appropriation be used--otherwise, why make it?--an alternative explanation is that Congress intended the funds to be used pursuant to a new authorization. Perhaps because repeal must be explicit or manifest, it has become fairly common to insert the phrase "notwithstanding any other provision of law" into legislation.

A third principle is that when two laws are in conflict, the more recent statute governs. Inasmuch as the normal sequence is for appropriations to follow authorizations, direct conflict between the two generally results in the application of appropriations law. Complications may arise if one of the laws passes Congress first but is signed by the president after the other. This situation occurred in 1992 with the annual defense authorization and appropriations acts;

legal counsel representing Congress argued that the law that passed latest should prevail, regardless of the sequence of presidential action.

Conflict between laws is much less common than conflict involving report language. As is discussed in chapter 8, the appropriations committees write most of their legislative intent into reports, not into laws. Most appropriations earmarks are in report language, which is usually followed closely by the agencies affected. When an authorization law and an appropriations report conflict, legal interpretation may clash with political exigency. The authorization law should win out, but the agency may nevertheless feel pressured to abide by the dictates of the appropriations committees.

Direct Spending Legislation

Approximately two-thirds of the budget resources spent by federal agencies are provided or effectively controlled by authorization law. This type of authorization is called spending authority by the Congressional Budget Act and direct spending by the Budget Enforcement Act. It is also referred to informally as backdoor spending. The terms are not precisely synonymous, but they are sufficiently similar to be used interchangeably except when the special provisions of law pertaining to them are being applied. *Direct spending* is the term preferred here because it distinguishes this type of legislation from *discretionary authorizations*.

The classification of a program as discretionary or direct spending depends on which committee controls the expenditure, not on which finances it. Discretionary spending is controlled by annual appropriations; all other spending is classified as direct, even if the budget authority is provided in annual appropriations. For example, medicaid is financed by annual appropriations but is direct spending because the amount provided is mandated by authorizing legislation.

Entitlements are the most prominent form of direct spending. These are controlled by provi-

sions of law that mandate payments to eligible recipients. Direct spending may also be in the form of *borrowing authority* (provisions authorizing agencies to spend borrowed funds), *contract authority* (provisions authorizing agencies to incur obligations in advance of appropriations), and *authority to forgo the collection of user fees* or other charges. The Congressional Budget Act bars Congress–with exceptions for trust funds and certain other purposes–from considering new contract or borrowing authority legislation unless it is made effective only to the extent provided in appropriations acts. When contract or borrowing authority is conditioned on appropriations actions, it is classified as discretionary spending (exhibits 7-7 and 7-8 provide examples of entitlement and contract authority).

Entitlements are a form of direct spending that gives eligible recipients a legal right to payments from the government. The government is obligated to make the payments even if the budget and appropriations acts do not provide sufficient funds for them. Most entitlement laws are open-ended; they do not specify or limit the total to be spent. Instead, the authorizing law typically spells out eligibility criteria and establishes a formula for computing the size of payments. The total paid out depends on the number of eligible persons and the amount each is entitled to receive.

Some entitlements (such as social security) have permanent appropriations; the necessary payments are made without annual action by Congress. Most entitlement programs, however, go through the annual appropriations process, although Congress does not really control them at this stage. If the amount appropriated does not suffice, Congress will have to provide supplemental funds. A few entitlements are formally controlled by appropriations, but the effectiveness of this control is questionable. The legislation authorizing the food stamp program, for example, provides that the amount spent shall be limited by annual appropriations. But food stamp spending has never been regulated by the appropriations

Exhibit 7-7. Entitlement Programs

Entitlement legislation

> "ENTITLEMENT TO HOSPITAL INSURANCE BENEFITS
>
> "SEC. 226. (a) Every individual who—
> "(1) has attained the age of 65, and
> "(2) is entitled to monthly insurance benefits under section 202 or is a qualified railroad retirement beneficiary,
> shall be entitled to hospital insurance benefits under part A of title XVIII for each month for which he meets the condition specified in paragraph (2), beginning with the first month after June 1966 for which he meets the conditions specified in paragraphs (1) and (2).

Permanent appropriation

> "FEDERAL HOSPITAL INSURANCE TRUST FUND
>
> "SEC. 1817. (a) There is hereby created on the books of the Treasury of the United States a trust fund to be known as the 'Federal Hospital Insurance Trust Fund' (hereinafter in this section referred to as the 'Trust Fund'). The Trust Fund shall consist of such amounts as may be deposited in, or appropriated to, such fund as provided in this part. There are hereby appropriated to the Trust Fund for the fiscal year ending June 30, 1966, and for each fiscal year thereafter, out of any moneys in the Treasury not otherwise appropriated, amounts equivalent to 100 per centum of—

Annual appropriation

> PAYMENTS TO HEALTH CARE TRUST FUNDS
>
> For payment to the Federal Hospital Insurance and the Federal Supplementary Medical Insurance Trust Funds, as provided under sections 217(g) and 1844 of the Social Security Act, sections 103(c) and 111(d) of the Social Security Amendments of 1965, section 278(d) of Public Law 97-248, and for administrative expenses incurred pursuant to section 201(g) of the Social Security Act, $39,421,485,000.

Sources: *Social Security Amendments of 1965*, P.L. 89-97, 79 Stat. 290, 299; and *Fiscal 1993 Labor-HHS-Education Appropriations Act*, P.L. 102-170, 105 Stat. 1121.

(a) These entries pertain to medicare; the first provision established entitlement to medicare, the second made a permanent appropriation to the Medicare Health Insurance Trust Fund, and the third made an annual appropriation to the Medicare Supplementary Medical Insurance Trust Fund.

(b) The Congressional Budget Act defines entitlements as authority "to make payments (including loans and grants), the budget authority for which is not provided for in advance by appropriations acts, to any person or government if, under the provisions of law containing such authority, the United States is obligated to make such payments to persons or governments who meet the requirements established by such law."

(c) When an entitlement has a permanent appropriation and is financed through a trust fund, as in the case of the Health Insurance Trust Fund, all receipts of the trust fund become available for obligation without further action by Congress. Hence the receipts of these trust funds are scored as budget authority.

Exhibit 7-8. Contract Authority

Authorizing legislation

> (1) Out of Highway Trust Fund.—There shall be available from the Highway Trust Fund (other than the Mass Transit Account) the following sums:
>
>   (A) National magnetic levitation prototype development program.—For the national magnetic levitation prototype development program under this section $5,000,000 for fiscal year 1992, $45,000,000 for fiscal year 1993, $100,000,000 for fiscal year 1994, $100,000,000 for fiscal year 1995, $125,000,000 for fiscal year 1996, and $125,000,000 for fiscal year 1997.

Limiting appropriation

(LIMITATION ON OBLIGATIONS)

(HIGHWAY TRUST FUND)

None of the funds in this Act shall be available for the planning or execution of (81)*programs the obligation of which are in excess of $27,900,000 for* the National Magnetic Levitation Prototype Development program as defined in subsections 1036(b) and 1036(d)(1)(A) of the Intermodal Surface Transportation Efficiency Act of 1991.

Liquidating appropriation

(82)*(LIQUIDATION OF CONTRACT AUTHORIZATION)*

(HIGHWAY TRUST FUND)

For payment of obligations incurred in carrying out the National Magnetic Levitation Prototype Development program as defined in subsections 1036(b) and 1036(d)(1)(A) of the Intermodal Surface Transportation Efficiency Act of 1991, $27,900,000, to remain available until expended and to be derived from the Highway Trust Fund.

Sources: Sec. 1036, *Intermodal Surface Transportation Efficiency Act of 1991*, P.L. 102-40, 105 Stat. 1986; and *Fiscal 1994 Transportation Appropriations Act*, H.R. 2750, p. 30.

(a) This exhibit mentions three closely related but conflicting provisions. The first provides contract authority–note the phrase "There shall be available"; the second, in a subsequent appropriation, limits the amount that could be obligated according to that contract authority; and the third, in the same appropriations act, makes a "liquidating appropriation" to pay off obligations incurred according to the contract authority.

(b) The obligation limitation in the appropriations act is barely one-quarter of the amount of contract authority made available by the authorization act. If there were no obligation limitation in the appropriations act, the full amount of contract authority would be available.

(d) As explained in chapter 8, a liquidating appropriation is made when budget authority, in the form of contract authority, is provided in authorizing legislation. In this case the appropriation liquidates (provides funds) to pay off the obligation.

process, and the Budget Enforcement Act lists this program as direct spending. It may be feasible to control entitlements through the appropriations process if the law authorizing them caps total payments. When revenue sharing was operative during the 1970s and 1980s, it was a capped entitlement that was, in its later years, controlled by annual appropriations. Controlling entitlements paid to individuals, however, may be more difficult than controlling those such as revenue sharing that are paid to other governmental units.

BEA regulates entitlements and other direct spending by the pay-as-you-go process discussed in chapter 2. PAYGO requires that legislation that increases direct spending (or reduces revenues) be offset by reductions in other direct spending or increases in revenues. Failure to offset the required amounts would trigger sequestration of certain direct spending programs.

The Growth of Direct Spending

Chapter 2 discussed the transformation of the federal budget from a means of financing government programs and agencies into a means of financing American families and households. Whatever the reasons for this transformation, it has resulted in a steady expansion in the share of the budget defined as direct spending. Most discretionary authorizations are for the operations of federal agencies, national defense, and grants to state and local governments. These portions of the budget have shrunk relative to total spending, if only because entitlement programs have expanded so greatly.

Although the growth in direct spending has been remarkable, more than two-thirds of these expenditures are in three areas: social security, interest on the public debt, and medicare and medicaid. With the exception of medicaid, almost all the expansion in these programs has resulted from pre-1980s legislation, not from new congressional action. In fact, Congress has taken repeated steps since

1980 to cut back expenditures for these and other direct spending programs.

The increase in direct spending has had an enormous impact on federal budgeting and congressional operations. It has made control of federal spending much more difficult than was the case when most of the budget was governed by discretionary authorizations and annual appropriations. It has put Congress in the uncomfortable position of having to vote spending cuts rather than increases, and it has made the budget more sensitive to economic conditions and political demands. It is the main reason why balancing the budget has been such an unreachable objective.

The surge in direct spending has, by definition, shifted budgetary power in Congress from the appropriations committees to certain authorizing committees. Although the appropriators still have considerable budgetary influence–the more than $500 billion in financial resources they control is a lot of money by anyone's count–they review a shrinking percentage of total expenditures. Arguably, the growth in direct spending has been spurred by efforts of various authorizing committees to strengthen their budgetary power by freeing programs in their jurisdiction from appropriations control. This is not to say, however, that direct spending programs are free from annual congressional control. Some are, some are not. Social security has been, medicare has not.

The raid on appropriations committee control of spending has been slowed by the Budget Enforcement Act, which walls off the discretionary portions of the budget from direct spending programs. Under the rules now in effect, legislation converting a discretionary program into an entitlement would have to be fully offset by means of that act's PAYGO procedures. PAYGO does not control existing direct spending programs, which have continued to grow, but it has made it much more difficult to legislate new ones. It is highly unlikely that direct spending will shrink as a share of the federal budget in the years ahead.

Not only are defense expenditures (still the largest component by far of discretionary spending) decreasing, but the aging of the U.S. population will impel future increases in federal spending on pensions and health care.

Conclusion

In the few years that it has been in effect, the Budget Enforcement Act has had a mixed impact on direct spending. It has made the enactment of new direct spending measures much more difficult, but it has done nothing to control increases resulting from existing law. New direct spending legislation must run the gantlet of PAYGO rules; increases caused by past legislation are not limited, even when they exceed budgeted levels.

Increases in direct spending cannot be controlled easily because most of the money is spent on mandatory entitlements. Still, Congress and the president are inching toward measures that would subject entitlements to budget limits. During consideration of the 1993 deficit reduction package, the House inserted new procedures to control direct spending in excess of budgeted targets. But the Senate refused to go along with them, and they were dropped in conference. In his search for votes to pass the package, however, President Clinton agreed to issue an executive order establishing new direct spending controls. Executive order 12857, issued August 4, 1993, provided for annual targets on total mandatory spending (excluding interest payments and deposit insurance) for each year from fiscal 1994 through 1997. The targets are to be adjusted each year for increases in the number of beneficiaries, revenue legislation, emergency spending, and certain technical factors.

Each year the president must inform Congress concerning the status of the mandatory spending targets. If projected spending is higher than the adjusted targets, he must submit a special message recommending legislative actions to deal with the excess. These actions may include increases in revenues or decreases in direct spending or acceptance of higher spending. The House (but not the Senate) has procedures ensuring a legislative response to the president's recommendations.

Exhibit 7-9 is taken from the initial implementation of this new procedure in the fiscal year 1995 budget. It shows that the mandatory targets were raised by $38 billion from 1994 to 1997 because of increases in the number of beneficiaries, and that projections of outlays for direct spending programs under current law were $57 billion (over the four years) below the adjusted targets. Consequently, the president was not required by the new procedures to recommend legislative action to deal with excess spending.

Although these procedures have not been fully tested, they are not likely to have a major impact on trends in direct spending. The rules are biased to accommodate higher spending because they require adjustments in the targets for increases in the number of beneficiaries but not for decreases. In addition, the rules do not require any action to quell excess spending. The procedures do, however, endorse the principle that direct spending should be constrained. They are a first step in controlling it; additional steps may include dollar caps on certain programs. In fact, President Clinton proposed a number of capped entitlements in his health care reform legislation. These proposals may be harbingers of more strenuous efforts to limit the growth of entitlement expenditures in future federal budgets.

Exhibit 7-9. Direct Spending Report

TABLE 15–1. SUMMARY OF CHANGES TO MANDATORY TARGETS AND CURRENT LAW OUTLAYS
(In billions of dollars)

	1994	1995	1996	1997	1994–97
Changes to mandatory targets					
Initial mandatory targets (Executive Order 12857)	746.4	784.7	823.7	887.7	....
Adjustments for:					
Increase in beneficiaries	5.7	8.0	10.2	14.1	38.1
Changes in receipts	–0.1	–0.1	–0.2	–0.1	–0.5
Changes due to category shifts	0.0	–0.0	–0.1	–0.0	–0.1
Total adjustments	5.6	7.9	10.0	14.0	37.5
Current mandatory targets	752.0	792.7	833.7	901.7	....
Changes to outlays under current laws					
Outlays under current law as of August 1993	746.4	784.7	823.7	887.7	....
Adjustments for:.					
Increase in beneficiaries	5.7	8.0	10.2	14.1	38.1
Decreases in beneficiaries	–7.6	–4.1	–2.1	–2.1	–15.9
Cost of living adjustments	–1.4	–1.0	1.1	4.0	2.7
Other inflation	0.4	1.3	2.4	4.6	8.7
Other technicals	–8.9	–14.2	–9.0	–20.8	–52.8
Total adjustments	–11.8	–10.0	2.6	–0.1	–19.3
Outlays under current law as of January 1994	734.6	774.7	826.3	887.6	....
Amount over (+) or under (–) the current target	–17.4	–18.0	–7.4	–14.1	–56.8

Source: *Budget of the United States Government, Fiscal Year 1995, Analytical Perspectives*, p. 203.

(a) This report is required by a presidential order issued in 1993. The report shows projected direct spending under current law and adjusted spending targets.

(b) The initial targets (the first line in this table) were based on the assumptions used in preparing the congressional budget resolution for fiscal year 1994. Almost all the adjustments were due to increases in the estimated number of beneficiaries. These increases are detailed in tables accompanying the direct spending report.

(c) The mandatory spending reported here does not include interest payments. With interest added in, mandatory spending would be more than $200 billion higher.

(d) Because the report projects mandatory spending less than the adjusted target, the president did not have to recommend any legislative action.

Chapter 8

The Appropriations Process

An appropriations act is a law passed by Congress that authorizes agencies to incur obligations and the Treasury to make payments for designated purposes. Congress's power to appropriate derives from the Constitution, which provides that "No money shall be drawn from the Treasury but in consequence of appropriations made by law." An agency may not spend more than the amount appropriated to it, and it may use available funds only for the purposes of and according to the terms set by Congress. In contemporary times, appropriations have also come to be viewed as mandates that agencies use the funds to carry out the activities intended by Congress. This expanded concept of appropriations is reflected in impoundment rules (discussed in chapter 9) that severely restrict the president's power to withhold appropriated funds.

Although appropriations provide legal authority for payments, with few exceptions the amounts set forth in appropriations acts pertain to budget authority--the authority to obligate funds--not to outlays. In contrast to most state and local legislatures, which make appropriations to cover the government's cash needs, Congress does not normally require that appropriations be paid out during any particular fiscal year. In the federal government outlays often ensue years after the appropriation is made. This practice has made it difficult to use the appropriations process as a short-term spending control. (The relationship between budget authority and outlays is discussed in chapter 2.)

Appropriations are the principal means of providing budget authority, but the Constitution does not require that they precede the obligation of funds. In fact, some forms of direct spending legislation do provide budget authority in advance of appropriations, as explained in chapter 7. If the direct spending legislation provides a permanent appropriation, no further congressional action is required to authorize either obligations or outlays. But when the substantive legislation does not make appropriations, Congress has to appropriate funds annually to enable the Treasury to make disbursements.

The Constitution does not require annual appropriations, but since the First Congress, the practice has been to appropriate funds each year. The 1993 National Performance Review proposed that the federal government adopt a biennial budget, with appropriations made every other year. This proposal (which I will discuss later in this chapter) would require far-reaching changes in congressional practice and in relations with the executive branch.

Appropriations must be obligated during the fiscal year for which they are provided, unless the law expressly makes them available for a longer period of time. All provisions in an appropriations act, including any limitations on the use of funds or substantive provisions, expire at the end of the fiscal year unless the language of the act gives them a different period of effectiveness.

Types of Appropriations Acts

The Constitution does not prescribe the form in which appropriations are to be made. Established practice predating the Constitution (in colonial legislatures and the British Parliament) and recognized in the rules of the House and the Senate provides for them to be made in appropriations acts that are distinct from other types of legislation. This distinction was discussed in chapter 7 and is codified in rule XXI of the House and rule XVI of the Senate.

Congress produces three types of appropriations measures each year. *Regular appropriations* bills provide budget authority for the upcoming fiscal year or, if it has already started, for the year in progress. *Supplemental appropriations* provide additional budget authority for the current fiscal year when the regular appropriation is insufficient or when activities have not been provided for in the regular appropriation. *Continuing appropriations* (usually referred to as *continuing resolutions*) provide stopgap or full-year funding to agencies that have not received regular appropriations by the start of the fiscal year. Table 8-1 lists the various appropriations measures considered during the 1993 session of Congress.

In a typical session, Congress acts on fifteen or more appropriations measures. Thirteen–never more or less–are regular appropriations, one or more are supplementals, and (in most years) at least one is a continuing resolution. Jurisdiction over these measures is vested in the House and Senate Appropriations Committees, each of which is divided into thirteen parallel subcommittees. Each pair of subcommittees handles one of the regular appropriations bills, as well as the portions of the supplemental and continuing appropriations in its jurisdiction. Thus each regular appropriations bill is in the custody of a single

pair of subcommittees, but a supplemental or continuing appropriation may be handled by some or all of the subcommittees.

The number and size of supplemental appropriations have decreased during the past decade, principally because of constraints imposed by Gramm-Rudman-Hollings and the Budget Enforcement Act. By the time Congress takes up supplementals, virtually all funds available within the BEA caps have been spoken for. Congress can exceed the caps by designating (together with the president) the additional expenditure as due to an emergency, but it has been reluctant to do so except in crises such as the 1993 Midwest floods and the 1994 California earthquake. Typically, one supplemental enacted during the session is a catchall measure, covering an assortment of funding needs. But the temptation to Christmas tree supplementals with a great many appropriations has been dampened by strict budget limitations.

Because of recurring delays in the appropriations process, Congress typically passes one or more continuing appropriations each year. The scope and duration of these measures depend on the status of the regular appropriations bills and on the intensity of budget conflict between the president and Congress. In some years the conflict has been so great that the final continuing resolution has been turned into an omnibus measure for enacting most or all of the regular appropriations bills.

Congress sometimes makes appropriations in substantive legislation reported by an authorizing committee rather than in appropriations acts. These usually are permanent appropriations that become available each year without repeated action by Congress. Because of the growth of programs (such as social security) funded by permanent appropriations, only about half the budget authority made available each year requires congressional action. And a sizable portion of the budget authority provided in annual appropriations acts is mandatory, principally for entitlements.

Table 8-1. Appropriations Bills Enacted, 1993

Bill	House passage	Senate passage	House approves conference	Senate approves conference	Signed	Public law
Regular appropriations						
Agriculture	6/29	7/27	8/06	9/23	10/21	103-111
Commerce	7/20	7/29	10/19	10/21	10/27	103-121
Defense	9/30	10/21	11/10	11/10	11/11	103-139
District of Columbia	6/30	7/27	10/27	10/27	10/29	103-127
Energy and water	6/24	9/30	10/26	10/27	10/28	103-126
Foreign operations	6/17	9/23	9/29	9/30	9/30	103-87
Interior	7/15	9/15	10/20	11/09	11/11	103-138
Labor and Health and Human Services	6/30	9/29	10/07	10/18	10/21	103-112
Legislative branch	6/10	7/23	8/06	8/07	8/11	103-69
Military construction	6/23	9/30	10/13	10/19	10/21	103-110
Transportation	9/23	10/06	10/21	10/21	10/27	103-122
Treasury	6/22	8/03	9/29	10/26	10/28	103-123
Veterans Affairs-Housing and Urban Development	6/29	9/22	10/19	10/21	10/28	103-124
Supplemental appropriations						
Stimulus	3/19	4/21	. . .	. . .	4/23	103-24
Spring	5/26	6/22	7/01	7/01	7/02	103-50
Flood relief	7/27	8/04	8/06	8/06	8/12	103-75
Continuing resolutions						
H J Res. 267	9/29	9/29	. . .	. . .	9/30	103-88
H J Res. 281	10/21	10/21	. . .	. . .	10/21	103-113
H J Res. 283	10/28	10/28	. . .	. . .	10/29	103-128

Source: *Calendars of the United States House of Representatives: Interim 1*, 103 Cong. 1 sess. (GPO, 1993), back cover.

The Appropriations Committees have effective discretion over only one-third of each year's new budget authority.

The Appropriations Committees

That the Appropriations Committees control only one-third of budget authority should not mislead one to conclude that they are weak and have little voice in federal budgeting. Seats on these committees are among the most coveted assignments in Congress. Members rarely leave them for other committees, and they frequently give up other committee assignments, even when they have accumulated some seniority, to join Appropriations. Although it is true that the Appropriations Committees control a decreasing share of federal spending, they have jurisdiction over the portion that is influenced by annual congressional action. They handle more than $500 billion of discretionary money each year. Theirs is the part of the budget in which money is spent next year because Congress voted it this year. Almost all the rest is determined by statutory formulas and rules, not by current congressional action.

In most regards, the Appropriations Committees are similar to other congressional committees. Seniority is important in determining the influence of members, most of the work is done by subcommittees, and the staff takes a substantial part in the process. But the differences are even more telling, and they distinguish not only the Appropriations Committees from other legislative panels but also the House and Senate Appropriations Committees from one another.

The two most important differences from other committees are the bounded jurisdiction of the Appropriations Committees and the certainty of congressional action on their measures. For almost every other House or Senate committee, the most important decision each year is what legislation it should work on. For the Appropriations Committees this decision is predetermined by their jurisdiction. They focus on the thirteen regular appropriations bills and one or more continuing resolutions if their work is not completed on time. The committees have some room for maneuver in determining, for example, whether to produce supplemental spending bills, but most of their work is decided for them in advance. Almost every other committee that produces legislation has no guarantee that its measures will be enacted. The Appropriations Committees know that appropriations for the programs covered by the thirteen bills will be enacted. They may not know whether the bills will be completed on time or whether they will be enacted in normal fashion one at a time, but they do know that unlike other measures acted on by Congress each year, theirs is must legislation.

The must status of the regular spending bills shapes the behavior and operations of the Appropriations Committees. These committees are among the least partisan in Congress, markedly less so than the House and Senate Budget Committees. Even when friction over budget policy and spending priorities intervenes, as it has frequently since the early 1980s, most Democrats and Republicans on Appropriations strive to assemble bills that they can support. Their task is eased by the distributive function performed by these committees. Democrats get money for their projects or constituencies and so do Republicans.

The formulation of passable appropriations bills is also helped by the committees' penchant for turning big policy and priority matters into routine questions of a little more versus a little less. If one seeks to examine the U.S. role in alleviating malnutrition around the world, the best forum might be the Agriculture or the Foreign Relations Committees. They do not have must pass legislation, and they can probe in as much depth as it takes to comprehend the issue. But the Appropriations Committees must act, and so they concentrate on marginal questions--whether funds to combat hunger should be more or less than the president's request or more or less than the previous year's allocation.

Making appropriations depends on a division of labor among the thirteen pairs of subcommittees. Throughout Congress, legislative power has gravitated over the past twenty-five years from full committees to subcommittees, but the power and prominence of subcommittees has always been more marked on Appropriations. Each appropriations subcommittee is a legislative fiefdom that fiercely guards its independence. Each pair of House and Senate subcommittees has jurisdiction over a single appropriations bill, and jurisdictional lines have not changed significantly for decades, despite enormous changes in the scale of federal operations. Almost all Appropriations Committee staff are assigned to subcommittees, not the full committee, and do not usually depart when a new subcommittee chair is selected.

The chairs of the appropriations subcommittees are commonly referred to on Capitol Hill as cardinals, in recognition of their power. The power comes from their control of the purse strings and their influence in channeling funds to their favored activities. Becoming a cardinal depends on seniority earned on a particular subcommittee, not on the full committee. Thus Senator Barbara Mikulski became chair of the Veterans Affairs–Housing and Urban Development Appropriations Subcommittee during her first term in the Senate, even though she was outranked by others on the full committee. Two decades ago, House Democrats decreed that appropriations subcommittee chairs should be selected by the party caucus in the same manner that full committee chairs are selected. At the time, no other House subcommittees were subjected to this procedure.

One of the distinguishing features of the appropriations process is the perfect alignment of House and Senate committee and subcommittee jurisdictions. Every federal program or agency has an identical niche in the House and Senate appropriations processes. Yet the two committees are very different. The House Appropriations Committee is twice the size of its Senate counterpart, and most of its members do not serve on any other major committee. Every member of the Senate Appropriations Committee, however, serves on at least one authorizing committee; a few have positions on authorizing committees and appropriations subcommittees with overlapping jurisdictions. The most prominent example is Senator Bennett Johnston, who chairs both the Energy and Water Appropriations Subcommittee and the Energy and Natural Resources Committee.

Multiple committee assignments may divide the loyalties of those serving on the Senate Appropriations Committee and diminish their attention to the committee's work. But the more probable result is that senators who serve on several committees are likely to bring some of their authorizing business to the Appropriations Committee. They may dominate an issue in Congress by virtue of their influence in both the authorization and appropriations processes.

The sequence of congressional action also differentiates the House and Senate Appropriations Committees. Although the Constitution is silent on the matter, by precedent appropriations originate in the House. The Senate does not produce its own bill but amends the House-passed appropriations. At one time this sequence (and the demands of multiple committee assignments) spurred the Senate Appropriations Committee to concentrate on those matters in dispute after the House had completed its work rather than thoroughly review the entire measure. This role as a court of appeals often resulted in the Senate's voting higher appropriations than had been passed by the House.

Now, although the Senate still amends the House-passed appropriations, it is less inclined to serve as a forum for agencies seeking more than they got from the House. Tight budgets and tough budget enforcement rules severely limit the additional funds the Senate can provide. The House typically appropriates almost the allowable limit, putting the Senate in the position of having to take away from some to give more to others. This is not a comfortable role for Senate appropriators; they often evade

Figure 8-1. Path of an Appropriations Act through Congress[a]

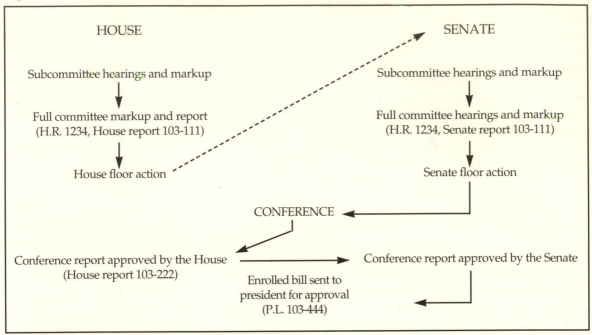

a. The broken line from House floor action to the Senate indicates that Senate subcommittee or committee activity often preceeds House passage.

pressure to redistribute by marking up (but not reporting) some spending bills before the House has completed action. After the House is done, the Senate inserts its version as an amendment.

Appropriations Procedures and Politics: Committee Action

Unlike authorizing committees, which typically take up legislation in response to the introduction of a bill, the appropriations process is initiated by the president's request for funds. The Appropriations Committees rarely act on their own initiative or pursuant to the introduction of a bill. In fact, there is no bill during the early stages of committee activity. Typically, an appropriations bill materializes only when the House Appropriations Committee marks up or reports the measure. Often the bill is introduced, referred to committee, and reported on the same day. Before

being reported the bill does not even have an H.R. number, and it cannot be tracked in legislative databases. Once the appropriations process is initiated, it follows the legislative path shown in figure 8-1.

Hearings

Soon after the president's budget goes to Congress, each Appropriations Committee conducts overview hearings at which the director of the Office of Management and Budget and others testify concerning overall budget policies and priorities. These are the only sessions in which OMB is formally involved (other than in hearings on its own appropriations) and the only hearings held by the full committee.

After the overviews, individual agencies defending their own budgets and individual subcommittees conduct their own hearings. Thus after the president's budget is submitted, it is split into thirteen parts and considered in a fragmented, decentralized manner. OMB does have a behind-the-scenes role clearing agency testimony (which is submitted to it in advance) and monitoring the progress of the appropriations bills. OMB also intervenes periodically in notifying the Appropriations Committees of any objections the president may have to pending measures.

During the hearings and in subsequent negotiations, OMB relies on agency officials to defend the president's request, even when it is at variance with their own preferences. Of course, there are ways of prying information from agencies on what they really want. Although they are not permitted to volunteer the information, agencies may do so in response to questions--some of which may be prearranged--from subcommittee members.

Most of the testimony is from agency officials who carefully prepare for the hearings by reviewing detailed briefing books, looking at the previous year's report language, and participating in mock hearings at which they are questioned on matters that might be raised by the subcommittee. Outside witnesses are also heard, but the sessions deal mostly with the internal operations and finances of the testifying agency.

Subcommittee Markup

Throughout the hearings stage, subcommittee members and staff informally discuss financial and operational issues with agency officials. By means of these discussions the subcommittees develop a sense of what the agency needs, what it can do without, and the funding levels that may be appropriate. The subcommittees are also assisted by investigatory reports prepared by their own staffs and persons detailed from the General Accounting Office and other agencies. By the time the subcommittee starts marking up its bill, it has a good idea of the changes it will make in the president's budget.

Before it can mark up its bill, each subcommit-

tee must be apprised of the total amount available for all accounts in its jurisdiction. For this purpose the subcommittees are guided by the Budget Enforcement Act discretionary spending limits and the allocations made to them pursuant to section 602 of the Congressional Budget Act. The discretionary spending limits (discussed in chapter 2) cap total budget authority and outlays. Inasmuch as all discretionary spending is by definition in the jurisdiction of the Appropriations Committees, the caps limit the amount that can be provided in annual appropriations acts.

Specific dollar limits on appropriations are also set, following adoption of a budget resolution, pursuant to section 602 (see chapter 6). Under this process the House and Senate Appropriations Committees receive total spending allocations that each then subdivides among its thirteen subcommittees. The rules bar the House and Senate from considering spending measures before the Appropriations Committees have filed the required section 602 report.

The discretionary spending caps and the 602 process have nudged the Appropriations Committees to coordinate the spending plans of their subcommittees. The subcommittees can no longer act wholly independently of one another and appropriate without regard for the total or for how much is available to all subcommittees. Before one subcommittee completes marking up its bill, all subcommittees must be informed of how much they have to spend. The way discretionary funds are divided among them varies from year to year and depends on the role of the chair of the full committee and the strength of fiscal stringency. In most years the chair consults with subcommittee leaders before subdividing the committee's discretionary funds. Once the allocations have been made, a subcommittee can enlarge its share only at the expense of other subcommittees.

This zero-sum competition pervades each subcommittee's markup. More for one account typically means less for others within that subcommittee's jurisdiction. Some subcommittees have such sprawling jurisdiction that programs

135

Exhibit 8-1. Agency Justification of Appropriations Request

CHILD NUTRITION PROGRAMS

Appropriations Act, 1993..$6,826,553,000
Budget Estimate, 1994...7,443,929,000
Increase in Appropriations..+617,376,000

JUSTIFICATION OF INCREASES AND DECREASES

The Fiscal Year 1994 request for the Child Nutrition Programs reflects an increase of $617,376,000.

(1) A decrease of $340,000 for administrative efficiency.

Need for Change. To promote the efficient use of resources for administrative purposes, in keeping with the President's Executive Order, total USDA baseline outlays for these activities will be reduced by 3 percent in Fiscal Year 1994, 6 percent in Fiscal Year 1995, 9 percent in Fiscal Year 1996, and 14 percent in Fiscal Year 1997.

Nature of Change. In order to achieve this savings, the Child Nutrition Programs will reduce non-salary administrative costs from Fiscal Year 1993 levels adjusted for inflation by $65,000 in the Summer Food Service Program, by $258,000 in Commodity Procurement, and by $17,000 in the Coordinated Review Effort by limiting travel and other administrative expenses.

(2) An increase of $216,442,000 in the appropriation for the School Lunch Program ($4,110,794,000 budgeted in 1993). On the basis of available funds, there is an increase of $196,789,183 ($4,131,424,817 available in 1993).

Need for Change. The total number of school lunches is expected to increase by 72 million in Fiscal Year 1994 due to increased school enrollment and an increase in the number of children applying for free meals. The number of free meals is projected to increase by 1.7% in Fiscal Year 1994. The projected rise in reimbursement rates on July 1 reflecting increases in the Consumer Price Index (CPI) for Food Away from Home contributes to the need for increased funding.

Source: House Agriculture Appropriations Subcommittee, *Hearings on the Fiscal 1994 Appropriations,* 103 Cong. 1 sess., pp. 438, 446.

(a) Each agency requesting appropriations submits detailed justifications to the appropriations subcommittees with jurisdiction over its budget. (The justifications are usually published as part of the committee's hearings.)

(b) Each subcommittee prescribes the form of the material submitted to it; the format displayed here is common. It compares the request for next year with the amount appropriated for the current year.

(c) The justification concentrates on proposed increases or decreases, not on the entire request. As is the case here, the request is usually higher than the current year's appropriation. But note that the first item justified is a tiny decrease.

(d) The justifications are formatted to highlight increases or decreases because these are the matters the appropriations committees concentrate on in reveiwing spending requests.

whose only relationship is that they are funded in the same appropriations bill are forced to compete against one another. One subcommittee, for example, has jurisdiction over veterans' programs, space exploration, environmental programs, housing and urban development, and more than a dozen other programs. Competition among programs is likely to intensify as the BEA discretionary caps become more stringent in the years ahead.

The Incremental Appropriations Process

In addition to assessing budget requests in light of the total resources available for allocation by it, each subcommittee closely reviews the voluminous material prepared by agencies to justify their budget requests. Although the format of these documents varies, most have characteristics that provide clues to the behavior of the subcommittees.

First, the justifications are very detailed, breaking down the agency's budget into discrete projects, activities, and line items. Second, most of the details pertain to personnel, equipment purchases, operating expenses, and other inputs rather than to programs and outputs. It is not common for the justifications to concentrate on objectives and performance, though there are typically some statements addressing these concerns.

Third and most important, the justifications are formatted so as to facilitate the comparison of current appropriations and next year's request. The justifications focus on spending changes between the current and upcoming fiscal years (exhibit 8-1). Although agencies ostensibly justify their entire request, the principal concern at the hearings is how much more (or less) the agency wants than it received for the current year and what the reasons for the changes are.

The Appropriations Committees are the only major participants in congressional budgeting that do not explicitly use baselines in measuring the financial impact of their actions.

Baselines depend on assumptions about future inflation, and the committees prefer instead to ground their decisions on actual amounts: the current year's appropriations and the next year's request. By eschewing baselines, they maintain control over incremental resources. They decide how much agencies should be compensated for inflation. They can thereby claim credit for increases due to inflation and avoid blame for increases that do not fully compensate for inflation.

The aversion to baselines and the focus on nominal year-to-year spending changes is maintained at all stages of committee and subcommittee action–from the initial hearings through final markup. The current year's appropriations and next year's request are the boundaries within which the committees operate. Item by item, and every step of the way, they compare their decisions to these reference points. They determine how much more or less they are recommending than they did for this year's appropriations and for next year's request. For every account and for each bill the committees publish the arithmetic difference between their actions and the two reference points (exhibit 8-2). They make these calculations because they need them to do their own work.

In normal times, when the president asks for more than was appropriated for the current year, most committee decisions fall between the two boundaries. This pattern breeds incrementalism, small changes rather than big ones, and lends somewhat greater weight to the president's budget than to authorizing legislation.

From the perspective of the Appropriations Committees, this behavior has several compelling advantages. First, it reduces conflict over spending decisions and facilitates the timely enactment of appropriations. Second, it reduces the workload by enabling the committees to concentrate on changes at the margins rather than on the total request. Third, it often enables the committees to take credit both for cutting the budget (below the president's request) and increasing expenditures (above the previous level). In view of the preference

Exhibit 8-2. Incrementalism in the Appropriations Process

House report

```
                    RURAL DEVELOPMENT GRANTS

1993 appropriation ...........................................................    $20,750,000
1994 budget estimate .......................................................     51,046,000
Provided in the bill .........................................................    35,000,000
Comparison:
     1993 appropriation ...................................................     +14,250,000
     1994 budget estimate ...............................................     − 16,046,000
```

Senate report

```
                    RURAL DEVELOPMENT GRANTS

Appropriations, 1993 .......................................................    $20,750,000
Budget estimate, 1994 .....................................................     51,046,000
House allowance ............................................................     35,000,000
Committee recommendation ...........................................     50,000,000
```

Comparative statement

COMPARATIVE STATEMENT OF NEW BUDGET (OBLIGATIONAL) AUTHORITY FOR 1993 AND BUDGET ESTIMATES AND AMOUNTS RECOMMENDED IN THE BILL FOR 1994—Continued

Agency and item (1)	Appropriated, 1993 (enacted to date) (2)	Budget estimates, 1994 (3)	Recommended in bill (4)	Bill compared with appropriated, 1993 (5)	Bill compared with budget estimates, 1994 (6)
State mediation grants	3,000,000	2,963,000	2,963,000	-37,000	
Rural water and waste disposal grants	390,000,000	535,571,000	450,000,000	+ 60,000,000	-85,571,000
Very low-income housing repair grants	12,500,000	30,679,000	25,000,000	+ 12,500,000	-5,679,000
Rural housing for domestic farm labor	11,000,000	11,157,000	11,000,000		-157,000
Mutual and self-help housing	12,750,000	12,932,000	12,750,000		-182,000
Supervisory and technical assistance grants	2,500,000	2,536,000	2,500,000		-36,000
Rural community fire protection grants	3,500,000	3,550,000	3,500,000		-50,000
Rural housing preservation grants	23,000,000	23,329,000	23,000,000		-329,000
Compensation for construction defects	500,000	508,000	500,000		-8,000
Rural development grants	20,750,000	51,046,000	35,000,000	+ 14,250,000	-16,046,000

Sources: *Agriculture, Rural Development, Food and Drug Administration, and Related Agencies Appropriations Bill, 1994*, H. rept. 103-153 and S. rept. 103-102, 103 Cong. 1 sess. (GPO, 1993), pp. 99, 164.

(a) The Appropriations Committees compare the amount recommended for each account with the current year's appropriations and the president's request for the next year. The Senate committee also compares its recommendation to the amount appropriated by the House. In addition, each report on a regular appropriations bill contains a "Comparative Statement of New Budget Authority" for all accounts funded in the bill.

(b) As occurred for the rural development grants displayed here, the Appropriations Committees often recommend more than the current appropriations but less than the president's request. Moreover, the amount recommended by the Senate committee usually differs from that provided in the House-passed appropriations.

(c) The Appropriations Committees do not compare their recommendations to baseline projections. These committees avoid baselines, which depend on assumptions about future economic and program conditions, and rely instead on the amounts actually appropriated or requested.

of Americans for smaller government and bigger programs, the committees' ability to satisfy both sentiments at the same time is no insignificant feat.

Incrementalism also promotes coordination in the decentralized appropriations process. If most appropriations fall between current spending and the president's request, the Appropriations Committees can be confident that the total will also fall between these reference points. For decades incrementalism enabled them to produce coordinated outcomes without trespassing on the autonomy of the subcommittees.

But incrementalism depends on a cooperative president, one who by asking for more enables the Appropriations Committees to give more while taking credit for cutting back. This condition did not prevail during the 1980s because Ronald Reagan demanded deep cuts in many established programs. Although he got his way at first, the Appropriations Committees quickly regrouped and managed to spend more while cutting the president's budget by transferring funds from defense to domestic programs. This tactic led to intense budget conflicts with the White House and to protracted delays in enacting the annual spending bills. George Bush also confronted Congress on the budget, but he did not have Reagan's early success. By the end of his term he took a more accommodating stance on congressional incrementalism, accepting spending increases while attacking Congress's ways.

In the first years of his presidency, Bill Clinton has requested big increases for his initiatives while trimming expenditures in many other accounts. The cuts have been numerous but generally small. The Appropriations Committees have endorsed only some of the increases and rejected many of the cuts. This behavior does not look very different from incrementalism, but continuing along this path may become more difficult as discretionary spending caps become tighter and the president proposes additional shifts in budget priorities.

Projects and Pork

Subcommittee members do more than look at the president's numbers and the agencies' justifications. They also listen to other members of Congress (especially colleagues on the Appropriations Committees) who want money earmarked for their districts or states. Subcommittees receive more of these requests than they can accommodate, but they satisfy enough of them to give the appropriations bill a solid base of support in the full committee and on the floor.

Typically, funds are earmarked to special projects or activities in committee reports rather than in the appropriations bill. Exhibit 8-3 shows project earmarks in one such report. The subcommittee chair, working with the ranking minority member, usually has the final say over which projects are funded, but widely shared distributive norms guide the process. First, subcommittee members get some of the prizes, with members of the full committee next in line. Second, the process is bipartisan; members from both parties take home some earmarks. Third, members of Congress who request and receive earmarked funds are expected to vote for the appropriations bill. The basic rule is, "don't ask for money if you are not going to vote for the bill."

Each subcommittee has its own idea about how much earmarking is acceptable. For years, the two largest appropriations bills have moved in opposite directions on this matter. The Labor, Health and Human Services, and Education bill has been relatively pork free; the Defense bill has been crammed with earmarks. Representative Bill Natcher, longtime chair of the House Labor, Health and Human Services, and Education Subcommittee until his death in 1994, did not like earmarks and kept most out of his bill. Defense, however, has long been a major pork barrel because of the thousands of military installations and contractors funded in it. If pork is, as some pundits have said, spending with a zip code attached, there are

Exhibit 8-3. Program Earmarks in Appropriations Reports

For rural development grants the Committee provides $35,000,000, an increase of $14,250,000 above the amount available for fiscal year 1993 and a decrease of $16,046,000 below the budget request.

The Committee restores bill language earmarking $500,000 for rural transportation systems technical assistance. The funds are designed to assist small rural communities in planning and developing transportation systems that promote a link between transportation and economic development initiatives.

The Committee is aware of a grant proposal from the State of Illinois Department of Agriculture for a pilot program to collect unwanted pesticides, both canceled and unknown, from Illinois farmers and dispose of them in a proper manner, and for a pilot program to design and implement a pesticide container recycling program. .

The Southern Kentucky Rural Economic Development Center in Somerset, Kentucky, is developing a rural technology facility in coordination with Kentucky Educational Television, a Statewide public television network. A grant proposal has been developed which involves funding for equipment for transmission and production. The Committee expects the Department to consider this proposal expeditiously.

A nonprofit community development corporation, Chicanos for LaCausa, provides many services to low-income residents in Yuma County, Arizona, including immigration and naturalization process counseling. The Committee is aware that its facilities are in need of expansion and rehabilitation and expects the Department to give high priority to the corporation's request.

Source: *Agriculture Appropriations Bill, 1994*, H. rept. 103-153, 103 Cong. 1 sess. (GPO, 1993), p. 99. The earmarks shown here pertain to the same account displayed in exhibit 8-2.

(a) The Appropriations Committees often earmark funds to designated projects or activities. Agencies are expected to adhere to these earmarks as well as to other guidance issued in the appropriations reports.

(b) The four earmarks displayed here were among the twelve issued for this relatively small account. Only the first earmark specifies an amount; in all the others the committee commended the project but left the amount to the agency. The more common practice is to earmark specific amounts.

(c) The committee varied the report language, in some cases urging consideration of the mentioned project, in others merely expecting consideration. Note that the first project earmark, pertaining to a grant proposal from Illinois, does not use any such wording. But since the chair of the appropriations subcommittee comes from Illinois and since this project is listed before any others, one can assume that the committee strongly expected funds to be forthcoming.

more zip codes in the defense budget than in any other appropriations bill.

The past trend has been to attach more earmarks, but appropriations reports for fiscal year 1994 indicate a downturn. The Clinton administration has argued against earmarking and, as noted, Natcher, who chaired the full House Appropriations Committee for the fiscal 1994 cycle, did not like them. Representative David Obey, his successor, is also a foe of extensive earmarking. Nevertheless, if two hundred years of appropriations history is a guide, earmarked projects are here to stay.

Hardly anyone has a nice thing to say about the practice. The president and executive agencies do not want earmarks because they tie their hands and divert funds from their priorities. Authorizing committees do not want them in appropriations bills because the committees would rather do the earmarking in their own bills. Members of Congress who do not get what they regard as a fair share of funds complain that the practice is wasteful and demeaning. Even those who come away winners will defend their actions only by saying that since everybody else is doing it, they have to stick up for their states and districts. The news media and critics of Congress see corruption and vote buying behind just about every earmarked project.

Earmarks flourish because members of the Appropriations Committees would rather decide where funds are to be spent than let executive agencies make the determination. They flourish because the chief political value of serving on the Appropriations Committees is to bring home the bacon, not to guard the Treasury. They flourish because a spending bill with a lot of projects spread across the country is easier to pass than is one without them. They flourish in good times, when incremental resources are bountiful, and, it seems, even more in hard times when the budget is tight.

The truth is that most earmarks are relatively cheap; many can be crammed into tight budgets. And when funds are scarce, pork is prized because it may be the only kind of benefit that members can bring home. Programs, by contrast, are expensive because they typically provide nationwide rather than local benefits. Consider, for example, a proposal to improve U.S. education by upgrading teaching material. Even if this program were to start modestly, with only $100 allotted per student, the total cost would exceed $5 billion. Suppose, however, that instead of a national program a member of Congress earmarks $1 million to a local school district for an education demonstration project. In the political arithmetic of budgeting, $100 may be too expensive but $1 million is affordable. Imagine that every member of Congress were to earmark $1 million. The total would be a bit more than $500 million, or barely one-tenth of 1 percent of discretionary appropriations, and only one-thirtieth of 1 percent of total federal spending.

To say that earmarking is cheap is not to justify the practice or to claim that all the money is well spent. But neither should one believe that the financial crisis in federal budgeting is due to pork. It is not.

Appropriations Procedures and Politics: Floor Action

The appropriations subcommittees are generally influential. It is not uncommon for the full committee to report bills prepared for it by the subcommittees without making substantive changes. The subcommittees also draft the reports that accompany the bills to the floor and establish much of the legislative history referred to in determining congressional intent.

Box 8-1 shows the main steps in House action on appropriations. Because general appropriations bills are privileged for floor consideration, they can be brought to the House without first obtaining a special rule through the Rules Committee. Nevertheless, most appropriations measures do come to the House under a rule (in the form of a House resolution) waiving one or more of the standing

Box 8-1. Sequence of House Actions on Appropriations Bills

Rule

Although appropriations bills are privileged and can be considered by the House at any time, the House normally considers them under special rules (in the form of a simple resolution) waiving certain points of order, such as the point of order barring unauthorized appropriations. After the House approves the rule, it takes up the bill.

Committee of the Whole

The House debates the bill in the Committee of the Whole, which has a smaller quorum requirement than that of the House. There are few substantive differences between the Committee of the Whole and the House.

General debate

Debate on the bill is opened by the floor managers: the chair and ranking minority member of the relevant appropriations subcommittee. Opening statements may also be made by the chair of the Appropriations Committee, who may remark on the overall status of appropriations bills, and by the chair of the Budget Committee, who may advise the House as to whether the bill conforms to section 602 allocations.

Amendments

Regular appropriations bills are usually considered under an open rule that does not preclude consideration of any floor amendments. An amendment must be offered in a timely manner, that is, when the portion of the bill to which it pertains is being considered.

Points of order

Points of order (which also must be timely) may be raised against either the committee bill or a floor amendment. In the House it is rare for the ruling of the chair on a point of order to be challenged.

Limitations

Floor amendments inserting limitations into an appropriations bill may be offered only after consideration of amendments affecting funding levels has been completed. At this point, any member can move that the Committee of the Whole "rise and report." If this motion, which is acted on at once, is adopted, there may be no opportunity to offer limitation amendments.

House passage

After the Committee of the Whole reports, final action is in the House itself. Under certain circumstances, the House may reconsider matters decided in the Committee of the Whole, but it usually concurs in the previous vote.

rules, such as the rule against unauthorized appropriations. The House first adopts the special rule (see exhibit 8-4), then takes up the appropriations bill.

Special rules on appropriations bills usually are open; they do not restrict floor amendments. Nevertheless, the rule is often crafted to protect only the bill reported by the Appropriations Committee, not floor amendments pertaining to the same matter. For example, unauthorized provisions in the reported bill may be protected against points of order, but floor amendments providing unauthorized appropriations may not be. (The rule in exhibit 8-4 does not provide a blanket waiver.) By waiving points of order only against specified portions of the bill, the rule may preclude certain floor amendments to provisions in the measure reported by the Appropriations Committee.

During House consideration of an appropriations measure, the Budget Committee usually compares the budget authority and outlays deriving from the bill with the amounts allocated to the relevant subcommittee under the section 602 process. Exhibit 8-5 shows one such comparison. Appropriations bills rarely exceed the subcommittee allocations, for doing so would indicate that the Appropriations Committee is fiscally irresponsible because it has violated congressional budget policy. Occasionally a bill exceeds the allocation for technical rather than substantive reasons, and the House waives the point of order.

The section 602 rules inhibit the passage of floor amendments that would change the amounts appropriated. Appropriations bills typically are slightly below the levels allowed by section 602, precluding amendments that would provide significant increases. Amendments reducing budget authority face challenges on the ground that Congress has already decided to appropriate at the reported level. The only other option would be to transfer funds from one account to another within the section 602 limits, but transfer amendments are likely to attract

strong opposition (and procedural impediments) from those whose programs would lose resources. Despite these impediments, there are times when an economizing mood takes hold on Capitol Hill and appropriations are cut by floor amendment below the allowed level. In 1993, for example, freshman representatives joined with fiscal conservatives to cut some spending bills on the floor.

Before voting on an appropriations measure, the House may be advised of issues raised by the White House or OMB. The advice takes the form of a statement of administration policy (exhibit 8-6). Each statement outlines the administration's concerns as the appropriations bill moves through the House and Senate. An SAP normally is issued at six stages of congressional action: House appropriations subcommittee markups; House Appropriations Committee markups; House floor action; Senate appropriations subcommittee action; Senate Appropriations Committee markup; and Senate floor action. An SAP is also usually issued before conference action. Each statement concentrates on items in the most recent version of the appropriations measure that the administration finds objectionable. It is carefully worded and structured to indicate the intensity of administration concern and the extent to which the objectionable matter might provoke a presidential veto.

The SAP process was introduced during the 1980s in response to two developments. One was the reorientation of OMB budget attention from agency operations to congressional actions. The other was extended conflict between the president and Congress on budget matters. The SAPs do not displace the give-and-take between presidential aides and legislative leaders, but they do suggest a formal, somewhat distant relationship between the president and Congress, one that impels the protagonists to put their differences down in writing and to threaten vetoes. Since the onset of the Clinton presidency, the tone of the statements has softened and the language has

Exhibit 8-4. Special Rule on Appropriations Bills

H. Res. 214

Resolved, That all points of order against consideration of the bill (H.R. 2520) making appropriations for the Department of the Interior and related agencies for the fiscal year ending September 30, 1994, and for other purposes, are waived. During consideration of the bill, all points of order against the following provisions in the bill for failure to comply with clause 2 or 6 of rule XXI are waived: beginning on page 4, line 22, through page 5, line 13; beginning on page 14, line 1, through "construction" on line 11; beginning on page 54, line 1, through line 4; beginning on page 58, line 14, through line 22; beginning on page 78, line 8, through page 80, line 10; beginning on page 85, line 15, through page 86, line 15; beginning on page 86, line 20, through page 87, line 3; and beginning on page 89, line 18, through line 21. Where points of order are waived against only part of a paragraph, a point of order against matter in the balance of the paragraph may be applied only within the balance of the paragraph and not against the entire paragraph.

Source: *Congressional Record*, daily edition, July 14, 1993, p. H4583.

(a) Although appropriations bills are privileged in the House and can be taken up at any time, the practice is to consider them according to a "special rule" (in the form of a House resolution) waiving certain points of order that would otherwise apply. The House acts first on the rule and then considers the appropriations bill.

(b) The rule exhibited here waives points of order on unauthorized appropriations and legislation in an appropriations bill. Note that points of order are waived only for certain specified provisions, not for the entire bill. These limited waivers do not protect other provisions or floor amendments (unless they are expressly protected) against points of order.

(c) This is an open rule; it does not limit floor amendments. Most rules on appropriations bills are open; however, in some recent sessions the House adopted rules restricting amendments to certain appropriations bills.

(d) The final sentence in the rule refers to the unnumbered paragraphs in appropriations bills, each of which (as explained in the text) constitutes one appropriations account. If a particular provision in an unnumbered paragraph is ruled out of order, the rest of the paragraph (account) is not affected.

Exhibit 8-5. Section 602(b) Statement

Mr. SASSER. Mr. President, the Senate Budget Committee has examined H.R. 2403, the Treasury, postal, and independent agencies appropriations bill and has found that the bill meets its 602(b) budget authority allocation and falls under its 602(b) outlay allocation by less than $500,000.

I compliment the distinguished manager of the bill, Senator DeConcini, and the distinguished ranking member of the Treasury, Postal, and Independent Agencies Subcommittee, Senator Bond, on all of their hard work.

Mr. President, I have a table prepared by the Budget Committee which shows the official scoring of the Treasury, postal, and independent agencies appropriations bill and I ask unanimous consent that it be printed in the Record.

SENATE BUDGET COMMITTEE'S SCORING OF H.R. 2403

FISCAL YEAR 1994 TREASURY-POSTAL SERVICE APPROPRIATIONS

(in millions of dollars)

Bill summary	Budget authority	Outlays
Discretionary total:		
New spending in bill	11,579	8,960
Outlays from prior years appropriations		2,729
Permanent/advance appropriations	0	0
Supplemental	0	11
Subtotal, discretionary spending	11,579	11,700
Mandatory total	11,494	11,493
Bill total	23,073	23,193
Senate 602(b) allocation	23,073	23,193
Difference	0	0
Discretionary totals above (+) or below (−):		
President's request	330	99
House-passed bill	311	173
Senate-reported bill		
Senate-passed bill		

Source: *Congressional Record*, daily edition, August 3, 1993, p. S10177.

(a) During debate on some appropriations bills, the chair of the House or Senate Budget Committee may provide a comparison of the amounts in the pending bill and the section 602(b) allocation to the relevant appropriations subcommittee. The current chair of the House Budget Committee, Representative Martin Sabo of Minnesota, issues these comparisons infrequently; his predecessor, Leon Panetta of California, issued them regularly.

(b) The Budget Committees are the official scorers of congressional budget action; hence the analysis issued by the Senate Budget Committee is authoritative in ruling on points of order concerning violations of the section 602 allocations.

(c) As in the case shown here, the Budget Committee statement usually reports that regular appropriations bills are within the subcommittee allocation. A point of order may be raised against an appropriations measure that would cause budget authority or outlays to exceed the subcommittee allocation.

(d) The Appropriations Committee typically uses all (or almost all) of the budget authority and outlays available under the section 602 process.

Exhibit 8-6. Statement of Administration Policy

STATEMENT OF ADMINISTRATION POLICY

(THIS STATEMENT HAS BEEN COORDINATED BY OMB WITH THE CONCERNED AGENCIES.)

H.R. 2686 -- DEPARTMENT OF THE INTERIOR AND RELATED AGENCIES APPROPRIATIONS BILL, FY 1992

(Sponsors: Whitten (D), Mississippi; Yates (D), Illinois)

This Statement of Administration Policy expresses the Administration's views on the Department of the Interior and Related Agencies Appropriations Bill, FY 1992, as reported by the Committee.

The Administration has several concerns about the bill. If these concerns are not addressed, the President's senior advisers will recommend that the bill be vetoed. The Secretary of the Interior addressed several of these concerns in more detail in his letter to the Committee of June 18th.

<u>Firefighting Scorekeeping</u>:

Although the Committee restored $213 million in discretionary funding for firefighting costs eliminated by the Subcommittee, the Administration strongly objects to the approach taken in the amendment. The bill, as amended, would preclude use of the funds unless the President declares an emergency, thus exempting all expenditures from applicable spending limits. This appears to be a gimmick designed to force the President to declare an emergency for clearly anticipated costs and thereby evade the domestic discretionary caps. As such, it is a violation of the budget agreement.

Source: Office of Management and Budget, June 24, 1991.

(a) A statement of administration policy (SAP) is issued for each of the thirteen regular appropriations bills, as well as for supplemental and continuing appropriations, at each stage of congressional action. The exhibited SAP was issued before House consideration; thus it commented on the bill as reported by the Appropriations Committee. The SAP is sometimes inserted in the *Congressional Record* and may be referred to during debate on the measure.

(b) Each SAP typically enumerates administration objections to provisions in the appropriations bills. The objections may pertain to either funding levels or substantive language.

(c) The SAP may threaten a veto, as it does here, but it rarely declares outright that the president will veto the bill unless the objectionable items are removed. The formula used here, "the President's senior advisers will recommend that the bill be vetoed," is a strong threat, for it indicates that both OMB and presidential aides have agreed to recommend a veto.

(d) With Democratic party control of both Congress and the White House during the Clinton presidency, the SAPs have become less confrontational and they rarely threaten vetoes.

Table 8-2. House and Senate Votes on Passage of Fiscal Year 1994 Appropriations Acts[a]

Bill	Senate	House
Agriculture	90-10	304-119
Commerce	87-13	327-98
Defense	Voice vote	325-102
District of Columbia	70-29	213-211
Energy and Water	89-10	350-73
Foreign operations	88-10	309-111
Interior	Voice vote	278-138
Labor and HHS	82-17	305-124
Legislative branch	85-7	224-187
Military construction	Voice vote	347-67
Transportation	90-9	312-89
Treasury	73-27	263-153
Veterans Administration-Housing and Urban Development	91-9	313-110

Sources: *Congresional Quarterly Weekly Report*, vol. 51, nos. 25-42; and *Calendars of the United States House of Representatives: Interim 1*, (GPO, 1993).

a. The votes listed here are on passage of the bill in the House and Senate, not on adoption of the conference report.

become more accommodating. It is not seemly for a Democratic president to openly threaten a Democratic Congress with vetoes because of quarrels over some of the details in appropriations bills. But the White House still needs to communicate its concerns to Congress, and the SAP has proven to be a convenient means of doing so.

SAPs provide talking points for negotiations between presidential aides and Appropriations Committee leaders. The veto threat issued in the statement says more about the intensity of administration concern than it does about the likelihood of a veto. In fact, both sides know that the appropriations must be made and that each will have to give ground to make that possible. Sometimes the negotiations break down and an appropriations bill is vetoed. But the White House is constrained in its ability to wield an effective veto by the knowledge that

most appropriations bills pass the House and Senate with lopsided margins and strong support from both Democratic and Republican members (table 8-2). A bill that passed the House by a 305-124 margin and the Senate by an 82-17 vote, as the fiscal year 1994 appropriations for the Departments of Health and Human Services and Labor did, is not going to be vetoed, even if the final version has some provisions that rankle the White House.

Senate Action

The Senate usually considers appropriations measures after they have been passed by the House. The sequence of Senate actions is outlined in box 8-2. Hearings conducted by the Senate appropriations subcommittees generally are not as extensive as those held by House subcommittees, but senators do not routinely defer to the actions of the House. In fact, the Senate Appropriations Committee typically makes numerous changes in the bill passed by the House, and this behavior continues on the floor. In acting on appropriations, as on other measures, the Senate puts few restrictions on the capacity of members to offer floor amendments. But it does present tough hurdles to provisions, whether in the reported bill or proposed on the floor, that would violate section 602 rules. These Senate rules, which are more stringent than those applied in the House, are discussed in chapter 5.

When either the Appropriations Committee or the full Senate changes a House-passed appropriations measure, it inserts a sequentially numbered amendment at the point where the change occurs in the bill (exhibit 8-7). The conference committee that resolves differences in the measures passed by the two chambers acts on each numbered amendment (exhibit 8-8). Congressional action on an appropriations bill is not complete until the House and Senate have agreed on all numbered amendments. After the conference, some amendments will be in technical disagreement, meaning that

Box 8-2. Sequence of Senate Actions on Appropriations Bills

Waiver motion (if necessary)

Section 303(a) of the Congressional Budget Act bars consideration of revenue or spending measures before the budget resolution has been adopted. This bar can be waived by a special Senate resolution.

Time limitation agreement

Major legislation in the Senate is often considered under a time limitation agreement (sometimes referred to as a unanimous consent agreement) that sets aside an amount of time for consideration of the measure and any amendments. The time limitation usually is propounded by the majority leader (after consultation with the minority leader and other interested senators) and agreed to by unanimous consent.

Managers' statements

The chair and ranking minority member of the relevant appropriations subcommittee provide an overview of the bill, usually comparing the amounts in it to the previous year's level, the president's request, and the House-passed bill.

Committee amendments

Changes recommended by the Senate Appropriations Committee to the House-passed bill are usually voted on en bloc and approved by voice vote. This procedure pertains only to appropriations bills, not to authorizing legislation.

Floor amendments

Unlike in the House, the entire appropriations bill is open to floor amendment at any time during consideration. However, the time limitation agreement often specifies the sequence in which amendments are to be taken up.

Points of order

Points of order also may be raised at any time. When a point of order is made that an item is legislation on an appropriations bill, another member may raise the defense of germaneness. If the Senate deems the item germane, the point of order fails.

Senate passage

After all amendments have been disposed of (or when the time for voting on final passage stipulated in the time limitation agreement arrives), the Senate votes on the bill. Some appropriations bills are agreed to by voice rather than recorded vote.

although the matter has been resolved, a separate vote is required in the House and Senate.

Supplemental and Continuing Appropriations

The route taken by supplemental and continuing appropriations corresponds in most regards to that taken by regular spending bills. There is no fixed number of these measures, but some are passed in each session of Congress.

Supplementals are assembled by the appropriations subcommittees affected, but not on their initiative alone and usually with more coordination than befits regular appropriations. The discretionary caps and section 602 rules preclude supplementals in which individual subcommittees, without regard for how their recommendations affect the totals, unilaterally decide on the amounts they will include. Producing a supplemental entails matters that only the full Appropriations Committee and its leaders can decide, such as the scope of the bill and the amount of additional resources that should be provided. Resolving these matters usually requires negotiations with the White House that range across the jurisdictions of various subcommittees.

Continuing appropriations, usually referred to as continuing resolutions or CRs, were important means of providing funds during the 1980s, and their scope was much broader than it had been earlier. In some years the major continuing resolutions covered all the regular appropriations bills for that year. And rather than just providing interim funding until the regular appropriations were enacted, some provided funds for the entire fiscal year. When this occurred, the continuing resolution was, in effect, an omnibus appropriations act (exhibit 8-9 shows the opening portions of a standard continuing resolution).

The transformation of the continuing resolution into an omnibus measure has been accompanied by two other changes. First, omnibus measures frequently provide funding at a level other than a continuing rate. Some contain the full text of regular appropriations bills or incorporate them by reference to the version passed by the House or Senate, or agreed to in conference. Some specify amounts for particular programs or accounts in the same manner as is done in regular appropriations acts. Second, omnibus continuing resolutions are often used to enact substantive legislation. The opportunity to do so arises out of several features of these measures. They are not deemed to be general appropriations bills by the House; therefore the rule excluding legislation from appropriations bills does not apply. And the manner in which these measures are considered–late in the session with the immediate threat that the government will have to suspend most domestic operations if the funds are not provided–invites their use of CRs as a vehicle for substantive legislation.

In the 1980s many observers considered massive continuing resolutions evidence of the breakdown of the appropriations process. During the 1990s, however, the resolutions have generally reverted to historical form, supplying stopgap funding when regular appropriations have been delayed. The problem in the 1980s was not so much in appropriations procedures but in sustained and intense conflict between the president and Congress over budget policy. Continuing resolutions enabled the two branches to enact appropriations through extraordinary procedures when normal means did not suffice. Now that the conflict has abated, their scope has shrunk.

Structure and Content of Appropriations Measures

Regular appropriations acts have three standard features: an enacting clause that designates the fiscal year for which the appropriations are made; an appropriation for each account, including provisions attached to particular accounts; and general provisions (exhibit 8-10).

The basic unit of appropriations is an account

Exhibit 8-7. Numbered Senate Amendments

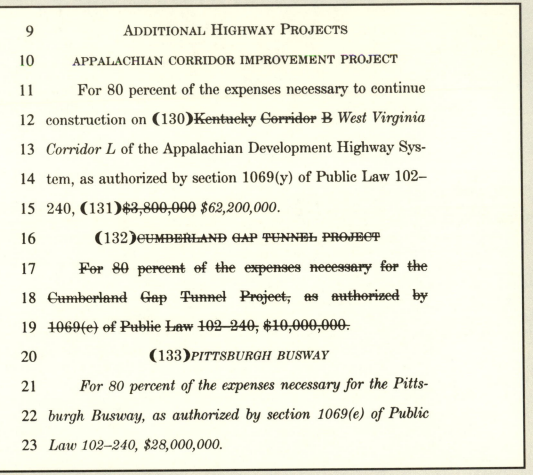

9   ADDITIONAL HIGHWAY PROJECTS

10   APPALACHIAN CORRIDOR IMPROVEMENT PROJECT

11   For 80 percent of the expenses necessary to continue

12   construction on (130)~~Kentucky Corridor B~~ *West Virginia*

13   *Corridor L* of the Appalachian Development Highway Sys-

14   tem, as authorized by section 1069(y) of Public Law 102–

15   240, (131)~~$3,800,000~~ *$62,200,000.*

16   (132)~~CUMBERLAND GAP TUNNEL PROJECT~~

17   ~~For 80 percent of the expenses necessary for the~~

18   ~~Cumberland Gap Tunnel Project, as authorized by~~

19   ~~1069(e) of Public Law 102–240, $10,000,000.~~

20   (133)*PITTSBURGH BUSWAY*

21   *For 80 percent of the expenses necessary for the Pitts-*

22   *burgh Busway, as authorized by section 1069(e) of Public*

23   *Law 102–240, $28,000,000.*

Source: *Department of Transportation Appropriations Act, Fiscal Year 1994*, with the amendments of the Senate numbered, H.R. 2750, 103 Cong. 1 sess. (GPO, 1993) p. 40.

(a) The Senate does not initiate its own appropriations bill. Instead, it amends (either in committee or on the floor) the House-passed appropriations bill.

(b) The numbers in parentheses designate Senate changes to the House-passed bill. Any change made by the Senate–deleting or inserting words or punctuation marks, or changing amounts–is a Senate amendment. The amendments are numbered sequentially and are referred to in the conference report on the appropriations bill (see exhibit 8-8).

(c) The lined-out text immediately following the numbered amendment is language in the House-passed bill struck by the Senate; the italicized text is language inserted by the Senate. The remaining text is House-passed language to which the Senate made no changes.

(d) As shown in exhibit 8-8, the conference report on an appropriations bill references the numbered Senate amendments. Hence it is necessary to have a copy of the Senate-passed appropriations bill to understand conference actions.

Exhibit 8-8. Conference Action on Appropriations Measure

CONFERENCE REPORT

[To accompany H.R. 2750]

The committee of conference on the disagreeing votes of the two Houses on the amendments of the Senate to the bill (H.R. 2750) "making appropriations for the Department of Transportation and related agencies, for the fiscal year ending September 30, 1994, and for other purposes," having met, after full and free conference, have agreed to recommend and do recommend to their respective Houses as follows:

That the Senate recede from its amendments numbered 28, 37, 40, 42, 43, 58, 61, 63, 64, 81, 82, 83, 84, 85, 113, 115, 117, 123, 146, 152, 153, 161, 162, 165, 166, 169, 170, 173, 174, 178, 179, 181, 183, 184, and 187.

That the House recede from its disagreement to the amendments of the Senate numbered 18, 19, 20, 22, 24, 25, 39, 44, 49, 55, 69, 75, 76, 77, 78, 79, 80, 86, 87, 89, 94, 95, 96, 97, 105, 108, 112, 116, 119, 120, 121, 126, 141, 148, 151, 156, 157, 160, 164, and 167, and agree to the same.

Amendment numbered 27:

That the House recede from its disagreement to the amendment of the Senate numbered 27, and agree to the same with an amendment, as follows:

In lieu of the sum proposed in said amendment insert: $2,570,000,000; and the Senate agree to the same.

Amendment numbered 30:

That the House recede from its disagreement to the amendment of the Senate numbered 30, and agree to the same with an amendment, as follows:

In lieu of the sum proposed in said amendment insert: $327,500,000; and the Senate agree to the same.

Source: *Making Appropriations for the Department of Transportation and Related Agencies*, H. rept. 103-300, Cong. 1 sess. (GPO, 1993), p. 1.

(a) The conference report sets forth the agreement of the conferees on all matters in disagreement between the House and Senate appropriations bills. To interpret the conference report (or to reconstruct the legislative history of an appropriations act), one must have a copy both of the conference report and of the Senate-passed bill. As shown in exhibit 8-7, the Senate-passed bill contains both the House-passed language and the Senate amendments.

(b) The conference resolves House-Senate differences in four ways, three of which are exhibited here: it can strike the Senate amendments (as it does here for amendments numbered 28, 37, 40, and so on); it can accept the Senate amendments (as it does here for numbers 18, 19, 20, and so on); it can devise a compromise by adopting new language (as it does here for numbers 27 and 30, or it can designate amendments as "reported in technical disagreement."

(c) Amendments in technical agreement have been resolved by the conferees, but they are so designated because a separate vote is required under the rules. These amendments are adopted by the House one by one immediately after it approves the conference report and en bloc by the Senate.

Exhibit 8-9. Continuing Appropriations

SEC. 101. (a) Such amounts as may be necessary under the authority and conditions provided in applicable appropriations Acts for the fiscal year 1993 for continuing projects or activities including the costs of direct loans and loan guarantees (not otherwise specifically provided for in this joint resolution) which were conducted in the fiscal year 1993 and for which appropriations, funds, or other authority would be available in the following appropriations Acts:

The Agriculture, Rural Development, Food and Drug Administration, and Related Agencies Appropriations Act, 1994;

The Departments of Commerce, Justice, and State, the Judiciary, and Related Agencies Appropriations Act, 1994, notwithstanding section 15 of the State Department Basic Authorities Act of 1956 and section 701 of the United States Information and Educational Exchange Act of 1948;

The Department of Defense Appropriations Act, 1994, notwithstanding section 504(a)(1) of the National Security Act of 1947;

The District of Columbia Appropriations Act, 1994;

The Energy and Water Development Appropriations Act, 1994;

The Department of the Interior and Related Agencies Appropriations Act, 1994;

The Departments of Labor, Health and Human Services, and Education, and Related Agencies Appropriations Act, 1994;

The Military Construction Appropriations Act, 1994;

The Department of Transportation and Related Agencies Appropriations Act, 1994;

The Treasury, Postal Service, and General Government Appropriations Act, 1994; and

The Departments of Veterans Affairs and Housing and Urban Development, and Independent Agencies Appropriations Act, 1994:

SEC. 106. Unless otherwise provided for in this joint resolution or in the applicable appropriations Act, appropriations and funds made available and authority granted pursuant to this joint resolution shall be available until (a) enactment into law of an appropriation for any project or activity provided for in this joint resolution, or (b) the enactment of the applicable appropriations Act by both Houses without any provision for such project or activity, or (c) October 21, 1993, whichever first occurs.

Source: *Continuing Appropriations for Fiscal Year 1994*, P.L. 103-88, 107 Stat. 977.

(a) A continuing appropriation is in the form of a joint resolution, which has the same legal status as a bill; these measures are often referred to as continuing resolutions.

(b) As shown here, the continuing resolution lists the regular appropriations measures covered by it. This was the first continuing resolution for fiscal 1994; it was enacted on the final day (September 30) of the preceding fiscal year. All but two of the thirteen regular appropriations bills were covered by it.

(c) A continuing resolution is superseded, as section 106 indicates, by enactment of regular appropriations bills. In this case the continuing resolution was effective for only three weeks, through October 21. When it expired, another continuing resolution was enacted.

Exhibit 8-10. Structure of a Regular Appropriations Act

Enacting clause

> Making appropriations for foreign operations, export financing, and related programs for the fiscal year ending September 30, 1994, and making supplemental appropriations for such programs for the fiscal year ending September 30, 1993, and for other purposes.
>
> *Be it enacted by the Senate and House of Representatives of the United States of America in Congress assembled,* That the following sums are appropriated, out of any money in the Treasury not otherwise appropriated, for foreign operations, export financing, and related programs for the fiscal year ending September 30, 1994, and for other purposes, namely:

Appropriations

> ### ASSISTANCE FOR THE NEW INDEPENDENT STATES OF THE FORMER SOVIET UNION
>
> For necessary expenses to carry out the provisions of chapter 11 of part I of the Foreign Assistance Act of 1961 and the FREEDOM Support Act, for assistance for the new independent states of the former Soviet Union and for related programs, $603,820,000, to remain available until expended: *Provided,* That the provisions of 498B(j) of the Foreign Assistance Act of 1961 shall apply to funds appropriated by this paragraph.

General provisions

> ### PROHIBITION AGAINST DIRECT FUNDING FOR CERTAIN COUNTRIES
>
> SEC. 507. None of the funds appropriated or otherwise made available pursuant to this Act shall be obligated or expended to finance directly any assistance or reparations to Cuba, Iraq, Libya, the Socialist Republic of Vietnam, Iran, Serbia, Sudan, or Syria: *Provided,* That for purposes of this section, the prohibition on obligations or expenditures shall include direct loans, credits, insurance and guarantees of the Export-Import Bank or its agents.

Source: *Foreign Operations Appropriations Act, 1994,* P.L. 103-87, 107 Stat. 931, 939, 946.

(a) An appropriations act has three main components: the enacting clause; appropriations to specified accounts; and general provisions.

(b) The enacting clause specifies the fiscal year for which appropriations are made. Unless otherwise stipulated, all funds provided in the act are available for obligation only in that fiscal year. All substantive provisions in appropriations acts expire at the end of the fiscal year unless the text gives them a longer period of effectiveness.

(c) Each unnumbered paragraph constitutes a single appropriations account. Most agencies have a single account providing for salaries and expenses; some have additional accounts for procurement or special activities. Provisions in an unnumbered paragraph pertain only to that account unless the text provides otherwise. Funds may be transferred between accounts only with the approval of Congress.

(d) The general provisions (which may limit the use of funds or contain new legislation) are numbered sections. These provisions apply to all accounts in the title or in the act, as specified.

153

(exhibit 8-11). A single unnumbered paragraph in an appropriations act comprises one account, and all provisions of a paragraph pertain only to that account, unless the text gives them broader scope. Any laws pertaining to spending out of particular accounts pertain to the relevant unnumbered paragraphs, and any provision limiting the use of funds provided in a paragraph is a restriction on that account alone, unless the language specifies otherwise.

Over the years, appropriations have been consolidated in a relatively small number of accounts. The budget now contains more than 1,000 accounts, but the 200 largest comprise more than 90 percent of all federal expenditures. It is typical for a federal agency to have a single account for all its operating expenses; some have additional accounts for special purposes such as procurement or construction. Most appropriations provide a lump sum for all the activities or projects encompassed by the account, though specific amounts may be earmarked in the Appropriations Committee report for particular uses.

In addition to the provisions associated with each account, each appropriations act has general provisions that apply to all the accounts in a title or in the entire act. These provisions appear as numbered sections at the end of the title or act (exhibit 8-12). Most are reenacted year after year with little or no change, though there has been a marked trend toward a greater number of general provisions.

An appropriation that does not mention the period during which the funds are available is a one-year appropriation; the funds have to be obligated during the fiscal year for which they are provided, and they lapse if not obligated by the end of that year. Congress also makes no-year appropriations by specifying that the funds shall remain available until expended. No-year funds are carried over to future years, even if they have not been obligated. Congress sometimes makes multiyear appropriations that provide for the funds to be available for two or more fiscal years. Exhibit 8-13 shows appropri-

ations with different periods of availability.

Appropriations measures also contain other types of provisions that serve specialized purposes. These include provisions to liquidate obligations incurred pursuant to backdoor contract authority (a form of direct spending legislation discussed in chapter 7), reappropriate funds provided in previous years, transfer funds from one account to another, rescind funds, limit the obligations that can be made or guaranteed, or limit the administrative expenses that can be incurred during the fiscal year (exhibit 8-14). Special appropriations also are made for the subsidy cost of direct and guaranteed loans (exhibit 8-15).

Legislation and Limitations in Appropriations Acts

Although the rules bar legislation in appropriations acts, many legislative provisions are included each year. (A provision is legislation if it changes existing law or makes new law.) In some cases entire laws have been enacted in appropriations measures; the more common practice has been to insert particular provisions.

Despite the rules, the House and Senate legislate in appropriations acts when they want to. They do so by ignoring or waiving the rules, by legislating in continuing resolutions, or by framing substantive provisions as limitations. These legislative maneuvers bypass the authorization process, but they sometimes are engineered with the consent, or at the behest, of authorizing committee members. Although the Appropriations Committees are often portrayed as interlopers who disregard jurisdictional boundaries and congressional rules, the truth of the matter is that they are frequently force-fed legislation sought by others.

Limitations are another matter, however. These provisions, which typically begin with the phrase "provided none of the funds shall be used for," have become the stock-in-trade of members who want to make policy through the appropriations process (exhibit 8-16). Hundreds of limi-

Exhibit 8-11. Structure of an Appropriations Account

UNITED STATES CUSTOMS SERVICE

SALARIES AND EXPENSES

For necessary expenses of the United States Customs Service, including purchase of up to 1,000 motor vehicles of which 960 are for replacement only, including 990 for police-type use and commercial operations; hire of motor vehicles; not to exceed $20,000 for official reception and representation expenses; and awards of compensation to informers, as authorized by any Act enforced by the United States Customs Service; $1,350,668,000, of which such sums as become available in the Customs User Fee Account, except sums subject to section 13031(f)(3) of the Consolidated Omnibus Reconciliation Act of 1985, as amended (19 U.S.C. 58c(f)(3)), shall be derived from that Account; of the total, not to exceed $150,000 shall be available for payment for rental space in connection with preclearance operations, and not to exceed $4,000,000 shall be available until expended for research: *Provided,* That uniforms may be purchased without regard to the general purchase price limitation for the current fiscal year: *Provided further,* That none of the funds made available by this Act shall be available for administrative expenses to pay any employee overtime pay in an amount in excess of $25,000: *Provided further,* That the Commissioner or the Commissioner's designee may waive this limitation in individual cases in order to prevent excessive costs or to meet emergency requirements of the Service: *Provided further,* That no funds appropriated by this Act may be used to reduce to single eight-hour shifts at airports and that all current services as provided by the Customs Service shall continue through September 30, 1994: *Provided further,* That not less than $750,000 shall be expended for additional part-time and temporary positions in the Honolulu Customs District.

Source: *Treasury, Postal Service Appropriations Act, Fiscal Year 1994,* P.L. 103-123, 107 Stat. 1229.

(a) This paragraph constitutes a single appropriations account; all provisions in the paragraph pertain only to this account unless otherwise indicated.

(b) It is common for a single account to cover all the salaries and expenses of an agency. In this case, the Customs Service received an appropriation of $1.35 billion to cover salaries and expenses, and other relatively small appropriations to cover special activities.

(c) The first part of the paragraph identifies the agency to which the appropriation is made and the amounts provided. Although a lump sum is provided for this account, the committee reports accompanying the appropriation, justification material, and other documents specify the particular projects and activities for which the funds are provided.

(d) The rest of the paragraph consists of assorted provisos that limit the use of the funds and prescribe or authorize certain activities.

Exhibit 8-12. Types of General Provisions

Limitation

> SEC. 9. None of the funds appropriated by this Act may be obligated or expended in any way for the purpose of the sale, excessing, surplusing, or disposal of lands in the vicinity of Norfork Lake, Arkansas, administered by the Corps of Engineers, Department of the Army, without the specific approval of the Congress.

Legislation

> SEC. 105. Notwithstanding any other provision of law, the Secretary of the Treasury shall establish an Office of the Undersecretary for Enforcement within the Department of the Treasury by no later than February 15, 1994.

Government-wide

> SEC. 609. No part of any appropriation for the current fiscal year contained in this or any other Act shall be paid to any person for the filling of any position for which he or she has been nominated after the Senate has voted not to approve the nomination of said person.

Source: *Treasury, Postal Service Appropriations Act, Fiscal Year 1994*, P.L. 103-123, 107 Stat. 1247, 1234, 1260.

(a) General provisions (usually numbered sections) pertain to all accounts in the appropriations act. (Some appropriations acts, including the one exhibited here, are divided into titles, which are designated as distinct appropriations acts. In these instances, the general provisions pertain only to the particular title in which they are found.)

(b) The number of general provisions has increased greatly over the past twenty years. Most are limitations on legislation; many are reenacted year after year.

(c) Limitations typically begin with language similar to that shown here, "None of the funds appropriated...."Some limitations pertain to broad policy matters, such as the use of appropriated funds to pay for abortions; some (such as the one exhibited here) pertain to very specific matters.

(d) Legislation often begins with the words "Notwithstanding any other provision of law...." The purpose of this phrase is to expressly override any existing provision of law that is contrary to the new measure.

(e) The annual Treasury–Postal Service Appropriations Act contains general provisions that pertain to all appropriations and all federal agencies. Note the words "in this or any other act."

Exhibit 8-13. Period during Which Funds Are Available

One year

> ### OFFICE OF THE ASSISTANT SECRETARY FOR CONGRESSIONAL RELATIONS
>
> For necessary expenses of the Office of the Assistant Secretary for Congressional Relations to carry out the programs funded in this Act, $1,325,000.

Multiyear

> #### COMMODITY SUPPLEMENTAL FOOD PROGRAM
>
> For necessary expenses to carry out the commodity supplemental food program as authorized by section 4(a) of the Agriculture and Consumer Protection Act of 1973 (7 U.S.C. 612c (note)), including not less than $8,000,000 for the projects in Detroit, New Orleans, and Des Moines, $104,500,000 to remain available through September 30, 1995: *Provided,* That none of these funds shall be available to reimburse the Commodity Credit Corporation for commodities donated to the program.

No year

> #### GREAT PLAINS CONSERVATION PROGRAM
>
> For necessary expenses to carry into effect a program of conservation in the Great Plains area, pursuant to section 16(b) of the Soil Conservation and Domestic Allotment Act, as added by the Act of August 7, 1956, as amended (16 U.S.C. 590p(b)), $25,658,000, to remain available until expended (16 U.S.C. 590p(b)(7)).

Source: *Agriculture, Rural Development Appropriations Act, 1994,* P.L. 103-111, 107 Stat. 1048, 1072, 1061.

(a) Appropriations differ in the period for which the budget authority is available for obligation. The three excerpts displayed here are one-year, multiyear, and no-year appropriations. Other variants are appropriations that become available during only a portion of a fiscal year or that become available in advance of the fiscal year for which they were made.

(b) When an appropriations account does not specify a period of availability (as in the first example here), the funds are available for only the fiscal year specified in the enacting clause of the appropriations act.

(c) The multiyear funds exhibited here are available for one fiscal year beyond the fiscal year for which the appropriation was made. Although these funds are available for two years, the entire amount is scored as budget authority in the year covered by the appropriations act.

(d) The phrase "to remain available until expended" provides a no-year appropriation that does not have to be obligated in a particular fiscal year. The availability of these funds carries over into subsequent fiscal years even if they have not been obligated.

Exhibit 8-14. Special Types of Appropriations

Liquidating
appropriation

> **(HIGHWAY TRUST FUND)**
>
> For payment of obligations incurred in carrying out section 21(b) of the Federal Transit Act, administered by the Federal Transit Administration, $1,000,000,000, to be derived from the Highway Trust Fund and to remain available until expended.

Transfer

> **(INCLUDING TRANSFER OF FUNDS)**
>
> For necessary expenses of the Nuclear Waste Technical Review Board, as authorized by Public Law 100–203, section 5051, $2,160,000, to be transferred from the Nuclear Waste Fund and to remain available until expended.

Limitation on
obligation

> **(HIGHWAY TRUST FUND)**
>
> None of the funds in this Act shall be available for the implementation or execution of programs the obligations for which are in excess of $17,590,000,000 for Federal-aid highways and highway safety construction programs for fiscal year 1994.

Sources: *Transportation Appropriations Act for Fiscal Year 1994*, P.L. 103-122, 107 Stat. 1214, 1206; and *Energy and Water Appropriations Act for Fiscal Year 1994*, P. L. 103-126, 107 Stat. 1333.

(a) A liquidating appropriation does not provide (and is not scored as) new budget authority. Rather, it pays off (liquidates) a contractual obligation made in accordance with substantive law.

(b) The second provision transfers funds from one account (or fund) to another. Transfers may be made only if authorized by Congress. Some agencies are given general authority to transfer up to a certain amount or percentage of their resources.

(c) The final example is of a limitation on the amount that may be obligated. This type of limitation is used for some programs financed by a trust fund. Without the limitation the agency would be permitted to obligate as much as was available in the trust fund. The limitation caps the amount of the trust fund that may be obligated during the fiscal year.

Exhibit 8-15. Appropriations for Credit Programs

Direct loans

VOCATIONAL REHABILITATION LOANS PROGRAM ACCOUNT

(INCLUDING TRANSFER OF FUNDS)

For the cost of direct loans, $53,000, as authorized by 38 U.S.C. chapter 31, as amended: *Provided,* That such costs, including the cost of modifying such loans, shall be as defined in section 502 of the Congressional Budget Act of 1974: *Provided further,* That these funds are available to subsidize gross obligations for the principal amount of direct loans not to exceed $2,387,000.

In addition, for administrative expenses necessary to carry out the direct loan program, $751,000, which may be transferred to and merged with the appropriation for "General operating expenses".

Guaranteed loans

INDIAN HOUSING LOAN GUARANTEE FUND

For the cost (as defined in section 502 of the Congressional Budget Act of 1974) of guaranteed loans authorized by section 184 of the Housing and Community Development Act of 1992 (106 Stat. 3739), $1,000,000. Such funds shall be available to subsidize guarantees of total loan principal in an amount not to exceed $25,000,000.

Source: *Veterans Affairs, HUD Appropriations Act for Fiscal Year 1994*, P.L. 103-124, 107 Stat. 1277, 1289.

(a) Congress maintains two types of controls on direct loans and loan guarantees through the appropriations process: it limits the gross obligations of direct loans and gross commitments of guaranteed loans that can be incurred for particular programs in a fiscal year; and it makes appropriations for the subsidy cost of direct and guaranteed loans. Both types of controls are combined in the appropriations language exhibited here.

(b) The cost of these loans is defined in section 502 of the Congressional Budget Act to include (on a present-value basis) the subsidized portion of direct and guaranteed loans. The Federal Credit Reform Act of 1990 requires Congress to make appropriations for the subsidy cost of these loans.

(c) The definition of subsidy cost excludes the expenses of administering loan programs; thus (as shown in the first example) a separate appropriation is made for administrative expenses.

(d) Appropriations language for direct and guaranteed loans has not been standardized, and there may be considerable variability in phrasing, even for accounts funded in the same appropriations act.

tations are enacted in appropriations measures each year. Many deal with relatively minor aspects of agency operations, such as the reorganization of field offices, but some affect truly major policies such as federal funding of abortions, the deployment of weapons, and the speed limit on interstate highways. Some are straightforward limitations on appropriations, but others have the barely disguised purpose of accomplishing via appropriations what has not been achieved via legislation.

The line between limitations and legislation is thin and depends on parliamentary precedents and interpretations. If a provision sets conditions on the use of funds or requires the government to take some action, it is likely to be ruled legislation; if it is negative, unqualified, and requires no action, it is likely to be ruled a limitation. Appropriations Committee members (and others) have become adept at wording provisions so that they are held to be limitations, even when the obvious purpose is to change existing policy. Although these limitations might not violate the rules, they do infringe on the role of authorizing committees.

Interpreting Appropriations Measures

In carrying out their functions, agencies need to know the amount they have to spend, as well as any restrictions on the use of funds and directives as to what the money is to be used for. The text of the appropriations act offers some guidance, but it rarely is sufficiently detailed to cover all the situations facing an agency. In addition to reviewing the act, the agency and other interested parties must consult authorization law, the supporting material submitted in justification of budget requests, and relevant reports of the Appropriations Committees.

Impact of Authorization Law

Chapter 7 noted that appropriations must be spent according to the terms and conditions set in substantive legislation. Accordingly, it does not suffice to review the appropriations act and pertinent legislative history; one must also examine relevant substantive law. Particularly difficult complications arise when the report on the appropriations bill specifies a somewhat different pattern of expenditure than is prescribed in substantive law. In sorting out conflicts between the two laws, seemingly slight differences in wording can spawn major differences in legal interpretation. One should not draw conclusions about how appropriated funds are to be spent without reviewing the actual texts of authorization and appropriations law and any accompanying committee reports.

Budget Justifications

Although an appropriations account often encompasses many activities, the detailed budget justifications typically break down the request by activity and items of expenditure. Agencies inevitably deviate from the detailed supporting schedules in spending available funds, but the appropriations subcommittees expect them to adhere to their justifications to the extent practicable. When an agency shifts funds from one program to another in the same account, it must go through the reprogramming procedures discussed in chapter 9. Less significant changes are handled informally or unilaterally by the agency, but there has been a pronounced trend for the Appropriations Committees to hold agencies more closely to the spending plans set forth in the budget justifications.

Appropriations Committee Reports

The Appropriations Committees provide detailed instructions on how funds are to be spent, along with other directives or guidance in their reports accompanying the various appropriations measures (exhibit 8-17). These reports do not comment on every item of expenditure. Comment is most likely when the Appropriations Committee prefers to spend more or less for a particular item than the president has requested,

Exhibit 8-16. Limits in Appropriations Acts

Appropriations account

> For National Defense Sealift Fund programs, projects, and activities, $1,540,800,000, to remain available until expended: *Provided*, That up to $50,000,000 shall be available for transfer to the Secretary of Transportation: *Provided further,* That none of the funds provided in this paragraph shall be used to award a new contract that provides for the acquisition of any of the following major components unless such components are manufactured in the United States: auxiliary equipment, including pumps, for all shipboard services; propulsion system components (that is; engines, reduction gears, and propellers); shipboard cranes; and spreaders

General provisions

> SEC. 8124. Notwithstanding any other provision of law, none of the funds appropriated in this or any other Act shall be used for the purchase of a totally enclosed lifeboat survival system, which consists of the lifeboat and associated davits and winches, if less than 50 percent of the entire system's components are manufactured in the United States, and if less than 50 percent of the labor in the manufacture and assembly of the entire system is performed in the United States.

Sources: *Department of Defense Appropriations Act, 1994*, P.L. 103-139, 107 Stat. 1435 and 1469.

(a) Although legislation is barred in general appropriations bills, limitations that preclude use of funds for certain purposes may be included in them. As shown here, the typical limitation begins with the phrase "none of the funds provided . . . ."

(b) The scope of a limitation depends on its wording and placement in an appropriations act. When placed in an unnumbered paragraph (the first example here), the limitation pertains only to the funds appropriated to that account, unless the language of the limitation gives it a broader effect.

(c) The second example shown here appears in the general provisions at the end of the appropriations act. Such a limitation normally covers all funds provided in the act. In this case, Congress gave the limitation even broader effect by applying to any funds regardless of their source.

161

when it wants to earmark funds for a particular project or activity, when it wants to emphasize its position on a matter, or when the two branches disagree on an issue. During the divided government of the 1980s, these instructions became more numerous and specific. Now that the Democrats control both the legislative and the executive branches, the White House is pressing Congress to give agencies more flexibility in using appropriated funds.

When it mentions a particular matter in a report, the Appropriations Committee expects the agency addressed to abide by its dictates. Because each committee comments only on those items that concern it, matters mentioned in one committee's report might not appear in the other's. When this occurs, the instructions of both committees are operative unless it is not feasible for the agency to carry out all of them. Thus if the House Appropriations Committee earmarks funds to certain projects and the Senate Appropriations Committee earmarks funds to other projects, both sets of earmarks are effective unless funds are insufficient to pay for both.

In Appropriations Committee reports, words matter. They are carefully selected to communicate the extent to which the committee may allow an agency some latitude in carrying out instructions. Words such as *assumes*, *requests*, *expects*, *directs*, and *requires* appear frequently. The words are not synonymous; each has its own meaning and nuance. But even the gentlest words offer guidance that should not be lightly disregarded.

What gives the appropriations reports special status is not law but the fact that the next appropriations cycle is less than one year away. An agency that willfully violates report language risks retribution the next time it asks for money. It may find this year's report language replanted into the text of the next appropriations act, thereby giving it even less leeway than before. The agency may have staffing levels converted into legally binding floors or ceilings. The Appropriations Committees can

punish uncooperative agencies by writing tough limitations into the appropriations act, by cutting an agency's favorite programs, by issuing more earmarks and cutting back on the agency's discretionary funds, or by dictating how the agency should be managed.

There is, however, a more accommodating side to the agency-committee relationship. When an agency maintains ongoing contact with appropriations subcommittee members and staff and consults with them on problems in implementing report language, it might gain more flexibility than an agency that acts unilaterally.

Conclusion

For two centuries making appropriations has been one of Congress's most stable activities, changing little, if at all, from one year to the next. The process has always been organized around the annual review of agency requests and congressional decisions on the amounts to be provided. In allocating resources the Appropriations Committees have looked ahead to what should be provided for the next year by looking back at what was provided for the current year.

The process has evolved incrementally, with a premium placed on procedural continuity. Even as the budgetary world in which they operate has been transformed, the Appropriations Committees have hardly changed, retaining the same subcommittee structure despite the vast expansion of government and allowing each subcommittee substantial autonomy. The committees have made concessions to the growth of government by consolidating accounts, to the advent of congressional budgeting by fitting spending decisions into predetermined amounts, to spending limits by paying greater attention to outlays, and to conflict with the president by resorting to omnibus measures.

The process leaves the Appropriations Committees in charge, at least insofar as discretionary spending is concerned. The fact that a shrinking portion of total spending is in their

Exhibit 8-17. Report Language: Guidance to Agencies

Amtrak thruway bus service.—The Committee is concerned that Amtrak's thruway bus service may be unfairly competing with private intercity bus operators in some cases. While Amtrak has a valid need to run short-haul feeder service in support of Amtrak train service, in some cases Amtrak is now operating long-haul bus routes without intervening rail segments. Since the Committee does not believe that federal funds should be used to provide service which competes with private industry, the bill includes a provision which states that Amtrak may not use federal funds to support, either directly or indirectly, intercity bus routes unconnected by a rail segment in its thruway bus service. Accordingly, the Committee directs the Secretary of Transportation to investigate the nature and extent of the Amtrak bus service and report back to Congress the effect of said bus service on unsubsidized, private sector bus service. The report should be submitted to the House and Senate Committees on Appropriations by January 1, 1994.

Release of older equipment.—Due to the projected arrival of significant amounts of new rolling stock over the next few years, Amtrak expects to begin releasing its older equipment for new service as early as fiscal year 1994. In order to provide Congressional oversight of Amtrak's decisions in this area, Amtrak is directed to notify the House and Senate Committees on Appropriations in writing prior to releasing older equipment from its current service to new routes or services, and to provide justification for the new routes or services selected.

Source: *Department of Transportation Appropriations Bill, 1994,* H. rept. 103-190, July 27, 1993, p. 123.

(a) The report of the Appropriations Committee, which is drafted by the relevant subcommittee, explains the committee's action and provides guidance to affected agencies. Although report language normally does not have legal effect, agencies heed these directives. The directives may be positive–telling them how appropriated funds are to be spent–or negative–telling them not to undertake certain expenditures or activities.

(b) The directives do not comment on all items in the appropriations bill. They typically concentrate on changes from the previous year's level, earmarks, restrictions on use of funds and disagreements with the agency.

(c) The language used here to convey the committee's position–"is concerned" and "the Committee directs"–is fairly strong. The committee may use other words to convey different messages.

(d) The increasing specificity of report language has led to charges that Congress micromanages federal agencies. As part of its drive to improve government performance, the Clinton administration has urged Congress to issue fewer directives in committee reports.

effective control is of less consequence to the Appropriations Committees than that they control the still large portion in their jurisdiction.

Three recent challenges have, however, been mounted to the commanding control of the committees over discretionary programs. The challenge from within Congress has come from proposals to merge the authorizing and appropriating committees. This reform is discussed below; the other two–a line item presidential veto and biennial appropriations–are examined in chapter 9.

Every discretionary program has the potential for duplication of effort in Congress and friction between the authorizing and appropriating committees. Duplication and conflict tend to be modest for programs that have permanent authorizations but significant for those that are reauthorized annually. The increase in temporary authorizations has raised the chances that congressional authorizers and appropriators will get in each other's way, even when going about their own business. Yet there are enormous differences in the relationship of the two kinds of committees, ranging from defense programs, where the Armed Services and the Appropriations Committees review the same budget material and decide many of the same spending issues each year, to some natural resource programs that often go for years without authorizing action and are considered only in the annual appropriations process.

Because of these differences, merging the authorization and appropriations processes would have little impact on some programs and a big impact on others. If merger were accomplished by abolishing the Appropriations Committees, congressional responsibility for spending would be even more dispersed than it is today. Some have argued that this would weaken congressional control of the totals, but

in view of the BEA procedures already in place, effective control can be maintained even when many committees share responsibility. A graver problem would be the likelihood that legislation and appropriations would be routinely combined in the same measure, giving rise to the problems that led to their separation in the first place. Combining the two processes might make for a more efficient Congress on paper but a less efficient one in operation. Appropriations actions would be hostage to conflict over substantive provisions, and the tendency of Congress to attach unrelated riders to spending measures would become more pronounced.

Understandably most of the pressure to merge the two processes has come from members of authorizing committees who feel that their jurisdiction has been violated by the Appropriations Committees. But the source of the problem has been the breakdown in the authorization process, not aggressive encroachment by the spending committees. An appropriate remedy, therefore, would be to repair the authorization process so as to give legislative committees a more substantive role. Proposals to reform the authorization process have moved in opposite, but compatible, directions. Some would decongest the legislative calendar by prescribing a minimum term for authorizing legislation; others would end permanent authorizations by requiring that all programs end or "sunset" every five years. Banning both annual and permanent authorizations would enable Congress to more clearly differentiate authorizing measures from appropriations bills and would compel legislative committees periodically to review all programs in their jurisdiction. Steps might also be taken to enforce the distinction in House and Senate rules between authorizations and appropriations, but these are likely to be only as effective as members want them to be.

Chapter 9

Managing Federal Expenditures

The fiscal year starts on October 1, about eighteen months after agencies start preparing their budgets and eight months after the president submits his budget to Congress. Many things will change during these long intervals. The cost of some goods and services will vary from initial projections, turnover rates among agency staffs will be higher or lower than expected, new problems and priorities will come to the fore. In spending appropriated funds, agencies must adhere to congressional intent while adjusting to changing conditions and emerging needs. They must be both compliant and flexible, responsive to the will of Congress and responsible for getting the job done.

Putting the budget into effect is a balancing act that begins the first day of the fiscal year and ends on the last day. During these twelve months, agencies make thousands of spending decisions; many are routine, but some reassess earlier plans in the light of current conditions. Although preparation of the president's budget and congressional action receive most of the public attention, those interested in particular programs should monitor implementation of the budget after appropriations have been made. Agency staffs spend more time and effort on this phase of the budget than on any other. They know that important matters are at stake.

Decisions made and problems faced during the implementation of one budget strongly influence future budgets. Agencies often free up some resources in their current budgets for seed money to initiate activities that may become priorities in future budgets. They often shift staff from old tasks to new ones and redirect contract money and other operating resources to fresh uses. They do the things that make sense to managers who must make ends meet while getting the job done.

Expenditure management is a far-flung, decentralized activity. The federal government is too big and its activities too diverse to permit centralizing of financial operations in a single agency. Each agency receiving appropriations or other financial resources from Congress has primary responsibility for ensuring the legality, propriety, and efficiency of its expenditures. Agencies generally make their own decisions on these matters, but they sometimes consult the General Accounting Office, which serves as the government's principal auditing and evaluation agency, or the Office of Management and Budget, which has broad responsibility for financial management. OMB's role is necessarily limited and selective. On any particular matter, it can intervene to influence the use of federal dollars, but it is much too small to oversee all government financial operations. Each agency has its own budget staff, and major units within departments also are staffed with budget specialists.

The next section in this chapter traces the normal sequence of implementation events, in which appropriations are spent as intended, and also considers variances due to reprogramming, impoundment, and other actions. The second section examines the structure of financial management in federal agencies, especially the relationship of budgeting and accounting, and recent efforts to improve it, including the ongoing implementation of the Chief Financial Officers Act of 1990 and the Government Performance and Results Act of 1993.

Spending Available Funds

Appropriated funds are not automatically available to agencies for their use. The Antideficiency Act requires that appropriations be apportioned for time periods (usually quarters) during the fiscal year or among the projects on which the funds are to be spent in order for them to become available for obligation. The purpose of apportionment is to prevent agencies from spending at a rate that would exhaust their appropriations before the fiscal year has been completed. In some instances (such as for national defense and certain emergencies) the Antideficiency Act permits apportionment at a rate that would necessitate additional appropriations.

Apportionment is managed by OMB using a standard form (exhibit 9-1). Agency requests for apportionment are reviewed by OMB, which may not apportion more resources than are available in each account. Funds withheld by OMB from apportionment must be reported to Congress under the impoundment procedures discussed later in this chapter. Although apportionment is largely a technical exercise, it does compel agencies to spread their funds over the entire fiscal year. At one time they could expect to receive supplemental appropriations if they faced a shortage during the year. But concern over the deficit and the budget enforcement rules enacted in 1990 now preclude supplemental funding except for emergencies.

At the start of each fiscal year, each agency compares the resources on hand with the amount projected for salaries, supplies, utilities, and other operating expenses. Because the fis-

cal year has just started and agencies are unsure of all the expenses they will face, they tend to be cautious. They assume that turnover will be low and that unbudgeted contingencies will occur. They often slow down spending for contracts, equipment purchases and other things directly under their control to ensure that they are not caught short before the year is over. They monitor spending rates closely, and as the fiscal year nears a close, they often find that they have been overly cautious. At this point they typically accelerate spending in areas treated more cautiously earlier, which may obligate a large proportion of contract and procurement money in the last months of the fiscal year. Although the year-end bulge in spending appears to be wasteful, it is often the result of prudent financial management.

Allotment

OMB makes a single apportionment for each appropriation or fund account; it does not subdivide the money among programs or organizational units. However, agencies need to inform program managers of the resources that will be available to them during the year. This information is provided through allotments, which distribute funds among each agency's bureau divisions, field offices, or other organizational units. The procedures for allotting resources vary among agencies, but the total amount allotted may not exceed the OMB apportionment.

Large agencies that have thousands of employees and dozens of units generally operate in a decentralized manner. The allotment gives each unit its budget for the fiscal year. Within the amounts allotted, each unit hires and pays staff, purchases supplies and equipment, and incurs other expenses. Of course, all units must adhere to agency (and government-wide) rules concerning personnel, procurement, and other administrative matters. But each unit is directly responsible for implementing its budget.

Exhibit 9-1. Apportionment and Reapportionment Schedule

STANDARD FORM 132
(Revised July 1976)
Office of Management and Budget
Circular No. A-34

Sheet _ _ _ of _ _ _
Fiscal year _ _ _ _ _ _

APPORTIONMENT AND REAPPORTIONMENT SCHEDULE

AGENCY	APPROPRIATION OR FUND TITLE AND SYMBOL
BUREAU	

DESCRIPTION	AMOUNT ON LATEST S.F. 132	AGENCY REQUEST	ACTION BY OMB
BUDGETARY RESOURCES			
1. Budget authority:			
A. Appropriations realized _ _ _ _ _ _ _ _ _ _ _ _ _ _ _ _ _			
B. Appropriations anticipated (indefinite) _ _ _ _ _ _ _ _ _ _ _			
C. Other new authority (			
D. Net transfer (+ or -) _ _ _ _ _ _ _ _ _ _ _ _ _ _ _ _ _			
2. Unobligated balance:			
A. Brought forward October 1 _ _ _ _ _ _ _ _ _ _ _			
B. Net transfers (+ or -) _ _ _ _ _ _ _ _ _ _ _ _ _ _ _ _			
3. Reimbursements and other income:			
A. Earned _ _ _ _ _ _ _ _ _ _ _ _ _ _ _ _ _ _ _			
B. Change in unfilled customers' orders (+ or-) _ _ _ _ _ _ _			
C. Anticipated for rest of year _ _ _ _ _ _ _ _ _ _ _ _			
4. Recoveries of prior year obligations:			
A. Actual _			
B. Anticipated for rest of year _ _ _ _ _ _ _ _ _ _ _ _			
5. Portion not available pursuant to P.L. _ _ _ _ _ _ _			
6. Restorations (+) and writeoffs (-) _ _ _ _ _ _ _ _ _ _ _ _			
7. TOTAL BUDGETARY RESOURCES _ _ _ _ _ _ _ _ _ _ _ _			

Source: Office of Management and Budget, standard form 132.

(a) A single apportionment is made for an entire appropriation of fund account (using standard form 132). Although OMB does not generally exercise formal control below the account level–except through impoundment procedures-- it has informal means of influencing particular expenditures and activities.

(b) The top part of the form (lines 1-7) itemizes the resources available for apportionment. These may include current or permanent appropriations, unobligated balances carried over from previous years, transfers from other accounts, and fees or other money deposited in the account.

(c) The amount apportioned (in the bottom part of the form, which is not shown) may not exceed the total of these resources. Category A apportionments allocate the funds among the quarters of the fiscal year; category B apportionments allocate funds to specific projects or activities.

(d) Funds withheld from apportionment must be reported on this form as rescissions or deferrals.

Obligation

Once funds have been allotted to a unit, it can obligate them. An obligation represents a legal commitment by an agency to another party. Each obligation has to be supported by documents attesting to the commitment of funds, such as completed purchase orders, signed contracts, payroll records, letters of credit, or any other documents binding the government to pay for goods or services or to transfer money to others. Funds may be obligated only during the period that they are available. However, once obligated, they carry over from year to year until the obligation is liquidated, even if the appropriation was available only for a single fiscal year.

Outlays

Once the goods or services for which funds were obligated have been provided, the ensuing outlay is normally a matter of administrative routine. Government funds are disbursed pursuant to vouchers (or, in some instances, invoices) that have sufficient information to enable payments to be audited. Before payment, the spending agency preaudits vouchers to determine, among other things, whether the payment is permitted by law and the amount of payment is correct, the goods or services were provided in accord with relevant contracts or other agreements, and the appropriation or fund from which payment is to be made is available for that purpose. Payments are made through disbursing offices operated by the Treasury.

Agencies prepare monthly budget execution reports (exhibit 9-2) showing, among other things, the amount of obligations incurred and outlays made during the latest month and cumulatively during the fiscal year. In addition to these reports, each agency keeps its own accounts, which are more detailed than those maintained on a governmentwide basis.

Although outlays are not an effective point of financial control, they cannot be ignored in managing federal dollars. For one thing, the timing

and rate of outlays is important for the Treasury in managing the government's cash and debt. For another, the difference between outlays and receipts determines the size of the budget deficit. As concern over the deficit mounted in the 1980s and 1990s, Congress paid closer attention to them.

Closing Accounts

The final step in the spending process is the closing of appropriation or fund accounts. Once an account is closed, all remaining balances are canceled and are no longer available for obligation or expenditure. Fixed accounts (those whose balances are available for obligation for a definite period of time) are closed according to a preset schedule. Accounts that have no-year funds (indefinite period) remain open until all balances have been depleted or canceled.

The procedures for closing accounts stretch over six fiscal years. During the period that funds are available for obligation—one year in the case of most appropriations—the account is open. When this period ends, the account is placed in expired status for five years, during which no new obligations may be incurred, but old ones are paid out as they become due. At the end of the five years, the account is closed and all remaining balances are canceled. From this point, 1 percent of unexpired appropriations granted for the same purpose are available to pay residual obligations of the closed accounts. In addition, Congress may appropriate new funds or provide other legislative authority to pay old obligations.

Transfers and Reprogrammings

The sequence of events from apportionment through the closing of accounts often occurs as planned in the budget or (if changes have been made) as approved by Congress. Sometimes, however, spending plans are altered during implementation of the budget and resources are moved from one purpose to another. These changes are classified as *transfers* when funds are moved from one account to another and as

Exhibit 9-2. Budget Execution Report

STATUS OF BUDGETARY RESOURCES			
8. Obligations Incurred_____($)			
9. Unobligated balances available:			
A. Apportioned, category A_____			
B. Apportioned, category B_____			
C. Other balances available_____			
10. Unobligated balances not available:			
A. Apportioned for subsequent periods*_____			
B. Withheld pending rescission*_____			
C. Deferred*_____			
D. Unapportioned balance of revolving fund*_____			
E. Other balances not available_____			
11. TOTAL BUDGETARY RESOURCES_____			
RELATION OF OBLIGATIONS TO OUTLAYS AND ACCRUED EXPENDITURES			
12. Obligations incurred, net (8—3A—3B—4A)_____			
13. Net unpaid obligations:			
A. Obligated balance, as of October 1_____			
B. Obligated balance transferred, net (+ or —)_____			
C. Obligated balance, end of period_____			
14. Outlays (12+13A+13B—13C)_____($)			
15. Change in accounts payable, net:			
A. Accounts payable, net, as of October 1_____			
B. Accounts payable transferred, net (+ or —)_____			
C. Accounts payable, net, end of period_____			
16. Accrued expenditures (14—15A—15B+15C) ($)			

*From S.F. 132   133-107

☆ GPO : 1977 O - 241-530 (3259)

(Authorized officer)

Source: Office of Management and Budget, standard form 133.

(a) Each agency is required to submit a budget execution report within twenty days after the close of each month. One form is submitted for each appropriation or fund account.

(b) The report is divided into three sections. The entries in the first section, "Budgetary Resources (not shown)," correspond to the first part of the apportionment schedule. The middle section of this form, "Status of Budgetary Resources," reports on obligations incurred, resources available but not yet obligated, and unobligated resources not available for obligation. The final part relates obligations to outlays and to accrued expenditures. Accrued expenditures are monies owed that have not yet been paid out.

reprogrammings when funds are switched from one activity to another within the same account.

Inasmuch as an account is a legal limit on expenditure, transfers may be undertaken only pursuant to statutory authority. Congress sometimes authorizes particular agencies, such as the Defense Department, to transfer up to a certain amount or percentage of their appropriation. An agency granted this general transfer authority is usually required to notify relevant congressional committees when it moves funds from one account to another. When funds are transferred, the receiving account (whose resources are augmented) must use the money in accord with any restrictions or conditions pertaining to the originating account.

Transfers are relatively easy to monitor because one or more accounts lose resources and others gain. Reprogrammings, however, may be difficult to identify. Reprogramming practices are affected by the definition of programs and structure and content of appropriations acts. At one time, appropriations were extremely detailed: they listed the various positions to be filled and items to be purchased, and agencies had virtually no discretion in spending available funds. As the government grew, appropriations were progressively consolidated to the point where many agencies now receive a lump sum for all salaries and operating expenses. As noted in chapter 8, the Appropriations Committees often earmark or direct the use of funds in their reports, and they generally expect agencies to adhere to the detailed spending schedules submitted in justification of their budget requests. Nevertheless, agencies have considerable flexibility in using their appropriations. They may, for example, experience less turnover than expected and shift some of the money budgeted for travel or equipment to personnel. At what point do adjustments such as these become reprogrammings? In implementing their budgets agencies make many minor adjustments in the use of funds without bringing formal reprogramming rules into play. In a

typical year they report fewer than a thousand reprogrammings. If all adjustments were reported, the number would run into many thousands.

Clearly, movement of funds from one discrete activity or project to another would constitute a reprogramming, as would any significant deviation from spending instructions in an Appropriations Committee report. Agencies must report these reprogrammings, following the rules promulgated by their appropriations subcommittees. The rules vary considerably among congressional committees and executive agencies. In some instances, only the relevant appropriations subcommittees are notified; in others, authorizing committees also participate. Some reprogrammings require advance approval of the participating congressional committees; in other cases, the reprogramming takes effect if it is not disapproved by congressional committees during a preset waiting period; in still other instances, the reprogramming becomes effective immediately after Congress is notified. Exhibits 9-3 and 9-4 provide information on reprogramming practices in two federal agencies.

Reprogrammings occur in a murky area of executive-legislative relations. Many entail House or Senate committee reviews that sometimes veto the proposed shift of funds. This arrangement occurs despite the 1983 Supreme Court ruling in *INS* v. *Chadha* that all legislative vetoes violate the Constitution. A legislative veto gives the House or Senate the power to block a pending executive action. Arguably, if vetoes by the House or Senate do not pass constitutional muster, vetoes by congressional committees should not either. But committee review of reprogrammings, along with many other committee vetoes, has become increasingly common during the decade since the *Chadha* decision.

Committee vetoes flourish because they are part of a quid pro quo in which Congress gives agencies discretion in exchange for the opportunity to review and disapprove certain actions

Exhibit 9-3. Reprogramming Rules: Veterans Affairs-Housing and Urban Development Appropriations Subcommittee

REPROGRAMMING AND INITIATION OF NEW PROGRAMS

The Committee continues to have a particular interest in being informed of reprogrammings which, although they may not change either the total amount available in an account or any of the purposes for which the appropriation is legally available, represent a significant departure from budget plans presented to the Committee in an agency's budget justifications.

Consequently, the Committee directs the Departments of Veterans Affairs and Housing and Urban Development, and the agencies funded through this bill, to notify the chairman of the Committee prior to each reprogramming of funds in excess of $250,000 between programs, activities, or elements unless an alternate amount for the agency or department in question is specified elsewhere in this report. The Committee desires to be notified of reprogramming actions which involve less than the above-mentioned amounts if such actions would have the effect of changing an agency's funding requirements in future years or if programs or projects specifically cited in the Committee's reports are affected. Finally, the Committee wishes to be notified regarding reorganizations of offices, programs, or activities prior to the planned implementation of such reorganizations.

The Committee also expects that the Departments of Veterans Affairs and Housing and Urban Development, as well as the Corporation for National and Community Service, the Environmental Protection Agency, the Federal Emergency Management Agency, the Federal Deposit Insurance Corporation, the National Aeronautics and Space Administration, and the National Science Foundation, will submit operating plans, signed by the respective Secretary, administrator, or agency head, for the Committee's approval within 30 days of the bill's enactment. Other agencies within the bill should continue to submit them consistent with prior year policy.

Source: Senate Appropriations Committee, *Department of Veterans Affairs and Housing and Urban Development, and Independent Agencies Appropriation Bill, 1994*, S. rept. 103-137, 103 Cong. 1 sess. (GPO, 1994), p. 8.

(a) There are no governmentwide reprogramming rules. Each pair of appropriations subcommittees issues directives for the programs and agencies in their jurisdiction. Pursuant to these directives, each agency maintains its own procedures for initiating reprogrammings and submitting them to the Appropriations Committees (and in some cases the authorizing committees as well) for review.

(b) The rules exhibited here manifest a pronounced trend in Congress toward more stringent notification and review procedures. In this case the subcommittee has insisted on being informed of any significant departure from the agency's budget justification.

(c) The subcommittee has established a low threshold--$250,000--above which it must be notified of reprogramming actions. Some agencies such as Defense are allowed thresholds as high as $10 million for some reprogrammings. As has become typical, the subcommittee has also insisted that it be notified of actions affecting programs or projects cited in Appropriations Committee reports.

Exhibit 9-4. Reprogramming Actions: Defense Department

BASE FOR REPROGRAMMING ACTIONS
(Dollars in Thousands)

Appropriation Account Title: Research, Development, Test and Evaluation, Defense Agencies, 1993/1994			Fiscal Year Program: 1993	
Line Item	**Changes Reflecting Congressional Action/Intent**		**Revised Program Base for Reprogramming**	
	Quantity	Amount	Quantity	Amount
<u>Defense Advanced Research Projects Agency</u>				
Advanced Development				
Eup. Eval. of Maj. Innv. Tech.		32,400		303,267
Light Contingency Vehicle		(-6,200)		(0)
Multi funct. Self Aligned Gate		(10,000)		(10,000)
Gallium Assex. Hdband Mod Dev				
Gamma-Gamma Resonance Imaging		(5,000)		(5,000)
Electric Vehicles		(17,500)		(17,500)
Electric Vehicles in Hawaii		(5,000)		(5,000)
Electric Veh. in Sacramento		(2,500)		(2,500)
ASTOVL		(5,000)		(5,000)
SAR Dig. Terr. Magging [IFSAR]		(16,000)		(16,000)
Earth Conservancy		(20,000)		(20,000)
Advanced Sonar Automation Sys		(5,000)		(5,000)
Wingship		(5,000)		(5,000)
ASTEC				
CAMEO				
ATSSB				
SENATECH		100,000		100,000

Source: Adapted from Department of Defense, *Budget Guidance Manual*, DOD7710-1-M (May 1990), form DD 1414.

172

(a) Because of its size and complexity, the Defense Department probably has the most elaborate reprogramming rules in the federal government. These rules take more than twenty pages in the department's budget guidance manual. In addition, the department has a series of forms (one of which is displayed here) for handling reprogramming actions.

(b) Form 1414 establishes the base from which reprogramming actions may be taken. It identifies each line item in defense appropriations acts. These line items include the several thousand procurement and research and development items funded in the defense budget. The first six columns (the first four are omitted here) show the quantity of items and the funding requested and provided by Congress for each line item. The final columns establish the program base against which reprogrammings are calculated.

(c) To reprogram funds, the Defense Department also files form 1415, "Reprogramming Actions," with separate forms for reprogramming requiring congressional approval or notification. A final set of forms, "Report of Programs" (form 1416), is prepared semiannually to show the results of reprogrammings and other changes to the program base.

such as the reprogramming of funds. If Congress were barred from reviewing agency actions, it would probably withhold discretion. Agencies would not face committee vetoes of reprogrammings, but they would probably have less flexibility in implementing the budget.

Impoundment

In addition to limiting the amounts that may be spent, appropriations establish the expectation that the funds provided by Congress will be used to carry out planned activities. When an agency impounds–fails to use–all or part of an appropriation, it deviates from the intentions of Congress. In the past, impoundments were a battleground between the president and Congress. Some presidents claimed an inherent power to refuse to spend appropriated funds. Some members of Congress insisted that the president has no choice but to use these funds. To resolve conflicts between the two branches, the Impoundment Control Act of 1974 prescribes rules and procedures for instances in which the president or an executive agency withholds the obligation or expenditure of budget resources.

This law was enacted during the final month of the Nixon presidency. Its language is exceedingly broad, defining impoundment as any "action or inaction" that delays or withholds funds. In operation, however, impoundment has been narrowly applied to practices that deliberately curtail expenditures; actions that only incidentally affect the rate of spending are not treated as impoundments. For example, if an agency withholds a contract because of a dispute with a vendor, the delay would not be classified as an impoundment; if the delay is simply to reduce expenditures, it would be an impoundment. The line between routine administrative actions and impoundments is not always clear, and disputes sometimes arise as to how particular actions should be classified.

The 1974 act divides impoundment into two categories and prescribes distinct procedures for each. A *deferral* delays the use of funds; a *rescission* requests Congress to cancel an appropriation or some other budget authority. Deferrals and rescissions are exclusive and comprehensive categories: an impoundment must be classified as either a deferral or a rescission; it cannot be both or something else.

Deferrals

When the president defers funds, he submits a message to Congress setting forth the amount, the account and program affected, the reasons for the deferral, the estimated fiscal and program effects, and the length of time the funds are to be deferred (exhibit 9-5). The president may not defer funds beyond the end of the fiscal year nor for a length of time that would cause the funds to lapse or otherwise prevent an agency from spending them prudently. Unobligated funds that remain available beyond the fiscal year may be deferred again in the next year.

The original Impoundment Control Act permitted the president to defer funds for any reason. He was able to defer funds for policy reasons, for example, because he opposed a particular program or wanted to curtail federal spending. In exchange for giving the president this broad power, Congress reserved to itself the power to disapprove any deferral by vote of the House or Senate. This arrangement was one of the legislative vetoes invalidated by the *Chadha* decision. In response to the loss of its legislative veto, Congress took away most of the president's deferral power. At present, the president may defer funds only for the limited reasons set forth in the Antideficiency Act: to provide for contingencies or to achieve savings made possible through changes in requirements or efficiency of operations. The president may not defer funds for policy reasons.

The deferral rules demonstrate reciprocity in executive-legislative relations. If Congress has the capacity to uphold its position on matters in dispute, it may grant the president power to

Exhibit 9-5. Presidential Impoundment Message

DEFERRAL OF BUDGET AUTHORITY
Report Pursuant to Section 1013 of P.L. 93-344

AGENCY: Funds Appropriated to the President	New budget authority............... * 2,364,562,000 (P.L. 103-87)
BUREAU: International Security Assistance	Other budgetary resources...... * 418,050,660
Appropriations title and symbol: Economic support fund 1/	Total budgetary resources....... * 2,782,612,660
113/41037 * 114/51037 11X1037 *	**Amount to be deferred:** Part of year............................. * 1,582,462,660 2/ Entire year.................... _____

OMB identification code: 11-1037-0-1-152	**Legal authority (in addition to sec. 1013):** [X] Antideficiency Act
Grant program: [X] Yes [ ] No	[ ] Other _____

Type of account or fund: [ ] Annual [X] Multi-year: September 30, 1994 / September 30, 1995 (expiration date) [X] No-Year	**Type of budget authority:** [X] Appropriation [ ] Contract authority [ ] Other

Coverage:

Appropriation	Account Symbol	OMB Identification Code	Deferred Amount Reported
Economic support fund...............	11X1037	11-1037-0-1-152	* 74,812,507
Economic support fund...............	113/41037	11-1037-0-1-152	* 343,088,153
Economic support fund...............	114/51037	11-1037-0-1-152	1,164,562,000
			* 1,582,462,660

JUSTIFICATION: This account provides economic and counternarcotics assistance to selected countries in support of U.S. efforts to promote stability and U.S. security interests in strategic regions of the world. This account also includes contributions to the International Fund for Ireland. This action defers funds pending review and approval of specific loans and grants to eligible countries. This interagency review process will ensure that each approved transaction is consistent with the foreign and financial policies of the United States and will not exceed the limits of available funds. This action is taken pursuant to the Antideficiency Act (31 U.S.C. 1512).

Estimated Program Effect: None

Outlay Effect: None

Source: *Message from the President of the United States Transmitting a Report of 4 Revised Deferrals and 27 New Proposed Rescissions of Budget Authority, Pursuant to 2 U.S.C. 685(c) and 2 U.S.C. 638(a) (1)*, H. Doc. 103-205, 103 Cong. 2 sess. (GPO, 1994), p. 7.

(a) The president notifies Congress of every rescission or deferral in a message that sets forth the reasons for the action and the estimated financial and program effects. The form here is used to report deferrals; a similar one is used for rescissions. If the president fails to report a deferral or rescission, the comptroller general may notify Congress. The notification has the same effect as a presidential message.

(b) Every deferral and rescission is assigned a unique alphanumeric identification. Deferrals are prefaced with the letter *D*, rescissions with the letter *R*. Rescissions and deferrals are numbered sequentially by fiscal year. The deferral here, D-94-1B was the first reported for fiscal year 1994.

The *B* indicates that this was the second time during the fiscal year that the deferral has been revised.

(c) Deferrals are permitted only for the purposes set forth in the Antideficiency Act unless they are expressly authorized by some other statute. The Antideficiency Act permits deferrals to provide for contingencies or to achieve savings made possible by efficiency or changes in requirements. Policy deferrals are not authorized by this act.

(d) The deferral message indicates the period of time during which the funds are to be withheld. The president may not defer funds beyond the current fiscal year or for a period that would prevent their obligation.

act. If Congress is denied that opportunity, it will curtail presidential power and both branches will be weak.

Rescissions

The relationship between the two branches is different in the case of rescission and so, too, are the rules. The president proposes a rescission by submitting a message to Congress specifying the amount to be rescinded and the reasons, the accounts and programs involved, and the estimated fiscal and program impacts. After receiving the message, Congress has forty-five days of continuous session (usually a larger number of calendar days) during which it may pass a rescission bill. Congress has the option of approving all, part, or none of the rescission proposed by the president.

If Congress does not rescind the funds by the end of the forty-five days, the president must make them available for obligation. The comptroller general, who reviews all proposed rescissions and deferrals and advises Congress of their legality and possible program and budgetary effects, may bring suit to compel the release of funds that continue to be impounded. This has been a rare occurrence, however.

The president's record on rescissions is a measure of his budgetary influence and of his relationship with Congress. Ronald Reagan proposed more than $15 billion in rescissions shortly after he became president in 1981, and Congress rescinded more than $10 billion (table 9-1). By the end of his presidency the volume of proposed rescissions had dwindled to negligible amounts, none of which were approved. George Bush had no success with Congress on rescissions. He proposed a sizable number in 1992, but Congress substituted some of its own for those he proposed. In one case it rescinded more than he had requested but took the money from his priorities rather than the areas he wished to cut.

Rescissions invite conflict between the president and Congress. Every one is a presidential demand that Congress cancel resources it had previously appropriated. By implication, rescissions tell Congress that it erred the first time around and that it wasted government funds. This is not a message that appeals to legislators, especially when it comes from a president who has different budget priorities.

Managing Agency Finances

Implementing the budget does not only mean spending the money provided by Congress; it also entails using resources efficiently and having timely and accurate information on the financial status of programs and accounts. Implementing the budget brings into play an agency's practices and procedures for managing its finances. OMB has defined financial management to include systems that collect, analyze, and report data for financial decisionmaking; process, control, and account for financial transactions and resources; and generate financial information in support of an agency's mission. Financial management goes beyond budget formulation and execution to include property and inventory control and the management of grants and contracts, debt and cash, personnel and payroll systems, and procurement practices. Only those features of financial management that relate directly to budgeting are discussed here. Table 9-2 sets forth the roles of major participants in financial management.

Accounting and Budgeting

The Budget and Accounting Act of 1921 conceived of budgeting and accounting as interdependent processes. The budget would provide the basis for the accounting structure, and data collected by the accounting system would provide the basis for the budget system. Over the years, however, budgeting and accounting drifted apart. They usually were located in separate units of an organization, and their data often were incompatible.

Table 9-1. Rescissions Proposed and Enacted, by President, Fiscal Years 1974-93
Millions of dollars unless otherwise specified

President	Fiscal Year	Rescissions proposed	Amount proposed	Rescissions approved by Congress	Amount rescinded
Ford	1974	2	496	0	0
	1975	87	2,722	38	386
	1976	50	3,582	7	148
	1977	13	1,135	7	718
Carter	1977	7	792	2	96
	1978	12	1,290	5	519
	1979	11	909	9	724
	1980	59	1,618	34	778
	1981[a]	33	1,142	0	0
Reagan	1981	133	15,362	101	10,881
	1982	32	7,907	5	4,365
	1983	21	1,569	0	0
	1984	9	636	3	55
	1985	245	1,856	98	174
	1986	83	10,127	4	143
	1987	73	5,836	2	36
	1988	0	0	0	0
	1989	6	143	1	2
Bush	1989	0	0	0	0
	1990	11	554	0	0
	1991	30	4,859	8	286
	1992	128	7,880	26	2,068
	1993	0	0	0	0
Clinton	1993	7	356	4	206
Total		1,019	69,629	354	21,585

Source: General Accounting Office, "Summary of Proposed and Enacted Rescissions, Fiscal Years 1974-93," and "Rescissions by Presidential Administration under the Impoundment Control Act," OCG-94-16 (1994).
[a] The thirty-three rescissions proposed by Carter for fiscal year 1981, which were converted by Reagan into deferrals, are not included in totals. This table does not include rescissions initiated by Congress.

Table 9-2. Major Financial Management Roles and Responsibilities, by Entity

Entity	Budget execution	Audit and evaluation	Financial management systems
Congress	Acts on supplementals, impoundments, and reprogrammings; sometimes monitors activities or expenditures	Imposes reporting requirements; conducts oversight; requests audits and evaluations from GAO and others	Establishes account structure; legislates policy on financial management systems and practices
Office of Management and Budget	Apportions budget resources; maintains FTE controls; monitors agency performance	Reviews agency spending and programs; focuses on high-risk areas; promotes performance measurement	Issues directives on internal control, accounting rules, and other management practices; oversees CFO and GPRA implementation
Agencies	Spend resources and carry out activities; report to Congress, OMB, and others	Conduct internal audits and evaluations; respond to congressional and executive requests; measure performance and results	Design and use financial management systems; maintain internal controls; report on material weaknesses
Treasury	Manages cash and debt; matches spending against resources	None	Maintains govermentwide accounting system
General Accounting Office	Reviews and reports on impoundments; settles certain claims	Reviews programs and operations; audits financial statements of government corporations	Approves agency accounting systems; advises Congress on material weaknesses in internal control systems
Agency chief financial officer	Monitors financial execution of budget	Prepares auditable financial statements, including data on performance	Promotes integration of accounting and budgeting systems
Inspector general	None	Audits financial statements; investigates spending and other actions	Recommends changes to improve systems and performance
Federal Accounting Standards Advisory Board	None	None	Formulates accounting standards and principles

177

In recent years renewed efforts have been made to link budgeting and accounting in integrated agency financial management systems. A key development has been the designation of a chief financial officer in all major federal departments and agencies. As prescribed by the Chief Financial Officers Act of 1990, each agency's CFO should be responsible for developing and maintaining an integrated accounting and financial management system, overseeing all financial operations relating to the agency's programs and operations, and monitoring the financial execution of the budget (box 9-1). The act does not expressly mention the participation of the CFO in formulating agency budgets, but most have become directly involved. OMB has reviewed each agency's plans for implementing the CFO legislation, and it has generally insisted that the officer be given responsibility for virtually all financial matters. The law also created within OMB the position of deputy director for management (to serve as CFO for the federal government) as well as the Office of Federal Financial Management.

Other developments in accounting practices have promoted the integration of budgeting and accounting. These include the ongoing standardization of accounting practices under the aegis of the Federal Accounting Standards Advisory Board (FASAB) and the requirement in the 1990 CFO law that federal agencies prepare auditable financial statements. The board is a joint activity of OMB, GAO, and the Treasury, each of which had claimed lead responsibility for accounting standards. In 1990 they established FASAB and agreed to cooperate in devising new accounting standards for the federal government.

One of the early issues faced by FASAB has been whether the standards should apply to budget documents and related material. The general rule is that accounting standards must be used in financial statements issued to outsiders such as stockholders or bondholders but that each entity can decide how to keep its books for internal use. In the private sector the budget is an internal document and is not bound by accounting standards; in the public sector, however, it is one of the principal means by which the government communicates its plans and results to citizens. In 1993 FASAB issued a statement that identified four principal objectives of federal financial reporting pertaining to budgetary integrity, operating performance, stewardship, and systems and control (box 9-2).

Although budget documents will not be immediately affected by new accounting rules, the likelihood is that in the future they will give greater attention to cost, in addition to their traditional focus on obligations and cash payments. Actually, cost-based budgeting and accounting are not new; they were mandated by legislation enacted in 1956, but this requirement has not been taken seriously. Cost-based budgets record revenue when it is earned rather than when it is received and expenditures when costs are incurred rather than when bills are paid (exhibit 9-6). This type of budget is useful in measuring the full cost of carrying out an activity or providing a service.

The linking of accounting and budgeting has also been given impetus by provisions in the 1990 Chief Financial Officers Act that direct federal agencies to prepare financial statements for their revolving and trust funds and, to the extent practicable, for any units that carry out substantial commercial operations. The act also provides for federal agencies to set up pilot projects to test comprehensive financial statements that report on their overall financial position, results of operations, and cash flows or changes in financial position and reconcile these statements with relevant budget documents. Although only six agencies were selected for the tests, many more have developed financial statements since the CFO legislation was enacted. Exhibit 9-7 presents OMB findings on the accuracy and completeness of certain statements. As in many other cases, monitors found serious deficiencies in financial statements and in related practices.

Box 9-1. Provisions of the Chief Financial Officers Act of 1990

Organization   Establishes in OMB a deputy director for management to be the chief official responsible for financial management in the federal government, and the Office of Federal Financial Management, headed by the controller.

Provides for the appointment in twenty-three major federal department and agencies of a chief financial officer, sixteen of whom are appointed by the president and confirmed by the Senate.

Establishes a CFO council headed by the OMB deputy director for management and including the twenty-three agency chief financial officers.

Functions   The responsibilities of agency CFOs include

--overseeing all financial management activities relating to the agency's programs and operations

--developing and maintaining an integrated accounting and financial management system that complies with accounting and internal control principles, standards, and requirements

--ensuring that the agency's system provides complete, reliable, consistent, and timely information, including cost information and information that facilitates the systematic measurement of performance

--monitoring the financial execution of the budget.

Reports   Reports include

--agency five-year plans (initially for the 1992-96 fiscal years) setting forth the agency's financial management strategy, including planned accomplishments and target dates

--a governmentwide five-year plan submitted by OMB describing steps to be taken in improving federal financial management

--annual reports by agencies analyzing the status of financial management and including required financial statements and a summary of reports on internal accounting and administrative control systems

--annual financial statements, supported by relevant financial and program performance data, audited by the agency inspector general (or an outside auditor).

Source: *Chief Financial Officers Act of 1990*, P.L. 101-576.

Box 9-2. Objectives of Federal Financial Reporting

Budgetary integrity	Federal financial reporting should assist in fulfilling the government's duty to be publicly accountable for monies raised through taxes and other means, and for their expenditure in accordance with the appropriations laws that establish the government's budget for a particular fiscal year and related laws and regulations.
Operating performance	Federal financial reporting should assist report users in evaluating the service efforts, costs, and accomplishments of the reporting entity; the manner in which these efforts and accomplishments have been financed; and the management of the entity's assets and liabilities.
Stewardship	Federal financial reporting should assist report users in assessing the impact on the country of the government's operations and investments for the period and how, as a result, the government's and the nation's financial condition have changed and may change in the future.
Systems and control	Federal financial reporting should assist users in understanding whether financial management systems and internal accounting and administrative controls are adequate to ensure that --transactions are executed in accordance with budegtary and financial laws and other requirements, are consistent with the purposes authorized, and are recorded in accordance with federal accounting standards; --assets are properly safeguarded to deter fraud, waste, and abuse; and --performance measurement information is adequately supported.

Source: Office of Management and Budget, *Objectives of Federal Financial Reporting: Statement of Federal Financial Accounting Concepts*, no. 1 (September 1993), pp. 4-6.

Exhibit 9-6. Accounting for Financial Transactions

Transaction	Obligation	Accrued expenditure	Cost accrual	Outlay (cash)
Order is placed	Obligation is recorded as an undelivered order and as a decrease in budgetary resources			
Order is received		Bill is recorded as a liability, as a charge to inventory, and a decrease in undelivered orders		
Materials are used			Cost is recorded as a decrease in inventory and a charge to program or activity	
Payment is made				Outlay is recorded as a reduction of liability and a reduction in cash

Source: General Accounting Office, *Policy and Procedures Manual for Guidance of Federal Agencies, Title 2 (Accounting)* (August 1987).

(a) This shows four types of accounting entries for financial transactions: obligation, accrued expenditure, cost, and outlay. Outlays may precede or account for costs.

(b) Obligatons and outlays are routinely accounted for in federal budgeting, but accrued expenditures and costs are not. With the development of accounting standards and increasing emphasis on accruals, the federal budget is likely to give more attention to accrued expenditures and costs in the future.

(c) An accrued expenditure is recorded and a liability is incurred when goods are received or when other transactions requiring payment occur. A cost (sometimes referred to as an expense) is recorded when goods or materials are consumed or when capital investments are depreciated. Cost-based budgeting is used to ensure that programs and operating units are charged the full cost of operations.

Exhibit 9-7. Audit of Agency Financial Statements and Practices

Agencies, Activities, and Organizations For Which FY 1991 Audited Financial Statements Were Prepared	Summary of Audit Reports
Department of Agriculture o Department of Agriculture (USDA) Organization-wide Financial Statements	*Financial Statements* The auditors reported that the consolidated financial statements were not fairly presented. The auditors cited material inaccuracies and inconsistencies in the consolidated financial statements that occurred during the consolidation process, the lack of sufficient accounting records to support amounts contained in the financial statements, the inability to properly account for subsidized loan agreements and loan modifications, improper accounting for Commodity Credit Corporation (CCC) price support program losses, and inaccurate estimates for CCC contingent liabilities. *Internal Controls* The auditors reported several material weaknesses in internal controls relating to the agency as a whole. They reported the need for USDA to improve security and control over computer operations to prevent unauthorized access, establish detailed policies and procedures for consolidating financial statements, strengthen agency oversight to ensure uniform accounting policies, adequately train financial management personnel, and resolve weaknesses identified through the Federal Managers' Financial Integrity Act (FMFIA) process. *Compliance with Laws and Regulations* The auditors reported several instances of noncompliance. Sufficient written policies and procedures were not in place to effectively prepare accurate financial statements, adequate financial statement preparation guidance was not provided to individual agencies, and narrative and statistical sections of the annual financial statement contained material errors. The IG also reported that CCC did not comply with the 1988 Appropriations Act in the use of their appropriation.

Source: Office of Management and Budget, *Federal Financial Management Status Report and 5-Year Plan*, appendix 1 (August 1993), p. 61.

(a) The Chief Financial Officers Act requires audited financial statements from trust funds, revolving funds, and accounts with substantial commercial activity. The auditors typically comment on the accuracy and completeness of financial statements, the effectiveness of internal controls, and compliance with relevant laws and regulations.

(b) When auditors identify deficiencies, they may issue a qualified opinion or no opinion. An unqualified opinion indicates that the accounting records provide sufficient basis for the representa-tions made in financial statements.

(c) Auditors do not review every transaction. Instead, they audit the entity's systems and procedures and sample transactions to determine whether the system operates as designed.

Internal Control

Financial management in the federal government is guided by the doctrine of internal control (sometimes referred to as management control). Under this doctrine each spending agency has primary responsibility for ensuring that resources are used properly and efficiently. An agency does not have to obtain outside approval before spending money, but before making the expenditure, it must ensure that funds are available for the intended purpose. Each agency keeps its own books, audits its transactions, and prepares periodic financial statements. The Federal Managers' Financial Integrity Act of 1982 requires each agency to establish systems of internal control, in accordance with standards prescribed by the comptroller general, so as to provide "reasonable assurance" that obligations and costs are in compliance with applicable law; that funds, property, and other assets are safeguarded against waste, loss, or abuse; and that revenues and expenditures are properly recorded.

Both OMB and GAO have oversight responsibility for internal control, and both act when agency management control systems break down. OMB circular A-123 sets forth policies and procedures to be followed by federal agencies in developing and reporting on their internal control systems. These guidelines require each agency to develop a management control plan that assesses the extent to which various activities are subject to waste or loss and identifies material weaknesses in agency internal control systems. Agencies must periodically evaluate these systems and take corrective action when necessary.

In addition to agency self-evaluations, OMB closely monitors programs that it has identified as high risk. Each year it compiles a list of high risks and reports on progress in correcting them. The fiscal 1995 budget lists eighty-four high risks and assesses the progress made in each.

As required by law, GAO reviews internal control systems and reports on any material weaknesses. In determining whether a particular shortcoming constitutes a material weakness, GAO advises agencies to consider the amount and sensitivity of the resources involved, conflicts of interest, and violations of statutory requirements. Recent GAO reports have concluded that many federal agencies still lack reliable internal control and accounting systems. According to GAO, long-standing deficiencies have resulted in billions of dollars of waste. Exhibit 9-8 is taken from a GAO assessment of an agency's internal controls.

Conclusion

The management of expenditures has always involved a tug-of-war between the executive branch and Congress. Executives want flexibility, Congress wants control. During the nineteenth century, Congress generally was dominant as it wrote detailed appropriations and restricted the authority of spending agencies to transfer funds. The balance tilted in favor of the executive branch from the New Deal years through the Great Society. Congress voted lump sum appropriations and greatly expanded the discretion of executive agencies in spending available funds. But the tide turned in the Vietnam-Watergate era as Congress enacted numerous restrictions on executive actions, imposed (for the first time) controls on the impoundment of funds, and issued numerous directives in committee reports. Congress was responding to real or perceived abuses by the executive branch, but as the controls and restrictions multiplied, it was accused of micromanagement, excessive and costly intervention in the details of administration.

The charge that Congress has micromanaged the executive branch indicates that the present period is a turning point in relations between the two branches. The president and federal agencies are striving to reclaim some of the policy and operating discretion surrendered during the 1970s and 1980s, and Congress is retreating from some of the controls imposed during years of legislative dominance. This reversal has been fueled

Exhibit 9-8. GAO Review of Agency Financial Management Practices

Comptroller General
of the United States

B-253124

April 27, 1993

The Honorable Les Aspin
The Secretary of Defense

Dear Mr. Secretary:

We have reviewed the Department of Defense's (DOD) fiscal
year 1992 report mandated by the Federal Managers' Financial
Integrity Act of 1982 (FMFIA). This report asserts that
DOD's internal controls and financial systems, when taken as
a whole, provide reasonable assurance that the objectives of
the FMFIA are being achieved.

These assertions are inconsistent with details in DOD's
report and with findings presented in a number of audit
reports by GAO and others on DOD's financial management
systems and operations. These reports highlight long-
standing management, internal control, and accounting system
deficiencies that weaken DOD's ability to safeguard, manage,
and control the hundreds of billions of dollars of resources
entrusted to it.

Source: Letter from Charles A. Bowsher, comptroller general, to Les Aspin, Secretary of Defense, AFMD-93-61R, April 27, 1993, p. 1.

(a) The Federal Managers' Financial Integrity Act (FMFIA) requires each agency to submit an annual self-assessment of its internal control and accounting systems. These reports must identify any material weaknesses in internal control as well as instances of nonconformity with the comptroller general's accounting principles or standards. The report must also describe corrective actions to deal with material weaknesses and noncompliances.

(b) GAO reviews agency FMFIA reports and issues its own reports assessing progress in improving financial management systems and in meeting the requirements of the law.

(c) In this case, GAO has challenged the self-assessment of the Defense Department; however, it cannot require the affected agency to alter its financial management practices or its FMFIA assessment.

by the end of divided government, strong presidential leadership, and efforts such as the National Performance Review to streamline government. The extent to which the president and agencies regain financial power will depend on progress in implementing reforms currently under consideration.

The 1993 report of the National Performance Review headed by Vice President Al Gore provided anecdotal evidence that federal managers dutifully follow every rule and spend just about every federal dollar provided to them. They have little flexibility and take few risks, and even when they see opportunities to spend money more wisely, they have little discretion to do so. Whether or not this is a true picture of federal management, it appears to be the basis on which many federal agencies implement their budgets.

Paradoxically, this wasteful situation is itself a by-product of campaigns against waste. The typical political response to reports of abuse has been to layer another set of controls (and controllers) on top of those already in place. The result has been an accumulation of regulations and reporting requirements that infringe on the principle of internal control. Although agencies have been told that they must be accountable for their programs and expenditures, managers often feel so constrained by the regulations that they are unwilling or unable to take much initiative. They see their job as spending the money provided by Congress according to rigid rules that preclude initiative or discretion.

The National Performance Review proposed a series of financial management reforms to loosen these controls (box 9-3). The most important of these include authority for agencies to carry funds over from one year to the next, elimination of ceilings or floors on personnel levels, increased flexibility for managers to implement their budgets, simplification of financial reporting requirements, revision of appropriation accounts to reduce the itemization of expenditures, and reduction in the volume of earmarks and restrictions in appropriations acts and committee reports.

As a quid pro quo for relaxing controls, the National Performance Review recommended that the government use budgeting as a means of improving program effectiveness and results. It urged the president to negotiate performance agreements with agency heads, specifying what would be accomplished with expected resources over a multiyear period. The NPR recommendations have been reinforced by the Government Performance and Results Act of 1993, whose provisions are summarized in box 9-4. The act calls on federal agencies to measure outcomes and results and to move toward performance-based budgeting.

This is not the first time that performance budgeting systems have been recommended for the federal government. Similar proposals were advanced by the Hoover Commission in 1949 and were implemented by some federal agencies in the 1950s. OMB instructions for the fiscal 1996 budget encourage agencies to submit performance measurements along with their budget requests. Exhibit 9-9 is a sample form added by the Department of Justice to the material prepared in support of its fiscal 1996 budget. The performance data do not reduce the amount of input detail that agencies must submit, but they represent an effort to give greater attention to outputs than has been customary. It remains to be seen whether the current efforts will be more successful than the earlier ones.

Box 9-3. Financial Management Recommendations of the National Performance Review

Performance agreements	The president should develop performance agreements with agency heads, and agencies should devise performance agreements committing themselves to achieve organizational goals and objectives.
Performance measures	Accelerate planning and measurement efforts in every federal agency and incorporate performance objectives and results as key elements in budget and management reviews.
Appropriations controls	Restructure appropriations accounts to reduce overitemization and align them with programs. Reduce detailed restrictions and earmarks in appropriations hearings and report language.
Personnel controls	Eliminate employment ceilings and floors and hold managers accountable for operating within budget.
Managerial discretion	Permit agencies to carry over 50 percent of their unobligated year-end balance in operating funds into the next fiscal year. Convert more appropriations to multiyear or no-year status and expedite the reprogramming of funds.
Biennial budgeting	Move from an annual to a biennial budget cycle for the president's budget, the congressional budget resolution, and appropriations. Evaluate program effectiveness and refine performance measures in the off-year.
Rescission authority	Enact expedited rescission procedures.
Accounting standards	Expedite the issuance of federal accounting standards, either through FASAB or a new independent board.
Budgeting and financial management	Fully integrate budget, financial, and program information and clarify the roles of OMB and Treasury in financial management.
Innovation funds	Allow agencies to establish innovation capital funds from retained savings, enabling them to plan and make multiyear investments that improve the quality and efficiency of services.

Source: National Performance Review, *From Red Tape to Results: Creating a Government That Works Better and Costs Less* (1993).

Box 9-4. Major Features of the Government Performance and Results Act of 1993

Purpose	To shift the focus of government management from inputs to outputs and outcomes, from process to results, from compliance to performance, and from management control to managerial initiative.
Basic requirements	All agencies must define long-term goals, set annual performance targets derived from these goals, and annually compare actual performance to the targets.
Pilot tests	Three sets of pilot tests: performance plans and reports, enhanced managerial accountability and flexibility, and performance budgeting.
Implementation schedule	Eight-year implementation schedule to provide feedback from pilot tests.
1993	Selection of at least ten agencies as pilot sites for testing performance plans and reports.
1994	At least five of these agencies selected as pilot sites for testing managerial accountability and flexibility.

1997	OMB reports to Congress on results of pilot tests and GAO reports to Congress on agency readiness for full implementation.
	    Agencies submit five-year strategic plans (to be updated every three years).
	    Agencies submit annual performance plans for fiscal year 1999, with annual plans each subsequent fiscal year.
	    Selection of at least five agencies as pilot sites for tests of performance budgeting.

1998	OMB submits governmentwide performance plan as part of fiscal year 1999 budget, with annual update thereafter.
2000	Agencies submit annual performance reports for fiscal year 1999, with annual updates thereafter.
2001	OMB reports to Congress on pilot test of performance budgeting.

187

Source: *Government Performance and Results Act of 1993*, P.L. 103-62.

Exhibit 9-9. Performance Budget Request Form

ORGANIZATION:

PROGRAM DECISION UNIT:

GENERAL GOAL/OBJECTIVE SUPPORTED:
 [Please reference the general goal/objective this decision unit most directly supports.]

ANNUAL PERFORMANCE GOALS:

State the target level(s) of performance toward which this program is striving.

- there should be no more than 3 or 4 annual performance goals, per operating program decision unit
- make them as specific, measurable and quantifiable as possible
- overall purpose is to establish the direction and focus of the program, i.e., definable targets
- target level must address FY 1996, but may also include FY 1995 targets
- any program change request must be supported by an annual performance goal

PERFORMANCE INDICATORS:

List indicators that will best measure progress made toward meeting the decision unit's annual performance goal(s). The number of indicators should be limited to 2 or 3 per goal, and it should be clear to which annual goal the indicators are related. Components must also provide actual FY 93 and estimated FY 94 performance data for those old indicators that are considered consistent with the new focus on results and outcome, and for any new indicators for which data are already available.

- indicators should be as output- and outcome-oriented as possible
- existing data sources should be used to develop and report on indicators, although over the long term new data sources and performance measurement experience will be used to report on program performance.

Source: Adapted from, "FY 1996: Spring Call for Budget Estimates," Department of Justice, April 8, 1994, p. 13.

(a) Federal budgeting has traditionally been oriented to the amounts to be spent on personnel, supplies, equipment, and so forth. The 1949 Hoover Commission recommended that the federal government develop a performance budget that focuses on accomplishments and objectives. Despite some progress, including the introduction of planning-programming-budgeting (PPB) systems in the 1960s, much budgeting, especially congressional appropriations, is still oriented around the items to be purchased.

(b) As noted in box 9-4, the Government performance and Results Act of 1993 requires federal agencies to develop performance plans and to issue annual performance reports. It also authorizes pilot testing of performance budgeting in selected federal agencies. After these tests are completed, the Office of Management and Budget will make recommendations to Congress on governmentwide implementation of performance budgeting.

(c) The implementation of performance budgeting depends on the development and use of performance measures. Toward this end, the Office of Management and Budget has prepared a primer that distinguishes among various types of measures–outputs, outcomes, impacts, goals, and indicators–along with examples of how these may be applied in budgeting.

Chapter 10

Controlling the Budget

This book has demonstrated that federal budgeting has many rules and procedures. It is not the case that anything goes in budgeting, that claimants get whatever they want, and that politicians have no means of saying no. Budgeting is a regulated process, with controls and checkpoints at various stages of executive and legislative action. Yet the budget often seems to be out of control, with outcomes that vary significantly from planned levels of spending and deficits that are much higher than elected officials say they want.

The anomaly of controls without control has given rise to proposals for still more rules and procedures. Some would amend the Constitution to require that the budget be balanced or to allow the president to veto line items in spending legislation. Others would revise federal laws to strengthen the president's power to impound funds, to establish a two-year budget cycle, or to tighten budget enforcement rules. This chapter assesses the potential effects of these and other procedural reforms on budget control.

Making this assessment requires a clear understanding of how budgeting works and especially why the many controls do not add up to sufficient control. To do so, it is necessary to distinguish discretionary spending controlled by annual appropriations from direct (or mandatory) spending governed by the PAYGO rules discussed in chapter 2. Figure 10-1 compares the shares of the budget accounted for by these categories of expenditure in 1963 and 1993. During these thirty years, the ratio of discretionary to mandatory spending (including interest payments) has been reversed. In the early 1960s the government spent more than two dollars on discretionary programs for every dollar of mandatory spending; today it spends almost two mandatory dollars for every discretionary one.

This transformation of federal spending is the source of the control problem. The loss of control is concentrated in the mandatory portion of the budget. Discretionary spending is effectively controlled; the amounts spent are determined by budget decisions. If discretionary programs still had the same share of federal spending that they had three decades ago, the budget would be controlled.

Proposed reforms would have different effects on discretionary and mandatory expenditure. It would be appropriate, therefore, to consider possible reforms from the vantage point of each category of expenditure. To do so, it is necessary to spell out the ways in which discretionary and direct spending differ.

Controlling Discretionary and Direct Spending

Discretionary and direct spending converge at two key points in federal budgeting: the president's budget and the congressional budget resolution. But the two categories of spending differ in regard to other vital budget procedures. Although there

Figure 10-1. Composition of Federal Outlays, Fiscal Years 1963, 1993

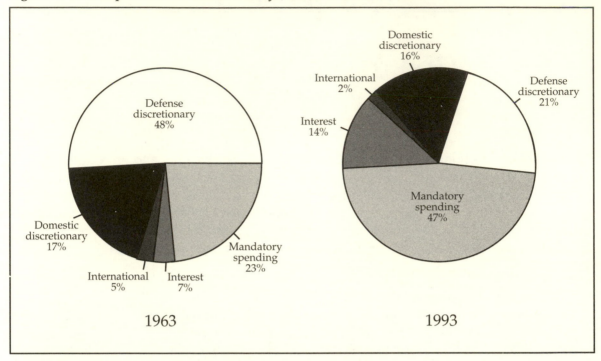

Source: *Budget of the United States Government, Fiscal Year 1995, Historical Tables*, table 8.3.
a. These classifications follow Budget Enforcement Act rules. All undistributed offsetting receipts have been deducted from mandatory out-lays. Inasmuch as these receipts include some asset sales, the share of the budget spent on mandatory programs has been slightly understat-ed. Deposit insurance is excluded from the totals in calculating budget shares.

are some exceptions to the distinctions presented in table 10-1—some features associated with direct spending apply to certain discretionary programs, and vice versa—the generalizations provide a useful summary of why one category of spending is effectively controlled and the other is not.

Budgetary Impact of Authorizing Legislation

An authorization of discretionary spending is only a license (required by House and Senate rules) to consider an appropriation. The amount authorized can be spent only to the extent that funds are appropriated. An authorization of direct spending (usually entitlement legislation) either provides funds or effectively mandates the appropriation of budget resources. Budget control is likely to be weaker when authorizing legislation dictates the amount to be spent because

authorizing committees tend to be advocates for the programs in their jurisdiction. The job of the veterans committees, for example, is to look after the interests of veterans; they and other authorizing committees are not responsible for the fiscal condition of the federal government.

Budget Role of the Appropriations Committees

The Appropriations Committees have effective control of discretionary spending. The amounts available are the amounts provided in annual appropriations acts. These committees do not control mandatory expenditures. Some mandatory programs bypass the Appropriations Committees altogether, but most are funded in annual appropriations acts. In these cases, however, the committees have little or no control over the amounts they provide. They cannot adjust

Table 10-1. Control of Discretionary and Mandatory Spending

Feature	Discretionary spending	Mandatory spending
Authorizing legislation	Authorizes consideration of appropriations measures	Provides budget resources
Appropriations Committees	Provide budget resources	Little or no control over budget resources
Frequency of control	Annual	Irregular, no fixed schedule
Basis of control	Spending caps	PAYGO rules
Means of enforcement	Section 602 allocations	Reconciliation procedures
Calculation of budget impact	Amount appropriated compared to current year's level and president's request for next year	Baseline projections and estimated effects of policy changes
Congressional choice	How much should spending be increased?	How much should spending be cut?
Economic sensitivity	Low, indirect	Direct, often automatic
Political sensitivity	Variable; high for some programs, low for others	Often very high
Correspondence of budgeted to actual spending	Usually high	Sometimes low

the amounts appropriated to the particular year's budget condition.

Frequency of Control

Discretionary appropriations are, with few exceptions, made annually for the next (or current) fiscal year. In the past, when most spending was discretionary, annual control enabled the Appropriations Committees to keep expenditures in line with receipts. Direct spending programs typically are established in permanent law that continues in effect until revised or terminated by subsequent legislation. The fact that many entitlements have annual appropriations does not diminish the permanence of the laws govern-

ing the amounts spent. Permanent control is inherently weaker than annual control because it gives politicians incentives and opportunities to underestimate future costs and does not provide a ready mechanism for adapting to changing financial circumstances. It should be noted, however, that some permanent direct spending programs, such as medicare, have been subject to frequent legislative changes.

Basis of Budget Control

Discretionary spending is controlled by the spending limits set in the Budget Enforcement Act. These caps are effective because they are enforced through congressional budget procedures. Moreover, the caps constrain–they do not merely accommodate–discretionary spending. The caps in effect for 1994 and subsequent fiscal years are significantly lower than the totals at which Congress would appropriate in the absence of discretionary spending limits. Mandatory spending is not capped, but operates under the PAYGO rules that control new revenue or direct spending legislation that would add to the deficit. PAYGO does not control direct spending due to existing law, which often rises automatically from one year to the next, regardless of the condition of the budget.

Means of Enforcing Budget Policy

The discretionary spending totals are distributed by the House and Senate Appropriations Committees to their subcommittees pursuant to section 602 procedures of the Congressional Budget Act. The total allocated by each committee to its thirteen subcommittees cannot exceed the discretionary spending caps. Congress relies on reconciliation procedures to enforce budget policies with respect to revenues and direct spending; it does not apply reconciliation to discretionary spending. Although reconciliation can be a strong instrument of budget control, it is not used every year. When it is used, it does not always have a significant effect on spending under existing law.

Basis of Calculating Budget Impact

Virtually all discretionary appropriations are for definite amounts. The amounts appropriated can be added up to ascertain whether they are within that year's discretionary caps or subcommittee allocations. Although outlays are not specified in appropriations acts, they can be calculated by means of the spendout rates ascribed to appropriations accounts. The Appropriations Committees sometimes stretch the caps a bit by imposing user fees, delaying obligations, transferring funds, rescinding some idle budget authority, and other means, but they still must operate within the discretionary limits.

PAYGO, reconciliation, and other means of controlling direct spending depend on baseline assumptions and estimates of the amounts by which changes in law would cause spending to vary from the baseline. Most mandatory spending is open ended; the law establishing the entitlement does not usually specify or limit the amount to be spent. Calculations of the budget impact of direct spending legislation are almost always based on assumed rather than actual impacts. The manner in which the assumptions are applied may make it appear that spending is more effectively controlled than it really is.

Congressional Choice

In making discretionary appropriations, the typical decision facing Congress is the amount by which spending should be changed from the current year's level or from the amount requested by the president for the next year. In the past the decision has often boiled down to a question of how much more should be provided for next year than was provided for the current year. As explained in chapter 8, the Appropriations Committees could increase spending while cutting appropriations to less than the president's request. By asking for more, the president enabled the Appropriations Committees to give more while taking credit for cutting the budget. Although this behavior accommodated a progressive increase in spending, the rate of increase was measured and incremental, and was capped by the president's budget. Today the discretionary caps supplement (and in some ways replace) the president's, with the result that spending control is even tighter. Because the effect of appropriations on the budget is calculated in nominal dollars, Congress can cut real (inflation-adjusted) resources while claiming that it is increasing them.

In mandatory programs, most spending increases are not at the discretion of Congress but are prescribed by existing law and are built into baseline projections. The typical budget decision for Congress is whether it should hold spending below the level mandated by existing law. If it does, the legislative action is counted as a spending cut, even if actual spending is higher than the previous year's level. In terms of budget control, it makes a great deal of difference whether the question facing Congress is framed as "how much should spending be increased?" as it is for discretionary programs, or as "how much should spending be cut?" as it usually is for mandatory programs. In the former, Congress takes credit for increasing resources; in the latter, it is blamed for cutting benefits. The political will of Congress to control spending is weakened when the increases are automatic (because of indexation) or assumed (in baseline projections) and the only viable option is to cut the size of the increase.

Economic Sensitivity

All budgets are sensitive to changes in economic conditions, but the response may be weaker or slower in discretionary programs than in mandatory ones. Discretionary spending is not directly or automatically adjusted for economic changes. When prices rise, Congress may appropriate more discretionary funds or it may compel agencies to absorb the inflation. But there often is an automatic adjustment in direct spending. Rising prices trigger cost-of-living adjustments in various payment formulas; rising unemployment adds to the number of persons receiving unemployment benefits or food stamps. By being hostage to the performance of the economy, the budget is less sensitive to the will of government.

Political Sensitivity

All budgets are affected by political pressure. Both discretionary and direct spending programs have constituents who benefit from federal dollars and guard their interests. Many agencies work (usually informally) with clients and other supporters to defend or expand their budgets. Because discretionary spending depends on the amount appropriated each year, beneficiaries

have a strong incentive to mobilize in support of their programs.

Although discretionary spending elicits political action because it is at risk each year, direct spending is politically sensitive because it affects the interests of so many Americans. The fact that so much of the budget is spent on entitlements speaks to a transformation in its role in American life. For many people the budget is the main determinant of their financial well-being. Almost one of every nine Americans receives food stamps; one of every eight participates in medicaid; one of every seven is enrolled in medicare; one of every six receives a social security check each month. Cutting entitlement payments has just about the same impact on household income as cutting the pay of workers. It is as visible, direct, and immediate, and is likely to provoke the same kind of protest.

It is not only their size that augments the political prominence of mandatory programs. When Congress establishes an entitlement, it gives recipients rights to the money; when it indexes entitlements, it gives them rights to automatic increases in payments. These rights have political value; they strengthen claims on the budget, and they weaken the resolve of budget officials to constrain spending. When Congress cuts an entitlement, it not only takes money from recipients, it also infringes on their rights. This is why Congress has been so reluctant to cut back cost-of-living increases.

Correspondence of Budgeted and Actual Spending

The final distinction in table 10-1 arises out of some of the other differences between discretionary and mandatory spending. The amounts spent on discretionary programs are usually close to appropriated or budgeted levels. In any particular year, outlays may diverge from the amounts estimated in the budget because the actual rate at which budget authority spends out may differ from the projected rate. But over a period of years, actual outlays will come in at just about budgeted levels. This is because discretionary spending is controlled by fixed appropriations.

The amounts spent on mandatory programs, however, sometimes diverge significantly from budget estimates. Variances may be due to estimation errors, unexpected changes in economic conditions, or new legislation or other policy changes. Changes in legislation usually account for much less of the difference between budgeted and actual spending than do the other two. When spending veers out of control, it is not likely to be because of congressional action but because of other circumstances that destabilize the budget.

This condition characterizes the contemporary problem of budget control. At its core, budgeting is a process for determining how much should be spent. For mandatory programs, about all the budget can do is to project the amounts to be spent. If the projections are wrong, there is little that the budget can do about it.

When the budget controls spending, individual transactions are linked to the totals by a sequence of actions (table 10-2). This chain of control is designed to ensure that the sum of the many millions of obligations or outlays made each year does not exceed the discretionary spending caps. Each action specified in table 10-2 is governed by "not to exceed" rules. For example, the amounts allotted by an agency to administrative units may not exceed the amounts apportioned to the agency by OMB. The controls are not quite as airtight as these rules suggest, but the sequence keeps discretionary spending within or very close to the established limits.

There is no comparable chain of controls for mandatory programs because the amounts spent each year on existing entitlements are not limited by current budget decisions. These amounts are open-ended; they are determined by the requirements of existing laws. In mandatory spending, control is inverted. Spending on individual entitlements determines total spending on entitlements.

The Principle of Budget Control

Entitlements are the big gap in budget control. Even when entitlements are cut, as has repeated-

ly happened to medicare since 1980, the totals are not effectively controlled. Almost all the cutbacks in medicare and other entitlement programs pruned by Congress have been achieved through the reconciliation procedures described in chapter 7. These procedures do not directly constrain spending on affected entitlements; rather they establish dollar targets for the amounts by which projected spending is to be cut. Reconciliation is a means of cutting assumed spending; it is not a means of determining the actual amount spent. In some years Congress has achieved the reconciliation targets, but spending on affected programs has nevertheless been above budgeted levels.

Just because the budget does not control entitlement spending does not mean that Congress should do something about it. Budget control is not the only value that Congress must consider, nor is it always the most important. In fact, control is not even the sole purpose of budgeting. The loss of budget control usually occurs because it conflicts with other important objectives. Congress has weakened annual budget control by giving workers some security about their financial well-being when they retire. It established the unemployment insurance program to assure workers that even if they lose their jobs they will have some income. It operates medicare and medicaid to give elderly and low-income households access to health care. It operates food stamps and other assistance programs to enable low-income households to maintain a decent standard of living. Through cost-of-living adjustments, it promises recipients of various entitlements that they will be protected against inflation.

The values that underlie the major entitlement programs are widely shared by most Americans. Public opinion polls show overwhelming support for social security, medicare, and other entitlements. These polls indicate that many Americans do not like welfare programs, but they also show that a majority wants the government to assist the poor. Americans may not favor every entitlement program, but the bigger the bite it takes out of the budget, the more sup-

Table 10-2. Discretionary Spending Control

Control or limitation	Method of control
Discretionary spending limits	Caps on total discretionary budget authority and outlays, as set by the Budget Enforcement Act and adjusted periodically by OMB. Caps are effective through fiscal year 1998.
Budget resolution aggregates	Ceilings on total budget authority and outlays (covering both discretionary and direct spending). These aggregates may not assume more for discretionary spending than is allowed by the limits.
Section 602(a) allocations	Total budget authority and outlays in the budget resolution are allocated to committees with spending jurisdiction. All discretionary spending is allocated to the Appropriations Committees.
Section 602(b) subdivisions	Each Appropriations Commitee subdivides its allocation of budget authority and outlays among its thirteen subcommittees. The total allocated to these subcommittees may not exceed the amount allocated to the full committee.
Appropriations	The budget authority provided and outlays deriving from each appropriations bill are compared to the relevant subcommittees' 602(b) allocation. A point of order may be raised in the House or Senate against an appropriations bill that would cause the relevant 602(b) allocation to be exceeded.
Apportionment	Appropriations and other available budgetary resources are apportioned by OMB to each account, either by projects or by quarters of the fiscal year. The total apportioned may not exceed available resources.
Allotment	Each department or agency allots apportioned resources to its subunits. The total allotted may not exceed the amount apportioned.
Obligation	Obligations by federal agencies that commit the government to future payments. Agencies may not (with few exceptions) obligate in excess of available budget resources.
Outlay	Payment by the Treasury to liquidate obligations incurred by agencies.

port it is likely to garner. Americans may be concerned about the cost of entitlements, but they are not eager to sacrifice income stability and other values for budget control.

If the government had perfect budget control, each year's budget would be unencumbered by past decisions; no commitments would spill over from one year to the next. Congress would annually decide how much to spend on pensions, medical assistance, veterans' pensions, food stamps, disability aid, unemployment insurance, and so on. The good old days would be back; all spending would be discretionary.

However, a world of perfect budget control would not be a perfect world. Social insecurity would be rampant. Workers, employers, and others would not be able to face the future with much certainty. Retired workers would have to go through the annual budget process to know what next year's social security payments or pension would provide. Persons enrolled in medicare or medicaid, and those providing health services, would have to operate under a great deal of uncertainty as to who would be protected and what would be covered.

A strong case can be made that the country is better off because of the entitlements in place. They cushion households against the cyclical shocks of recession and temporary disability, and the secular shocks of old age and infirmity. They ease anxieties about inflation, unemployment, illness, and the affordability of health care. But saying that a budget dominated by entitlements does good does not imply that all mandatory spending is equally valuable or essential or that all features of each entitlement are worth the cost. The big entitlements are big, however, because the values they reflect and the benefits they provide are widely shared. These are the programs that do the most damage to budget control.

In principle, entitlements are incompatible with budget control; in practice, the two must be reconciled. The reconciliation process first used in 1980 gives Congress a modicum of budget control without infringing on the core benefits provided by the programs. Not a single entitle-

ment program has been terminated by reconciliation, and only one–farm price supports–has been significantly restructured. After fifteen years of cutting (by official account) well over $100 billion from medicare, this program is pretty much the same as it was in 1980. In fact, the most important change in medicare–from retrospective reimbursement to prospective payment--was enacted in ordinary legislation, not in a reconciliation bill. Precisely because it does not take a hatchet to entitlements, reconciliation is valued. It saves both money and programs by trimming expenditures at the margins and shifting some costs from government to individuals or businesses. But when all is done, the entitlement program is intact and the budget has made it through another deficit reduction drive.

Congress can continue to muddle through from one budget crisis to the next, patching together reconciliation packages that whittle down the deficit to manageable size. But projections of the long-term imbalance of revenues and expenditures indicate that this tactic will not suffice in the next century, when entitlement spending will surge as a consequence of the aging population. Even in the face of escalating budget stress, there is little chance that Congress will roll back entitlements to the point where they claim as small a share of the budget as they did a generation ago. It will be impelled by rising deficits to restructure some entitlement programs more boldly than it has done by means of reconciliation.

Options for Strengthening Budget Control

In addition to cutting back, Congress and the president are likely to seek new means of budget control. This search will lead them to consider changes in the rules of budgeting. They can choose from a menu of proposals that includes a constitutional amendment to require a balanced budget, line-item veto authority for the president, stronger power for the president to impound funds, a biennial (or longer) budget cycle, a statutory budget resolution that would be signed or vetoed by the president, and caps on entitlement spending. These are not the only reforms on the agenda–others were discussed in previous chapters–but they are the ones that deal most directly with the problem of budget control.

Balanced Budget Amendment to the Constitution

In 1994 a constitutional amendment to require a balanced budget was approved by a majority in the House and Senate but fell short of the two-thirds margin required to submit it to the states for ratification. If, as is likely, deficits persist, efforts to amend the Constitution will be renewed.

Balanced budget amendments come in several forms. Some would merely require a planned balance; the version considered in 1994 would have required an actual balance. Outlays could not exceed revenues during a fiscal year. Most balanced budget amendments would waive the requirement during wartime or by a super majority (such as a three-fifths vote) in the House and Senate. Rather than consider textual differences among the various proposals, the discussion here focuses on two overriding questions. Do inadequacies in budget control justify a constitutional restriction? What would be the likely impact of an amendment on budget practice and outcomes?

The case for amending the Constitution to require a balanced budget rests on the conviction that all deficits are irresponsible, regardless of their size or cause, and that statutory remedies do not work. A constitutional remedy would not distinguish between big deficits and small ones; all would be proscribed. Nor would it distinguish between deficits that result from temporary weakness in the economy and those that are embedded in a structural imbalance between revenues and outlays.

Throughout American history, the prevailing sentiment has been that deficits are injurious to the well-being of the country. The main complaint has been that by spending beyond its income, the government burdens future generations, which have no voice in making the decision and do not directly benefit from it. At times the issue has been couched in moral terms, as if it were utterly wrong for the government to finance its operations with borrowed funds. This moral stance has been relaxed during wartime, when the need to finance military operations has been deemed to be of a higher order than making ends meet.

The contemporary drive for a balanced budget amendment has been spurred by the extraordinarily high deficits that have persisted since the early 1980s. These deficits do reflect a breakdown in budget control, but it does not necessarily follow that the remedy must be an amendment to the Constitution. Statutory approaches have enormous advantages that should not be overlooked. They can more readily distinguish between big deficits and small ones, between those stemming from cyclical conditions and those based on structural causes, between those that occur in one year and those that recur in several, and between those based on willful error and those due to conditions that the president and Congress could not foresee when the budget was made. Statutory requirements can be adjusted as experience accumulates, as political leaders learn about what works and what does not.

One such adjustment–the evolution from the Gramm-Rudman-Hollings (GRH) Acts of the 1980s to the Budget Enforcement (BEA) Act of 1990–speaks to the value of experimenting with statutory controls. The GRH laws were not effective; BEA has been. GRH required a balanced budget but never met its target; BEA does not require a balanced budget but has spurred a significant drop in the deficit. GRH barred politicians from adjusting the deficit targets, so they lied instead. BEA permits the president to adjust the target, with the result that budget projections now are more honest than they were when GRH was in effect.

Congress should not tamper with the Constitution until it has exhausted legislative remedies. If BEA does not get the budget sufficiently close to preferred outcomes, Congress should consider changes in the budget enforcement rules. It might make BEA more stringent by restricting the types of adjustments the president is allowed to make in the deficit targets and in the discretionary spending caps. It might also explore means of controlling mandatory spending that are inherent in existing law, perhaps by capping expenditures in the manner discussed later in this chapter.

The implementation of a balanced budget amendment will inevitably depend on legislation that defines the scope of the budget, establishes accounting rules for receipts, outlays, and other transactions, and establishes procedures for dealing with unplanned deficits. Implementing legislation will have to take account of faulty estimates, changing economic conditions, emergencies, and other occurrences that were not foreseen when the budget was prepared. It will have to prescribe rules for determining which entities are federal agencies and which are not. And it will have to determine the treatment of capital investment in the budget. It will not be hard to devise loopholes in ordinary laws that enable the federal government to balance its books while piling up additional debt.

Chapter 2 noted that the economy often has the last word in determining the fate of presidential and congressional budgets. The economy will also have the final say in determining whether a constitutional requirement of budgetary balance will be achieved. The odds are overwhelming that the Constitution will have to retreat in the face of economic realities. In fact, most versions of a balanced budget amendment permit the requirement to be waived in time of emergency. If a balanced budget rule may be suspended for economic necessity, it will also be suspended for political expedience. The fact that waivers would require a super majority would invite paralysis and hostage taking. Finally, the rule could open the door to situations in which Congress would lack both a majority to produce a balanced budget and a super majority to permit deficit spending.

Ultimately, a balanced budget amendment would violate the fundamental principle that elected officials should be responsible for government policy. If the political process spawns unwanted

deficits, then statutory rules should be changed to increase the prospect of reducing them.

Line-Item Veto

The Constitution empowers the president to veto any measure presented to him by Congress, but it does not authorize him to veto parts of a bill. He must either veto or sign the entire measure. The line-item veto would enable the president to disapprove particular sections or other parts of appropriations acts. Although there are scattered dissents, the accepted view is that it would take a constitutional amendment to give the president a line-item veto.

Those who favor a line-item veto note that the governors of more than forty states have this power and use it to expunge items added by the legislature and restrain expenditures. Proponents argue that the line-item veto is even more urgently needed in the federal government because each appropriations bill contains many billions of dollars, typically including both spending that is essential to the ongoing operations of government agencies and disputed items such as funds earmarked to particular projects and activities. The president often is compelled to accept spending he does not want in order to provide funds needed by agencies. The president's position is weaker yet when Congress combines some or all of the regular appropriations bills in an omnibus measure.

The line-item veto is an old idea that has a negligible chance of being enacted. It would in any event have little impact on total spending, though it would, of course, have a strong impact on the particular items to which it was applied. First, the veto would pertain only to discretionary spending, not to the two-thirds of the budget that is outside the control of the appropriations process. Second, most discretionary spending either is not disputed by the president or is appropriated at levels below the president's request. The loudest disputes between the two branches tend to involve relatively small amounts of money. Although Congress frequently allots more to specific activities or projects than the president wants, it can blunt his veto threat by underfunding some of his priorities. When Congress wants added funding for some items and the president wants more funding for others, the outcome depends more on negotiations than on vetoes. True, the president's bargaining position might be bolstered by the threat of a line-item veto, but Congress still can withhold funds from presidential priorities until he accepts some of its priorities.

The prospective impact of a line-item veto is further diminished by Congress's practice of putting most earmarks and other special funding into committee reports rather than appropriations acts. The president cannot veto report language, which means that he would not be able to veto most congressional add-ons. He can take a stand against report language, refusing to spend according to its dictates even if he does not have a line-item veto. But he should do so only if he is prepared to face up to Congress by vetoing appropriations bills that deviate significantly from his policy preferences.

Although the line-item veto would not have much impact on budget control, it might have a marked impact on political relationships between the two branches. It would augment the president's power at the expense of Congress's, which is why presidents want it and why Congress will not give it to them.

Enhanced Rescission Authority

When he campaigned for the presidency in 1992, Bill Clinton advocated a line-item veto. But when he became president and learned that Congress would not accede to this request, he indicated interest in a stronger rescission power instead. In its strongest form, rescission authority would be a more potent weapon than a line-item veto.

The impoundment rules in effect since 1974 give Congress the upper hand when the president proposes the rescission of funds (see chapter 9). If Congress does not approve a proposed rescission within forty-five days, the president must release the funds. Congress prevails by doing nothing. Two changes have been proposed; each would

give the president some advantage vis-à-vis Congress. The first—usually referred to as enhanced rescission authority—would provide for impounded funds to be canceled if Congress fails to disapprove the rescission within a certain period. This arrangement would tip the balance so overwhelmingly in favor of the president that it has virtually no chance of enactment. Congress would almost always lose when its spending preferences differed from those of the president. There is little prospect that Congress will enable the president to rescind funds without express legislative approval. On what constitutional basis should the president be empowered unilaterally to rescind funds duly appropriated by Congress? If the president opposes an appropriation, he has the option of vetoing the measure. If he signs the measure, or if Congress overrides his veto, the president should not be permitted to cancel the appropriation by rescinding the funds.

A more balanced approach would require Congress to vote on proposed rescissions within a fixed period of time. The president would be guaranteed an up or down vote, but funds would be canceled only if they were rescinded by Congress. Congress would have the final say but, in contrast to the current rules, it could not prevail by inaction. Some members of Congress argue that this expedited rescission authority would also give the president undue advantage.

A stronger impoundment power would retrench spending on projects or programs opposed by the president. But the overall impact would vary greatly, depending on the president's popularity and the extent to which he and Congress clashed on budget policy. Like the line-item veto, greater rescission authority would affect discretionary appropriations but would not apply to entitlements. But unlike the line-item veto, it could reach projects earmarked in committee reports as well as discrete elements in appropriations accounts. Also, unlike the line-item veto, rescissions could be proposed throughout the year, not just during the period when appropriations bills were under consideration.

Properly used, the power to rescind could provide year-round flexibility in implementing the budget. Circumstances do change as the fiscal year unfolds–emergency and other unanticipated spending needs emerge and economic conditions deviate from the projected course. It would be a good idea for the president and Congress to have the option of scaling back some previously voted funds in response to these or other changes. Bolstering the president's rescission authority might make the budget more responsive to changing conditions, but it would not have a dramatic impact on total spending unless it were used to reopen major matters decided in the appropriations process.

Biennial Budgeting and Appropriations

A biennial cycle has been a recurring goal of budget reformers. This cycle would establish a two-year minimum for authorizing legislation and would provide for the president to submit a budget every other year. Congress would switch to a biennial schedule for its budget resolution and it would enact regular appropriations bills every two years. Both the president and Congress would have the option of making supplementary budget decisions. The discussion here concentrates on biennial appropriations.

Advocates in both the legislative and executive branches have advanced a barrage of arguments in favor of a two-year cycle. Most have to do with the internal operations of Congress or federal agencies, especially the congestion of legislative calendars and agency budget schedules. The 1993 National Performance Review welcomed biennial budgeting as a means of liberating the budget process from the details of expenditure and orienting it to larger policy issues. Freed from the tight deadlines of the annual cycle, NPR reasoned, agencies would devote less time and resources to formulating detailed budget requests and would have more time for program planning and policy guidance.

Legislative supporters of a biennial budget complain about the amount of time taken by the annual appropriations bills and the conflicts they generate. They blame the appropriations process for crowding out authorizing legislation, and the Appropriations Committees for trespassing on the jurisdiction of authorizing committees. They view appropriations as a grinding process that is often completed behind schedule and appropriations bills as pork barrels for those who control the purse strings. Congressional reformers anticipate a two-year schedule in which substantive legislation would be considered in the first year and spending bills in the second. This arrangement would, they believe, encourage fuller congressional oversight of government programs and performance.

In terms of budget control, the argument for a biennial budget rests on expected changes in the focus of appropriations actions. A one-year appropriations process controls the small matters–the items of expenditure–but gives little attention to the long-term direction in federal spending. A two-year (or longer) cycle would surrender some congressional control of the details but gain more effective control of the government's financial future. The longer process would be less incremental and more change-oriented, less oriented to inputs and details and more to outputs and performance, less interested in micromanagement and more concerned about policies and priorities.

Are these expectations realistic? Not if past reforms, such as the planning-programming-budgeting system, introduced in the 1960s, and the zero-base-budgeting system, tried in the 1970s, are a guide. Reformers insist that the results will be more favorable this time because changes will be made in congressional operations and not just in the executive branch, and because the biennial process is part of a larger set of innovations moving forward under the aegis of the National Performance Review and the Government Performance and Results Act of 1993.

Despite these strong arguments, a critical process that has operated on an annual basis from the very start of American democracy should not be radically changed without considering possible implications and alternative means of accomplishing the objectives sought. A biennial cycle would ripple well beyond the appropriations process to the overall operations of Congress and its relations with the executive branch. Congress would still have the power of the purse, but it would hold the strings more loosely. How loosely would depend on the extent to which two-year appropriations would bring about the behavioral changes anticipated by its advocates.

If the government were to shift to biennial appropriations, the United States would be the first industrial democracy to take this step, although not the first to establish a multiyear budget cycle. Governments in some countries have stretched the cycle by giving agencies discretion to carry funds over from one year to the next, an idea that has been endorsed by the National Performance Review and is being pilot-tested in various agencies. Some rely on multiyear budgets that specify the resources some agencies will receive for a number of years and the programs they will carry out during that period. Significantly, however, interyear flexibility and multiyear arrangements coexist with annual appropriations. The lesson from other countries is that it is feasible to reduce the work burdens of annual budgeting and to increase managerial flexibility while continuing to make appropriations each year.

In fact, Congress has already moved substantially away from annual appropriations. For one thing, these appropriations control barely one-third of federal spending; for another, a sizable portion of discretionary funds is appropriated on a no-year basis and therefore remains available for obligation beyond the budget year. Moreover, Congress has effectively determined total discretionary appropriations for each year from 1993 through 1998 by capping this portion of the budget.

Should Congress go a big step further and formally embrace biennial appropriations for all accounts? The answer to this question depends on answers to others. Would a biennial cycle impair Congress's capacity to rein in spending when political or fiscal conditions warranted smaller appropriations than were made at the start of the cycle? Would agencies and Congress tend to regard the second-year (of a two-year) appropriation as a floor from which to provide additional funding in supplemental measures? Would Congress make such substantial use of supplemental appropriations that the process would be biennial in name only? What legislative changes should accompany biennial budgeting to ensure that congressional oversight would be vigorous and that legislative control of the purse would remain effective? These questions lead to one concluding comment. Biennial appropriations should be considered in tandem with other matters, including cyclical fiscal policy, the conditions under which supplemental appropriations may be provided, and relations among Congress, the president, and federal agencies.

Strengthening the Congressional Budget Resolution

For reasons discussed in chapter 5, the congressional budget resolution has had a troubled existence since it was introduced in 1975. There are plenty of ideas about what should be done, but no consensus. Some would abolish the congressional budget process, including the budget resolution; others would invest the process with greater importance by making the resolution into a law signed by the president. This can be accomplished by converting the measure into a joint–rather than a concurrent–resolution. Although its content would remain the same, a joint budget resolution would formally involve the president in congressional budget decisions and would give these decisions legal effect. On paper these changes would appear to augment budget control; in practice they probably would not make much difference.

The notion that the president should formally participate in congressional budgeting emanated from the White House, which claimed during the Reagan-Bush years that Congress could not be trusted to control federal spending. I believe this claim to be of little merit, for reasons that will be argued in the concluding section. Regardless of how one thinks on this matter, it is important to note that the president is informally involved in congressional budgeting and that the adopted budget resolution often reflects agreement between the two branches on key budget policies. This was as true during the Reagan and Bush presidencies as it has been during the Clinton administration. A formal role would add little when the White House can influence congressional budget decisions through negotiations with legislative leaders. And presidential participation might block adoption of the resolution when the two sides are far apart on budget policy. In the latter circumstance, a statutory budget resolution might mean no resolution, for the president might get a better deal through individual spending and revenue measures than through a comprehensive congressional budget.

Although a statutory budget process would enable Congress to enact revenue or spending legislation in the resolution, there would be little improvement in budget control if it did. Congress already has three instruments of budget control discussed earlier in this chapter: caps on discretionary spending, PAYGO rules for revenue and spending legislation, and reconciliation procedures for revenues and mandatory spending under existing law. All three are enforced through congressional rules and procedures, not through statutory controls.

The controls now in place leave one big gap: actual revenue and spending often deviate from budgeted levels without occasioning any reaction. In contrast to the advisory budget resolution Congress now uses, a statutory resolution could limit revenue or spending outcomes. It could put a floor on revenues or a ceiling on expenditures, but without an enforcement mechanism these limits would not control the amounts collected or paid out during a fiscal year. Statutory controls are not inherently superior to those operating through congressional procedures; both are only as effective as their enforcement is.

Entitlement Caps

Enforcement is most needed in mandatory spending, where it is most difficult to achieve. (These comments are addressed to mandatory spending, but they also pertain to revenues. The two have similar budgetary characteristics, as PAYGO recognizes.) The leading candidate for filling this hole in budget control is a cap on entitlement spending. The cap could be applied to total entitlement spending or to specific programs. Either would operate through automatic cuts triggered by excess spending or by legislative action taken pursuant to notification that the cap was exceeded.

If the control were to be automatic, the conditions under which it would be triggered and the manner in which spending would be cut must be spelled out in law. Automatic savings can be achieved through across-the-board cuts in payments to recipients (or, in health care programs, to providers) or according to some other formula. The formula might require that the cuts offset all or only part of the excess spending, it might impose the cuts in a single fiscal year or spread them over several, or it might spread the cuts among all entitlement programs or confine them to a few. Or the formula might trim payments to all recipients or only to those with incomes above a certain level, it might require that some portion of the excess spending be offset by revenue increases, or it might have the cuts take effect after a waiting period, during which Congress would be able to substitute other savings. These are the most obvious options, but many others are feasible.

All these options would be available if, instead of automatic cutbacks, the matter were placed before Congress for its decision. This is the arrangement promulgated by executive order in 1993 and described at the end of chapter 7. One of Congress's options would be to do nothing, that is, to accommodate the excess spending. The fact that Congress can choose to do nothing has stimulated demands for automatically enforced caps on entitlements. Interest in entitlement caps has also been stimulated by the health reform legislation pending in Congress when this book was completed.

Although the federal government has very little experience with entitlement caps, these can be made to work. The important question, however, is whether they make good policy. An automatic cap would probably have hidden side effects, such as rationing of health services or a reduction in the income of dependent persons. Spending in excess of the caps would most likely occur during a recession, when personal incomes are depressed and federal spending has increased. This would not be the most appropriate time to cut income support or other payments in accord with a preset formula.

Automatic cuts uphold budget control at the expense of other objectives pursued by entitlement programs. The only way to balance these competing goals would be to let Congress decide what to do when entitlement spending exceeds the cap. As required by the 1993 executive order, the president would recommend a course of action, but Congress would not be bound by the advice. The exact procedures for congressional review of excess entitlement spending need not concern us here, but they would include a timetable for action. Even if Congress decided to do nothing, it would have to vote on the matter.

If Congress eschews cutbacks and permits spending to exceed the caps, its decision should not be viewed as a breakdown of budget control but as an affirmation of other objectives valued by Americans. The important thing is that competing values have a fair chance of carrying the day, not that the process be rigged for or against a particular outcome.

Conclusion

Claiming to strengthen budget control and actually doing so are different matters. Most of the proposals discussed here would affect discretionary spending, the portion of the budget that is effectively controlled, but would have little effect on mandatory spending, which is inadequately controlled. Only entitlement caps would expressly deal with mandatory expenditures.

This mismatch between budget reforms and the problem of budget control has several explanations. One is that Congress controls that which is controllable because it is easier to do. It is much harder to constrain entitlements than to trim discretionary spending. Another is the tendency of politicians to pander to the public perception that the budget is out of control because of lavish spending by federal

agencies on their own operations. Few Americans know that discretionary spending is controlled and that the year-to-year increase in federal spending is almost entirely due to entitlements.

At least four of the reforms discussed here would strengthen the president's budget powers at the expense of Congress. The line-item veto, enhanced rescission authority, biennial appropriations, and a statutory budget resolution would improve the president's chances of getting his way in budget clashes with Congress.

These reforms assume that Congress is the irresponsible branch and that it must be reined in for budgetary discipline to be restored. This view was actively promoted by the White House during the Reagan and Bush administrations. Yet a strong case can be made that presidents are more wont than Congress to brush aside budget controls. Ronald Reagan was not an exemplar of fiscal responsibility in 1981 when he used faulty projections to cajole Congress into hiking defense spending while slashing taxes. George Bush held onto his "no new taxes" pledge by submitting budgets that greatly understated the next year's deficit; he retreated only in the face of congressional pressure and overwhelming evidence that his projections were very wide of the mark. Bill Clinton's fiscal 1994 budget exceeded the discretionary spending caps and his fiscal 1995 budget has questionable estimates of the budgetary impact of health care reform. Congress enforced budget control by keeping appropriations within the discretionary caps and by relying on more cautious CBO estimates in developing health care reform legislation.

Proposed reforms will not do much good if they substitute Congress bashing for genuine control or if they concentrate on the portion of the budget that is already disciplined. As long as presidents plunge ahead with legislative agendas that break the budget but Congress gets blamed for the damage, Americans will get the programs they want and the deficits they do not want. And as long as the noose is tightened around discretionary spending while existing entitlements are left alone, the federal budget will have many controls and still be out of control.

203

Glossary

ACCOUNT. A reporting unit for budgeting, accounting for, and managing financial resources and transactions. An account is either an item for which an appropriation has been made or for which an account identification number has been assigned in the budget.

ACCRUED EXPENDITURES. Charges that reflect liabilities incurred for services received, goods or other property received, or amounts becoming owed under programs for which no current service or performance is required. Expenditures accrue regardless of when cash payments are made.

ADJUSTMENTS (to discretionary spending limits). Changes in discretionary spending limits for purposes specified in the Budget Enforcement Act of 1990. Adjustments may be made for (among other reasons) changes in budget concepts or definitions, differences between assumed and actual inflation, credit reestimates, or emergency appropriations.

ADVANCE APPROPRIATIONS. Budget authority provided in an appropriations act to become available in a fiscal year beyond the one for which the act is written. The amount is included in the budget totals for the fiscal year in which the amount will become available for obligation. *See also* Forward funding.

ADVANCE FUNDING. Budget authority that may be obligated or spent during the current fiscal year from the next year's appropriation. When obligated in advance, budget authority is increased for the current fiscal year and decreased for the next fiscal year.

ALLOCATION. In executive budgeting, allocations are budget authorities or other resources transferred to another account to carry out the purposes of the parent account. For use in congressional budgeting, *see* Committee allocation.

ALLOTMENT. A distribution by an agency to officials or administrative units authorizing them to incur obligations within a specified amount. The total amount allotted by an agency cannot exceed the amount apportioned by the Office of Management and Budget.

ALLOWANCE LETTER. A letter sent to each agency by the Office of Management and Budget after the president's budget has been submitted to Congress. The letter advises the agency of budget decisions and multiyear planning estimates, employment ceilings, and other significant policy and administrative matters.

ALLOWANCES. Amounts included in the budget to cover possible additional expenditures for statutory pay increases, contingencies, and other requirements.

ANNUAL AUTHORIZATION. An authorization of appropriations for a single fiscal year, usually for a definite amount of money. Ongoing programs with annual authorizations are supposed to be reauthorized each year. If they are not reauthorized, Congress often enables them to continue by providing appropriations.

APPORTIONMENT. A distribution made by the Office of Management and Budget of amounts available for obligation. Apportionments divide these amounts by time periods (usually quarters) or projects. The apportionment limits the amount that may be obligated. When an account is apportioned, some resources may be reserved pursuant to the Antideficiency Act or may be proposed for rescission pursuant to the Impoundment Control Act.

APPROPRIATED ENTITLEMENT. An entitlement whose budget authority is provided in annual appropriations acts instead of in substantive law. These entitlements are classified as direct spending by the Budget Enforcement Act.

APPROPRIATION. A provision of law providing budget authority that enables an agency to incur obligations and to make payments out of the Treasury for specified purposes. Appropriations are the most common means of providing budget authority. Annual appropriations are provided in appropriations acts; most permanent appropriations are enacted in substantive law.

APPROPRIATIONS ACT. A law making annual appropriations. The law may be a regular, supplemental, or continuing appropriation.

AUTHORIZATIONS ACT. A law that establishes or continues one or more federal programs or agencies, establishes the terms and con-ditions under which they operate, sets other policy requirements or restrictions, authorizes the enactment of appropriations, and specifies how appropriated funds are to be used.

BACKDOOR SPENDING. Budget authority provided in substantive legislation in advance of appropriations acts. The most common forms of backdoor spending are entitlement authority, borrowing authority, contract authority, and authority to forgo the collection of certain offsetting receipts. The Congressional Budget Act defines this type of provision as spending authority.

BALANCED BUDGET. A budget in which receipts equal or exceed outlays.

BASELINE ESTIMATE. A projection of future revenues, expenditures, and other budget amounts under assumed economic conditions and participation rates, and assuming no change in current policy. The baseline is usually projected annually by the Congressional Budget Office for each of the next five years. It is used in preparing the congressional budget resolution and reconciliation instructions and in estimating the amount of deficit reduction in reconciliation bills and the effects of legislation on the budget.

BIENNIAL BUDGET. A budget for a period of two years. The federal government has an annual budget, but proposals have been made that it adopt a biennial budget.

BORROWING AUTHORITY. A type of spending authority that permits a federal agency to incur obligations and to make payments for specified purposes out of funds borrowed from the Treasury or the public. Except for trust funds and certain other entities, borrowing authority is effective only to the extent provided in appropriations acts.

BUDGET AMENDMENT. A revision to a pending budget request submitted by the president before Congress has completed action on the original request.

BUDGETARY RESOURCES. The amounts available (regardless of source) for obligation in a fund or account. These resources include new budget authority, recoveries or restorations of budget authority provided in previous years, transfers from other accounts, fees and other collections deposited in the account, and unobligated balances. In the Gramm-Rudman-Hollings process, sequestrable budget resources are those subject to sequestration.

BUDGET AUTHORITY. Authority provided by law to enter into obligations that normally result in the outlay of funds. The main forms of budget authority are appropriations, borrowing authority, and contract authority. Budget authority also includes the subsidy cost of direct and guaranteed loans but not the unsubsidized portion. Budget authority may be classified by the period of availability (one year, multiyear, or no year), by the timing of congressional action (current or permanent), or by the specificity of the amount available (definite or indefinite).

BUDGET ENFORCEMENT ACT. A 1990 act of Congress that establishes limits on discretionary spending, maximum deficit amounts, pay-as-you-go rules for revenue and direct spending, new credit budgeting procedures, and other changes in budget practices.

BUDGET RESOLUTION. A concurrent resolution passed by both houses of Congress that does not require the signature of the president. It presents the congressional budget for each of the succeeding five fiscal years. The budget resolution sets forth various budget totals and functional allocations and may include reconciliation instructions to designated House or Senate committees. *See also* Reconciliation instruction.

BUDGETARY RESERVES. Funds withheld from apportionment by the Office of Management and Budget, as authorized by the Antideficiency Act. Unless expressly authorized by other laws, such reserves may be set aside only because of savings due to changes in requirements or efficiency of operation. Reserves are reported to Congress, as required by the Impoundment Control Act.

CAPITAL BUDGET. A budget that segregates capital investments from operating expenditures. Investment in capital assets is excluded from calculation of the surplus or deficit, but the operating budget is charged for depreciation or debt service or both. The federal government does not have a capital budget, but investment expenditures are shown in supplementary budget schedules.

CASH BASIS. The accounting method in which revenues are recorded when received and expenditures are recorded when paid, without regard to the accounting period in which the revenues were earned or the costs incurred.

CHIEF FINANCIAL OFFICER. An official appointed pursuant to the Chief Financial Officers Act of 1990 to oversee financial management activities relating to the programs and operations of an agency, develop and maintain an integrated accounting and financial management system, and monitor the financial execution of the agency's budget.

CLOSED ACCOUNT. An account whose balance is canceled and is no longer available for obligation or expenditure. A fixed account (such as a one-year appropriation) that is available for obligation for a limited period is closed five years after obligations may no longer be drawn against it. *See also* Expired account.

COMMITTEE ALLOCATION. The distribution, pursuant to sections 302 and 602 of the Congressional Budget Act, of new budget authority, entitlement authority, and outlays to House and Senate committees. The allocation, which may not exceed the relevant amounts in the budget resolution, usually is made in the joint explanatory statement that accompanies the conference report on the budget resolution.

COMPARATIVE STATEMENT OF NEW BUDGET AUTHORITY. A table in the report of the House or Senate Appropriations Committee on an appropriations bill. The table compares the amount recommended for each account with the amount appropriated for the previous fiscal year and the amount requested by the president.

CONCURRENT RESOLUTION ON THE BUDGET. *See* BUDGET RESOLUTION.

CONSTANT DOLLARS. The dollar value of goods and services, adjusted for changes in prices. Constant dollars are calculated by dividing current dollar amounts by an appropriate index, such as the consumer price index. Constant dollar figures are used to compute the inflation-adjusted level of budget receipts and outlays.

CONTINGENT LIABILITY. A conditional obligation that may become an actual liability if certain events occur or fail to occur. Contingent liabilities include loan guarantees, bank deposit insurance, and price guarantees.

CONTINUING RESOLUTION OR CONTINUING APPROPRIATION. A joint House-Senate resolution that provides budget authority for programs or agencies whose regular appropriation was not enacted by the start of the fiscal year. A continuing resolution is usually a temporary measure that expires at a specified date or is superseded by enactment of the regular appropriations act. Some continuing resolutions, however, are in effect for the entire fiscal year and serve as the means of enacting regular appropriations.

CONTRACT AUTHORITY. Legislation that permits obligations to be incurred in advance of appropriations. With certain exceptions, contract authority is effective only to the extent provided in appropriations acts. After contract authority is provided, Congress appropriates funds to pay off obligations incurred pursuant to it.

COST ESTIMATE. An estimate prepared by the Congressional Budget Office of the outlays that would ensue from reported legislation over a five-year period. The cost estimate, which is required by the Congressional Budget Act, usually is published in the report accompanying the legislation.

CREDIT BUDGET. The appropriate levels of total new direct loan obligations, total new primary loan commitments, and total new secondary loan guarantee commitments set forth in a budget resolution. The credit budget has largely been superseded by procedures established by the Federal Credit Reform Act of 1990.

CREDIT PROGRAM ACCOUNT. The budget account into which an appropriation is made to cover the subsidy cost or administrative expenses or both of a direct or guaranteed loan. The appropriated funds are then disbursed to a financing account.

CREDIT SUBSIDY COST. The estimated cost, over the duration of a direct or guaranteed loan, calculated on the basis of the net present value of the cash flows or the loan or guarantee, excluding administrative expenses. For direct loans the subsidy cost is the net present value of the following cash flows: disbursements, payments of interest and principal, recoveries, fees, and other payments. For loan guarantees the subsidy cost is the net present value of government payments for defaults, interest subsidies, and other payments less the estimated payments to the government for fees, other charges, and recoveries.

CURRENT DOLLARS. The dollar value of a good or service in terms of prices paid at the time the good or service is sold. *See also* Constant dollars.

CURRENT LEVEL. An estimate of the amounts of new budget authority, outlays, and revenues for a fiscal year that is based on enacted law. The estimates do not take into account pending legislation. The House and Senate Budget Committees estimate the current level once a month, or more often if necessitated by legislative activity. In making its section 602 allocations to committees, the House Budget Committee makes separate allocations for current levels; the Senate Budget Committee does not.

CURRENT SERVICE ESTIMATES. Estimates submitted by the president (usually in his budget) of the levels of budget authority and outlays that would be required in the next and subsequent fiscal years to continue existing services. These estimates reflect the projected cost of continuing federal programs if there are no policy changes. *See also* Baseline estimate.

DEFERRAL. An action or inaction that temporarily withholds, delays, or precludes the oblig-ation or expenditure of budget authority. Deferrals may be made only for the purposes authorized by the Antideficiency Act (or by another law), not for policy reasons. Unless it is renewed, a deferral may not extend beyond the fiscal year in which the funds have been withheld.

DEFICIENCY APPORTIONMENT. An apportionment (by the Office of Management and Budget) of available budgetary resources in an amount or rate that may compel the enactment of supplemental budget authority. Such apportionments may be made only under the conditions allowed by the Antideficiency Act.

DIRECT LOAN. A disbursement of funds (not in exchange for goods or services) that is contracted to be repaid. An appropriation is made to cover the subsidy cost and administrative expenses of each direct loan program.

DIRECT SPENDING. Budget authority and ensuing outlays provided in laws other than appropriations acts, including annually appropriated entitlements. Direct spending is distinguished by the Budget Enforcement Act of 1990 from discretionary spending. Direct spending is subject to pay-as-you-go (PAYGO) rules.

DISCRETIONARY SPENDING (appropriations). Budget authority, other than appropriated entitlements, and ensuing outlays provided in annual appropriations acts. The Budget Enforcement Act sets limits or caps on discretionary budget authority and outlays. *See also* Discretionary spending limits.

DISCRETIONARY SPENDING LIMITS. Ceilings on budget authority and outlays for discretionary programs set by the Budget Enforcement Act. These limits are currently in effect through the 1998 fiscal year, but

209

they may be extended by Congress. Appropriations causing budget authority or outlays to exceed the limit may compel a sequestration.

EARMARKING. Earmarked revenues are dedicated by law for a specific purpose or program. The revenues include trust funds, special funds, and offsetting collections credited to appropriations accounts. Earmarked expenditures are appropriations dedicated by an appropriations act or the accompanying committee report to a particular project or activity.

EMERGENCY APPROPRIATION. An appropriation that the president and Congress have designated as an emergency. An emergency appropriation causes an increase in the relevant discretionary spending limits to accommodate the additional spending.

ENTITLEMENT AUTHORITY. A provision of law that requires payments to eligible persons or governments. Entitlements constitute a binding obligation on the part of the federal government, and eligible recipients may have legal recourse if the obligation is not fulfilled. Entitlements require annual appropriations unless the appropriation is permanent.

EXPIRED ACCOUNT. An appropriation or fund account whose balances are no longer available for incurring new obligations because the time available for incurring such obligations has expired. Outlays may be made from expired accounts for previously made obligations. *See also* Closed account.

FEDERAL DEBT. The total amount of public debt and agency debt. The portion of the debt held by trust funds or other federal accounts is not counted in the debt held by the public.

FEDERAL FUNDS. All monies collected and spent by the federal government, other than those designated as trust funds. Federal funds include general, special, public enterprise, and intergovernmental funds.

FINANCIAL STATEMENTS. Statements reporting on the financial condition of agencies or other federal entities, including statements of financial condition, results of operations, cash flows, and a reconciliation to the budget. The Chief Financial Officers Act prescribes financial statements for trust and revolving funds, commercial operations, and certain other entities.

FINANCING ACCOUNT. An account established pursuant to the Federal Credit Reform Act of 1990 that receives disbursements from a credit program account and handles all other cash flows to or from the government resulting from direct or guaranteed loans. Financing accounts are not included in the budget totals.

FISCAL POLICY. Federal policies concerning revenues, spending, and the deficit intended to promote the nation's macroeconomic goals with respect to employment, output, prices, and the balance of payments.

FISCAL YEAR. The accounting period for the budget. The fiscal year for the federal government begins on October 1 and ends the next September 30. The fiscal year is designated by the calendar year in which it ends; for example, fiscal year 1995 begins on October 1, 1994, and ends on September 30, 1995.

FIXED ACCOUNT. An account whose funds are available for a definite period, in contrast to accounts that have no-year funds. Balances in fixed accounts expire (are no longer available for obligation) at the end of the period for which they are available.

FORWARD FUNDING. Budget authority that becomes available for obligation during one fiscal year and continues to be available through the next fiscal year. The budget authority is counted in the fiscal year for which the appropriation is made, not the succeeding fiscal year.

FULL FUNDING. The provision of budget authority to finance the full estimated cost of a project or activity, such as ship construction, that will be completed in subsequent years. Full funding also refers to the appropriation of the full amount authorized in authorizing legislation.

FUNCTION OR FUNCTIONAL CLASSIFICATION. A classification of budgetary resources (budget authority, outlays, direct loans, loan guarantees, and tax expenditures) in terms of the principal purposes they serve. A function may be divided into two or more subfunctions. The last three digits of an account's identification code represent the subfunction into which the account has been classified.

GOVERNMENT-SPONSORED ENTERPRISE. An enterprise established by the federal government but privately owned and operated. These enterprises are excluded from the budget totals because they are classified as private entities. However, financial information concerning them is included in the budget.

GRAMM-RUDMAN-HOLLINGS PROCESS. The process established by the Balanced Budget and Emergency Deficit Control Act of 1985 (commonly known as the Gramm-Rudman-Hollings Act). The process included fixed deficit targets and the sequestration of budgetary resources if the projected deficit was greater than the target. The Budget Enforcement Act of 1990 substantially revised these procedures.

GROSS DOMESTIC PRODUCT (GDP). The value of all final goods and services produced within the borders of a country in a given period of time. GDP can be expressed in current or constant dollars.

IDENTIFICATION CODE. The eleven-digit code assigned to each appropriation or fund account that identifies the agency, the account, the timing of the transmittal to Congress, the type of fund, and the account's functional classification.

IMPOUNDMENT. An action or inaction by a government officer or employee that precludes the obligation or expenditure of budget authority. *See also* DEFERRAL, RESCISSION.

INTERNAL CONTROL. The practices of an agency to safeguard its assets, ensure the accuracy and reliability of accounts, and foster compliance with prescribed financial management policies. Sometimes referred to as management control.

JUSTIFICATION MATERIAL. The documents and schedules submitted by an agency to the Appropriations Committees in support of its budget request. The material typically explains changes between the current appropriation and the amounts requested for the next fiscal year.

LINE-ITEM VETO. Authority to veto part of an appropriations act. The president does not now have line-item veto authority; he must sign or veto the entire appropriations act.

LIQUIDATING ACCOUNT. An account (established pursuant to the Federal Credit Reform Act of 1990) to handle all cash flows resulting from direct or guaranteed loans made before the start of fiscal year 1992.

211

LIQUIDATING APPROPRIATION. An appropriation to pay obligations incurred pursuant to substantive legislation, usually contract authority. A liquidating appropriation is not recorded as budget authority.

LOAN GUARANTEE. A commitment by the federal government to pay part or all of the loan principal or interest to the lender in the event of default by the borrower. The subsidy cost of new loan guarantees is included in the budget's computation of budget authority and outlays.

MANAGEMENT FUND. An account authorized by law to receive budgetary resources from two or more appropriations to carry out a common purpose or activity not involving a continuing cycle of operations.

MAXIMUM DEFICIT AMOUNT. The maximum deficit level set in the Gramm-Rudman-Hollings Act as amended by the Budget Enforcement Act. The maximum deficit amount is subject to certain adjustments. If the deficit for a particular fiscal year is estimated to exceed the adjusted level by more than a permitted margin, a sequester is required to eliminate the excess deficit.

MEANS OF FINANCING. Financial flows to the federal government that are not included in budget receipts or outlays. These include funds borrowed from the public, seigniorage, and the credit-financing accounts.

MIDSESSION REVIEW OF THE BUDGET. An updated summary of the budget containing revised estimates of revenues, budget authority, and outlays, as well as other information. The midsession review is supposed to be issued by July 15, but it is sometimes submitted later.

MONTHLY TREASURY STATEMENT. A summary statement issued each month by the Treasury presenting data on receipts, outlays, and the surplus or deficit for the latest completed month and for the fiscal year to date, with comparisons to the same period in the previous year.

MULTIYEAR APPROPRIATION. Budget authority provided in an appropriations act for a specified period in excess of one fiscal year. Multiyear appropriations may cover periods that do not coincide with the start or end of a fiscal year.

MULTIYEAR AUTHORIZATION. An authorization of appropriations for a specified period in excess of one fiscal year. Programs with multiyear authorizations must be reauthorized periodically.

NATIONAL INCOME AND PRODUCT ACCOUNTS. Quarterly and annual accounts providing data on aggregate economic activity in the United States. These accounts depict in dollar terms the composition and use of the nation's output and income. The budget presents a statement showing federal revenues and expenditures on a NIPA basis.

NO-YEAR APPROPRIATION. Budget authority provided in an appropriations act that remains available for obligation for an indefinite period. These funds do not lapse if they are not obligated by the end of the fiscal year.

OBJECT CLASSIFICATION. A classification identifying expenditures by the goods or services purchased (such as personnel, supplies, and equipment). An object classification schedule is included in the budget for each appropriation account.

OBLIGATED BALANCE. The amount of obligations incurred for which payment has not yet been made. This balance usually is carried forward until the obligations are paid.

OBLIGATION. An order placed, contract awarded, service received, or similar transaction that will require payment.

OFF-BUDGET. Budget authority, outlays, or receipts of federal entities that are excluded by law from the budget. These entities currently include the social security trust funds and the Postal Service.

OFFSETTING COLLECTIONS. Certain receipts that are not counted as revenues but are deducted from budget authority and outlays, and are classified as follows. *Proprietary receipts from the public*: collections from business-type or market-oriented activities such as interest and income from the sale of property or products. *Intragovernmental transactions*: flows between accounts or funds that may be intrabudgetary (both the payment and the receipt occur within the budget) or between on-budget and off-budget entities.

ONE-YEAR APPROPRIATION. Budget authority provided in an appropriations act that is available for obligation only during a single fiscal year, usually the fiscal year specified in the enacting clause of the appropriations act.

OUTLAYS. Payments made (usually through the issuance of checks or the disbursement of cash) to liquidate obligations. Outlays during a fiscal year may be for payment of obligations incurred in previous years or in the same year.

PAYGO (Pay-as-you-go). The procedure established by the Budget Enforcement Act to ensure that direct spending and revenue legislation do not cause an increase in the deficit. PAYGO requires that an increase in the deficit due to such legislation be offset by other legislation or by a sequester.

PERFORMANCE BUDGETING. A form of budgeting that relates resources provided in the budget to measurable results.

PERMANENT APPROPRIATION. Budget authority that becomes available without any current action by Congress. Budget authority is deemed to be permanent if it derives from legislation enacted in previous sessions of Congress.

PERMANENT AUTHORIZATION. An authorization of appropriations without a time limit and often without a limit on money. A permanent authorization continues in effect unless revised or terminated by Congress.

PROGRAM ACCOUNT. *See* CREDIT PROGRAM ACCOUNT.

PROGRAM AND FINANCING SCHEDULE. A schedule published in the president's budget for each appropriations account consisting of program by activities, financing, relation of budget authority to outlays, and adjustments to budget authority and outlays.

PROGRAM, PROJECT, OR ACTIVITY (PPA). An element within a budget account. For annually appropriated accounts, PPAs are defined by appropriations acts and accompanying reports and documentation. For accounts not funded by annual appropriations, PPAs are defined by the program listing in the program and financing schedules. Under sequestration procedures, except as otherwise provided, PPAs are reduced by an equal percentage.

213

PUBLIC DEBT. Funds borrowed by the Treasury (including the Federal Financing Bank) from the public or from another fund or account. The public debt does not include agency debt (funds borrowed by other federal agencies). The public debt is not the same as debt held by the public.

PUBLIC ENTERPRISE REVOLVING FUND ACCOUNTS. Expenditure accounts authorized by Congress to be credited with collections that are generated by and earmarked to finance a continuing cycle of business-type operations.

REAPPROPRIATION. Congressional action that continues the availability of all or part of the unobligated portion of budget authority that has expired or would otherwise expire. Reappropriations are counted as budget authority in the fiscal year for which the availability is extended.

RECEIPTS OR BUDGET RECEIPTS. Collections from the public, including payments by participants in social insurance programs. These collections consist principally of tax receipts and social insurance premiums. Budget receipts do not include various offsetting collections which are accounted for as negative outlays, not as revenues.

RECONCILIATION BILL. A bill containing changes in law recommended by House or Senate committees pursuant to reconciliation instructions in a budget resolution.

RECONCILIATION INSTRUCTION. A provision in a budget resolution directing one or more House or Senate committees to recommend legislation changing existing law so as to bring spending, revenues, or the debt limit into conformity with the budget resolution. The instructions specify the committees to which they are directed, the dollar changes

to be achieved, and a deadline by which the legislation is to be reported.

RECONCILIATION PROCESS. Procedures established in the Congressional Budget Act by which Congress changes existing laws to conform revenues and spending to the levels set in a budget resolution.

REPROGRAMMING OF FUNDS. Shifting of funds from one purpose to another within the same appropriations account, in contrast to a transfer, which involves shifting funds between accounts. Reprogramming sometimes entails formal notification and the opportunity for congressional committees to disapprove the action.

RESCISSION. The cancelation of budget authority previously provided by Congress. The Impoundment Control Act prescribes procedures for presidential notification and congressional action on rescission proposals.

RESCISSION BILL. A bill reported pursuant to a president's rescission message that cancels budget authority previously provided by Congress.

RESERVES. *See* BUDGET RESERVES.

REVOLVING FUND. An account or fund in which the income derived from its operations is available to finance the fund's continuing operations without fiscal year limitations.

SCOREKEEPING OR SCORING. The process of estimating the budgetary impacts of pending and enacted legislation and comparing them with limits set in the budget resolution or in law. For purposes of the congressional budget process, the Budget Committees and the Congressional Budget Office are responsible for scoring legislation. For purposes of sequestration, the Office of Management and

Budget scores legislation in enforcing the discretionary spending limits , the PAYGO rules, and the maximum deficit amounts established by the Budget Enforcement Act.

SECTIONS 302 AND 602. *See* COMMITTEE ALLOCATION.

SEQUESTRATION. The cancelation of budgetary resources pursuant to the Budget Enforcement Act. Once canceled, sequestered funds are no longer available for obligation or expenditure (except for special funds or trust funds). Sequestration may occur in response to the enactment of appropriations that cause a breach in the discretionary spending limits, the enactment of revenue or direct spending legislation that causes a net increase in the deficit, or the estimation of a deficit in excess of the maximum deficit amount. Sequestration can be classified in terms of when it is implemented– for example, as a within-session or an end-of-session sequester.

SPECIAL FUND. Funds earmarked by law for special purposes. There sometimes is little practical difference between a special fund and a trust fund, but special funds are classified as federal funds.

SPENDING AUTHORITY. The term designated by the Congressional Budget Act for borrowing authority, contract authority, entitlement authority, and authority to forgo offsetting collections, the borrowing authority for which is not provided in advance by appropriations acts. *See also* BACKDOOR SPENDING, DIRECT SPENDING.

SPENDOUT RATE. The rate at which new budget authority provided by Congress is spent by federal agencies; hence the rate at which out-

lays occur. Sometimes referred to as the outlay rate.

STATUTORY DEBT LIMIT. The maximum amount, established in law, of public debt that can be outstanding. The limit covers virtually all debt issued by the federal government, including borrowing from trust funds, but excludes some debt incurred by agencies.

SUBSIDY COST. *See* CREDIT SUBSIDY COST.

SUPPLEMENTAL APPROPRIATION. An act appropriating funds in addition to those provided in an annual or continuing appropriations act. Supplemental appropriations cover needs deemed too urgent to be postponed until enactment of the regular appropriations. Supplemental appropriations sometimes include items not provided in regular appropriations for lack of timely authorizations.

TAX EXPENDITURE. Revenue losses attributable to provisions of federal law that allow a special exclusion or deduction from income or that provide a special credit, preferential tax rate, or deferral of tax liability. Tax expenditures entail no payment from the government; rather, the Treasury forgoes some of the revenue it would otherwise have collected, and affected taxpayers pay lower taxes than they otherwise would have had to pay.

TRANSFER OF FUNDS. The transfer of budgetary resources from one appropriations account or fund to another, in contrast to reprogramming, which shifts resources within the same account. Funds may be transferred only when authorized by law.

TRANSFER PAYMENTS. Payments made by the government to individuals for which no current or future goods or services are provided in return. These payments include social

215

security, unemployment insurance, veterans' benefits, and various welfare payments.

TRUST FUNDS. Funds collected and used by the government to carry out specific purposes or programs according to the terms of a trust agreement or statute. Trust funds are not available for the general purposes of the government.

UNDELIVERED ORDER. The value of goods and services ordered and obligated but not yet received. The term is synonymous with unliquidated obligations.

UNDISTRIBUTED OFFSETTING RECEIPTS. Receipts that are budgeted as offsets against total spending rather than offsets against particular accounts or functions. These include income from the sale of major assets and from offshore oil leases.

UNIFIED BUDGET. A comprehensive budget that includes all receipts and outlays from federal funds and trust funds. Off-budget entities (the Postal Service and social security) are presently excluded from the unified budget, but data relating to them are presented in the budget.

UNOBLIGATED BALANCE. The portion of budget authority that has not been obligated. Unobligated balances are carried forward until the period for which they are available expires. No-year funds are carried forward until they are rescinded or until disbursements have not been made against the account for two consecutive years.

USER FEES. Fees, such as grazing fees or duck hunting licenses, charged to users of goods or services provided by the government. In levying or authorizing these fees, Congress determines whether the revenue should revert to the Treasury or should be available to the agency providing the goods or services.

VIEWS AND ESTIMATES REPORT. A report issued each year within six weeks after submission of the president's budget by each House or Senate committee with jurisdiction over federal programs. Each views and estimates report contains a committee's comments or recommendations on budgetary matters in its jurisdiction.

WORKING FUND ACCOUNTS. Funds established to receive advance payments from other agencies or accounts. Consolidated working funds do not finance the work directly; they reimburse the appropriation or fund account that finances the work performed.

Index

Accounting and budget arithmetic: allocations, 73, 88-91; appropriations, 158, 192; baseline projections, 22; budget resolution, 79; entitlements, 39-40; deficit calculation, 27-31; discretionary and direct spending, 123, 192-93; federal budget, 12-31, 178, 181, 192; incremental appropriations, 137; offsetting collections, 108; pay-as-you-go rules, 41, 79-80; revenues and receipts, 87-88, 108; standards, 186; tax expenditures, 101. *See also* Federal Accounting Standards Advisory Board

Accounts, 149, 154, 155, 168, 170, 177

AFDC. *See* Aid to families with dependent children

Agencies, federal: accounts, 154, 155, 168, 170, 177; allocations, 92; allotments and obligations, 166, 168, 195; apportionment, 166, 167, 195; audits, 47, 177, 178, 182; budget reforms, 55; budget timetables and schedules, 52, 53, 65-66, 165, 186; and Congress, 58, 168, 170-73, 183, 185; controls, 183, 184, 185, 186; direct spending, 113, 123-27; financial officers, 178, 179; financial statements, 178, 179; Government Performance and Results Act of *1993*, 187; history of the budget process, 49, 185; impoundments, 173; incremental and bottom-up budgeting, 52-54, 56; innovation funds, 186; and National Performance Review, 185, 200; object classification, 67; and Office of Management and Budget, 53,

54, 55, 56, 64; passback, 56; in president's budget, 53, 54-55, 58, 61, 63-69, 135; reprogrammings, 168, 170, 171, 186; substantive legislation, 113, 114, 115. *See also* Appropriations; Authorizations; Expenditure management; Government, federal

Agencies, role in budget process: *Book of Estimates*, 35; budget requests, 43; financial management, 36, 175-85; receipts, 19; spending process, 39, 47, 165-75; timetables and schedules, 44*t*, 45*t*

Aid to families with dependent children (AFDC), 38*t*

Airports and Airways Trust Fund, 105

Allocations. *See* Congressional budget resolution

Antideficiency Act of *1905-06*, 36, 166, 173, 174

Appropriations: accounts, 149, 154, 155-56, 166; agencies and, 58, 61, 110, 113, 120, 122-23, 129, 134, 136-37, 160, 162, 170; appropriating legislation, 45-46, 72, 129-35, 137; authorizations and, 117, 118, 120-23, 129; biennial budget and, 129, 200-01; Congress and, 19, 43, 44-46; continuing, 46, 130, 131, 149, 152; earmarks, 123, 170, 200; emergency spending, 130, 146, 166; entitlements and, 40, 123, 126, 130; House of Representatives actions, 141-47; incrementalism, 137-39, 192, 200; legislation and limitations in appropriations acts, 154, 156, 158, 160, 161; liquidating, 125, 158;

loans and loan guarantees, 159; National Performance Review and, 186; obligation limitation, 125; omnibus measures, 149; rules, 141, 143, 144; section *602* procedures, 72, 88, 135, 143, 145, 149, 192, 195; spending caps, 135, 192, 195; structure and content of appropriations acts, 149, 153-57; substantive legislation, 113, 114, 115, 122, 129, 130, 149, 160, 200; supplemental, 44*t*, 46, 130, 131, 149, 166; timeframe of, 113, 122, 129-30, 131, 133, 154, 157; unauthorized, 113, 119, 120-22. *See also* Budget process; Expenditure management

Appropriations and authorization committees: agencies and, 35, 55, 64, 136-37, 160, 162; allocations, 88, 92, 143, 145, 192; authorizations and appropriations, 122-23, 130, 133-35, 137-39, 147, 190-92; budget authority and, 132; budget resolution, 72, 77; chairmen, 133, 135, 139; Clinton, Bill and, 139; Congress and, 73, 76, 77, 111, 112, 120*t*, 133-34; direct spending, 126, 190, 191; discretionary spending, 190, 191, 192; earmarks, 120, 122, 139-41, 154, 170; entitlements, 40; functions, 43, 44-46, 126, 132-41, 154; hearings, 134-35, 137, 147; history, 34, 36, 162; legislative vetoes, 170, 173; markups, 135, 137, 143; program assumptions, 78; reconciliation, 83; reforms, 164; reports, 160, 162, 163; reprogramming, 168, 170, 171

Authorizations: agencies and, 110,

tion legislation, 162; authorization legislation, 118; defense spending, 7; deficit reduction, 8, 23, 40; earmarks, 141; statements of administration policy, 143, 147

Clinton, Bill: *1994* budget, 61, 203; *1995* budget, 55, 56, 57, 61, 203; campaign pledges, 3, 6, 8, 23, 50; compromises, 59, 62; congressional relations, 58, 59, 61, 79; deficit reduction, 3-4, 6, 7, 9, 22-23, 39; executive order, spending controls, 128, 202, 203; federal budget, 2, 3, 8-9, 13, 19-20, 43, 72, 79, 82, 127, 128; health care reform, 11, 13, 59; president's budget, 50, 51-52, 62, 139; rescissions, 176, 199; taxes, 6; use of television, 59

College Construction Loan Insurance Association (Connie Lee), 17

Congress: and agencies, 58, 168, 170-73; appropriations, 117; authorizing legislation, 110-23; biennial budgeting, 200-01; budget authority, 19, 20; budget control, 189-94, 202-03; budget negotiation and resolution, 59-61, 70-72, 73; budget process, 9-10, 13, 19, 20-24, 31, 37-39, 41, 43-46, 55, 164, 177; budget reconciliation, 83-85; and Clinton *1994* budget, 3-4; conference committee and reports, 80, 99, 147, 150-51; deferrals and rescissions, 173-75, 199-200; and deficits, 8, 22-23, 31, 41, 60; direct spending legislation, 123-28, 192-93; discretionary spending legislation, 192; expenditure transfers and reprogrammings, 168, 170-73; history of federal budgeting, 33-39, 183; impoundments, 173-75, 183; president's budget, 49, 55, 56, 58, 59-61, 71; revenue legislation, 98-99; spending caps, 8. *See also* Congressional budget resolution; House of Representatives; Senate; *and names of individual presidents*

Congressional Accounting Office, 47*t*

Congressional Budget Act of *1974*: budget authority, 74, 75; entitle-

ments, 124; history, 33, 37; revenue and spending aggregates, 87; section *502*, 159; section *602* rules, 72, 88-93, 135, 143, 145, 149; spending authority, 123

Congressional Budget and Impoundment Control Act of *1974*, 36, 173

Congressional Budget Office, 36; actual and budgeted deficits, 86, 87*t*; budget process, 44*t*, 47*t*, 77, 83; and Clinton deficit reduction, 6; and Clinton energy tax, 6; and Clinton health care reform, 13; cost estimates, 94; and federal deficit, 4, 30; federal spending, 11; monitoring effects on budget, 91; and Office of Management and Budget, 58; politics of budget arithmetic, 13, 22, 24; revenue estimates, 100, 101; spending caps, 8, 9; user charges, 106

Congressional budget resolution: aggregates, 60*t*, 72-75, 79, 87-88, 97; allocations, 73, 79, 87, 88-92; assumptions, 73, 77, 78, 83; budget deficits, 59-60, 93; conference committee, 80, 88; enforcement, 86-96, 202; formulation of, 77, 79-80; legislative process, 79-81, 86-97, 108; markup, 77, 79; partisanship, 79; president and, 201-02; and reconciliation, 82-86, 96; reforms, 96, 201-02; revenues and, 98-99, 107, 108; role of, 43, 70-72, 73, 81-82, 96; scorekeeping, 91-93, 107; section *602* procedures, 88-92; timetable, 72, 74, 80-81, 82, 84, 96. *See also* Budget Enforcement Act of *1990*

Congressional committees: agencies and, 55; allocations, 88-91; authorizations, 117-18, 120, 122; financial functions, 34, 43, 45, 46, 71; Office of Management and Budget and, 58; reconciliation, 83-85. *See also* Appropriations and authorization committees; House of Representatives, committees; Senate, committees

Congressional Record, 93, 146

Congressional Research Service (CRS), 47*t*

Connie Lee. *See* College Construction Loan Insurance Association

Consolidated Omnibus Budget Reconciliation Act of *1985*, 107

Constitutional issues: appropriations, 129; authorizations, 110-11; balanced budget amendment, 108, 189, 197-98; budget process, 33-34, 36, 44, 49; taxes, 98-99; vetoes, 170, 198

Continuing appropriations. *See* Appropriations

Customs Service, 155

Darman, Richard, 8, 50, 62

Debt, public: Congressional votes on, 73; increases, 75; interest on, 4, 5, 7, 11; limit, 73; paydown, 34; trends, 33*t*

Deferrals. *See* Expenditure management

Deficit, federal: *1993* deficit reduction package, 22-23, 61, 127; actual and budgeted, 86, 87*t*; amounts, 75; baby boomers and, 4; budget arithmetic and accounting, 19, 27-31, 85, 168; causes, 1, 4, 71; economic factors and, 26; effects, 3, 37, 71, 86, 98, 197; federal funds deficit, 28-29, 104; measurement of, 27-31; on- and off-budget, 14, 28; politics and, 25-27; projections, 3, 4, 22, 24-25; sequestration and, 39, 40-41, 44*t*, 100, 102, 126; taxes and, 6-7, 103; trends, 27*t*, 33*t*; user fees, 107. *See also* Budget Enforcement Act of *1990*; Budget, federal; Gramm-Rudman-Hollings Acts of *1985, 1987*; Pay-as-you-go rules

Deficit reduction: *1980s* deficit reduction legislation, 26, 37-41, 75; *1993* deficit reduction legislation, 3-7, 8-9, 75; baseline projections, 22; budget reconciliation and, 82; Byrd rule, 85-86; economic factors affecting, 26, 37-38; taxes, 101, 103; user charges and, 107. *See also* Budget